Lecture Notes in Economics and Mathematical Systems

Managing Editors: M. Beckmann and H. P. Künzi

Econometrics

165

Agustin Maravall

Identification in Dynamic Shock-Error Models

Springer-Verlag
Berlin Heidelberg New York 1979

Authors

Prof. Dr. Klaus Neumann
Institut für Wirtschaftstheorie
und Operations Research
Universität Karlsruhe
Kaiserstraße 12
D-7500 Karlsruhe

Dr. Ulrich Steinhardt
Broichstraße 17
D-5300 Bonn 3

AMS Subject Classifications (1970): 90-02, 90 B15

ISBN-13:978-3-540-09112-7 e-ISBN-13:978-3-642-95339-2
DOI:10.1007/978-3-642-95339-2

2142/3140-543210

PREFACE

Looking at a very simple example of an error-in-variables model, I was surprised at the effect that standard dynamic features (in the form of autocorrelation in the variables) could have on the state of identification of the model.[1/] It became apparent that identification of error-in-variables models was less of a problem when some dynamic features were present, and that the cathegory of "predetermined variables" was meaningless, since lagged endogenous and truly exogenous variables had very different identification properties. Also, for the models I was considering, both necessary and sufficient conditions for identification could be expressed as simple counting rules, trivial to compute. These results seemed somewhat striking in the context of traditional econometrics literature, and provided the original motivation for this monograph. The monograph, therefore, atempts to analyze econometric identification of models when the variables are measured with error and when dynamic features are present. In trying to generalize the examples I was considering, although the final results had very simple expressions, the process of formally proving them became cumbersome and lengthy (in particular for the "sufficiency" part of the proofs). Possibly this was also due to a lack of more high-powered analytical tools and/or more elegant derivations, for which I feel an apology coul be appropiate.

With some minor modifications, this monograph is a Ph.D. dissertation presented to the Department of Economics of the University of Wisconsin, Madison. Thanks are due to Dennis J. Aigner and Arthur S. Goldberger for their very valuable help, and to Richard H. Day for his helpful suggestions. Of course, if despite the numerous revisions errors still remain, the responsability is entirely mine. Thanks are also due to Susan Fay Eubank for doing the typing. Finally, I wish to express my thanks to the Fulbright Commission in Spain, the Ford Foundation and the University of Wisconsin Graduate School for their financial support in the

---

1/ The example is discussed in pp. 21-26.

form of fellowships, and to the Board of Governors of the Federal Reserve System, since this work was completed while I was an economist in their Division of Research and Statistics.

ABSTRACT

It is a standard econometric textbook result that the presence of errors in the variables (EIV) destroys identification of the contemporaneous linear regression model. The analysis of EIV models usually assumes the variables to be independent over time. In this work we study econometric identification of EIV models which have a dynamic structure. The dynamics of the model are reflected, on the one hand, in the presence of distributed lags in the structural equation (reflecting perhaps proxies for expectations, permanent components, etc.). On the other hand, autocorrelation between the exogenous variables and/or the shock is explained by autoregressive-moving average (ARMA) processes.

The analysis proceeds by considering a sequence of models. At each step, a new dynamic stochastic assumption is considered, and the necessary and sufficient conditions for the model under consideration to be identified are derived. In this way, the individual effect of each stochastic assumption can be isolated.

In analyzing identification, a time domain approach is followed. For a particular model, the prior information incorporates constraints for the parameters, as the ones implied by the stationarity and invertibility conditions of the stochastic processes involved, and defines an admissible parameter space. Under normality and zero-mean assumptions, the observational information is contained in the elements of the auto and crosscovariance functions of the observable variables. The model is identified if and only if all the unknown parameters of the model can be uniquely determined from the observational and prior information. The observational information is translated into a system of covariance equations, and the model is (locally) identified if and only if the Jacobian of this sytem with respect to the unknown parameters has (almost everywhere) rank equal to the number of these parameters. (Thus, for an identified model, a set of the covariance equations can be solved for the unknown parameters as functions of the observable covariances and consistent estimators can be computed).

For the class of models considered, the conditions for identification have a very simple expression, involving only a comparision of the orders of the lag polynomials for the equations. Thus their computation for any given model is trivial, and although "order" conditions, they happen to be necessary and sufficient.

Broadly speaking, we conclude that the information contained in the dynamic features of the model may be enough to bring identification depite the presence of errors in the variables. Yet different dynamic assumptions have in general, different identification effects. For example, while autoregressive shocks "help" identification, moving average ones have the opposite effect, and the overall effect of an ARMA shock depends on the relative orders of the autoregressive vs. the moving average polynomials. On the contrary autocorrelation of the exogenous variables, independently of the stochastic model that generates it, always helps identification. Also, models containing larger lags in the structural equation are more likely to be identified. In particular, for large enough orders of the polynomial lags in the structural equation, the model is always identified.

Some extensions are considered. It is seen that (homogenous) nonstationarity of the endogenous variable and/or contemporaneous correlation between exogenous variables also help identification, while autocorrelation of the errors of measurement may act in either direction. Finally, we show how the analysis can be extended to models with a priori zero restrictions on the coefficients (possibly due to the presence of seasonality).

TABLE OF CONTENTS

TABLE OF CONTENTS cont.

CHAPTER I

THE MODEL AND METHODOLOGY

1. INTRODUCTION

After an early period of interest in models containing unobservable variables, the attention of econometric theory switched to models where the stochastic disturbances were only in the form of "shocks" perturbating the structural equations. It is only in recent years that the interest in models with stochastic disturbances affecting the variables ("errors") has been revived. The evolution of errors-in-variables (EIV) models in the econometric literature is described in Goldberger [1972] [1974] and Griliches [1974]. Part of the unpopularity of EIV models was undoubtedly due to the identification problems that unobservable variables could create.1/ To formulate identified models, strong a priori information was required. For models with normal likelihoods it seemed that consistent estimators could only be found if some of the variances (or their ratios) were known, if additional instrumental variables were available, or, from a Bayesian approach, if informative prior distrubutions for the parameters were used (see Johnston [1965, chap. 6] and Zellner [1971, chap. V]).2/ None of this prior information seemed very appealing to econometricians.

Yet economic variables that cannot be directly observed, such as expectations or "permanent" components, are a part of a large number of economic theory models.3/ Resurgence of EIV models has also been the result of the realization that structural equation models familiar to several branches of the social sciences, and closely related to traditional econometric models, are such that identification

---

1/ As Goldberger remarks "we have come to associate errors in the variables with underidentification" [1974, p. 194].

2/ One distinctive feature of normal distributions is that they are fully characterized by the first two moments. When the distributions of the variables are not normal, moments of higher order may add information which affects the identification properties of the model (see Reiersøl [1950]).

3/ See, for example, the discussion in Nerlove [1967].

is preserved, despite the presence of unobservables.[4/] One of the things we know now is that a priori information already familiar in econometric models (the existence of overidentifying restrictions or of multiple indicators) may, in some situations, be sufficient to achieve identification of an EIV model.

Still most of the research along these lines has concentrated on analysing "contemporaneous" models. As pointed out by Geraci [1977, p. 107] when the model contains dynamic features the results obtained for contemporaneous models do not hold. Indeed, from the results reported by Hurwicz in 1949 until the recent attention, as evidenced in Hsiao [1976, 1977], Nowak [1977] Maravall [1974], and Maravall and Aigner [1977], little interest was paid to the problem of identification in dynamic EIV models.[5/]

Contrary to econometrics, dynamic models with unobservable variables have been familiar to statisticians and to engineers for quite sometime. The "signal extraction" literature, very closely related to the study of seasonal models, and the "state space" literature, with the development of the Kalman Filter, use models with variables that are not directly observed.[6/] Yet the standard format of these models, justified from empirical considerations, and the fact that on many occasions the parameters are set equal to predetermined constants, avoided the problem of identification.[7/]

The dynamic aspects of econometric models have become an area of intense research. In general, the structural relationships incorporate the theoretical dynamism of the model (or the proxies for the expectations) as distributed lags on

---

4/ Examples of this renewed interest are Zellner [1970], Jöreskog and Goldberger [1975] and Geraci [1977].

5/ Prior to the last two years, the only general approach is contained in Hurwicz [1949]; although the results were never published.

6/ See, for example, Whittle [1963] and Sorenson [1966].

7/ In a recent paper, Box, Hillmer and Tiao [1976] deal with an errors in variables model in the context of a trend-seasonal-noise statistical decomposition. The model is underidentified, and in order to achieve identification, they introduce an extra "ad hoc" assumption: the variance of the noise is to be maximized. A similar approach is found in Pierce [1976].

the variables. The necessity of reflecting time correlation among the residuals has led to the formulation of additional (nonstructural) equations that try to capture the patterns of the lagged covariances. Thus often, an econometric model combines structural equations with empirical ones, the latter borrowed in general from statistical models of the type presented in Box-Jenkins [1970].

The previous paragraphs serve to place the intention of this research: to analyse identification of dynamic shock-error models. The general model contains a structural equation with several exogenous variables, in which each one of the variables may appear with any number of lags. Also, the empirical equations consist of autoregressive-moving average processes for the exogenous variables and the shock. We consider identification of this model when stochastic disturbances affect the structural equation ("shocks") and each one of the variables ("errors").

Specifically, our attention focusses on how identification of the shock-error model varies according to the different dynamic features of the model. Thus we start by analysing a relatively simple model, where dynamics is only reflected in the distributed lags of the structural equation. Progressively, more dynamic stochastic assumptions are introduced into the model. For each case, we derive the necessary and sufficient conditions for identification.8/ These conditions can be always expressed by means of a very simple counting rule.9/

The rest of Chapter I develops the general methology and assumptions. Chapter II considers a model with a structural equation that has a distributed lag

---

8/ The term "identification" is used in the econometrics, statistics and engineering literature with somewhat different meanings. The econometrics meaning is described in section 4 below. A model is identified in the econometric sense when there are not two or more structures of the model that are observationally equivalent. Basic references are Koopmans [1953], Fisher [1966] and Rothenberg [1971]. In statistical time-series analysis the term is used to denote the specification of the model, within a purely empirical approach (see Haugh and Box [1977]). In engineering the term refers to the entire process spanning from specification to estimation (see Graupe [1972]). Some of the relationships between the different meanings is discussed in Mehra [1974]. In our analysis we use the term solely in its econometrics sense.

9/ Some of the results appeared in Maravall and Aigner [1977], although in that publication we committed a (slight) mistake. The Theorem stated in p. 355 should be modified to read exactly like Theorem 8 in this text.

structure. The exogenous variables and the shock are assumed to be independent white-noises. Chapter III and IV maintain the assumption of white-noise exogenous variables, but consider autocorrelated shocks. In particular, Chapter III analyses models with a pure autoregressive and a pure moving average shock, and Chapter IV deals with mixed autoregressive-moving average processes. Chapter V analyses the effect of autocorrelated exogenous variables, while maintaining the white-noise assumption for the shock. Chapter VI brings together the results of the previous chapters, and considers a model where the shock and any number of exogenous variables may or may not be correlated. Finally, Chapter VII considers some extensions of the analysis. First, a multivariate ARMA process is assumed to generate the exogenous variables. Second, the endogenous variable is allowed to be (homogenously) nonstationary. Third, a model with a priori zero constraints for the coefficients is analyzed (these zero constraints may be due to the presence of seasonality). The last extension considers a model with autocorrelated errors of observation. In all cases, the analysis is illustrated with some examples.

2. THE MODEL

2.1 Equations and Assumptions

We proceed to specify more rigorously the models that will be analysed in the next chapters.

The structural econometric equation is given by

$$G_p(L)\eta_t = B^{(1)}_{q_1}(L)\zeta^{(1)}_t + \dots + B^{(n)}_{q_n}\zeta^{(n)}_t + u_t \tag{1.1a}$$

where L is the lag operator and $G_p(L)$ and $B^{(i)}_{q_i}(L)$ are finite polynomials in L of order p and q_i, respectively:

$$G_p(L) = 1 - \gamma_1 L - \gamma_2 L^2 - \dots - \gamma_p L^p,$$

$$B^{(i)}_{q_i}(L) = \beta^{(i)}_0 + \beta^{(i)}_1 L + \beta^{(i)}_2 L^2 + \dots + \beta^{(i)}_{q_i} L^{q_i} ,$$

The endogenous variable η, the exogenous variables $\zeta^{(1)}, \dots, \zeta^{(n)}$, and the shock u are jointly stationary stochastic processes. A first implication of this stationarity is contained in the following assumption:

Assumption 1: The characteristic roots of the polynominal $G_p(L)$ lie outside the unit circle.

Also, the shock process is assumed independent of each one of the exogenous variables. In particular,

Assumption 2: The variable u is independent of the variables $\zeta^{(1)}, \ldots, \zeta^{(n)}$.

The endogenous and exogenous variables are assumed to be measured with error, according to the equations:

(1.1b) $x_t^{(i)} = \zeta_t^{(i)} + \delta_t^{(i)}, \qquad i = 1,2,\ldots,n$

(1.1c) $y_t = \eta_t + \varepsilon_t$

The stochastic specifications of the errors are contained in the following assumption:

Assumption 3: The variables $\delta^{(1)}, \ldots, \delta^{(n)}$ and ε are white-noise errors, independent of each other, and independent of $\zeta^{(1)}, \ldots, \zeta^{(n)}$, η and u.

Except for some of the extensions considered in Chapter VII, assumptions 1, 2 and 3 are common to all the models analyzed. These models differ in the assumptions made with respect to the exogenous variables and the shock processes.

Chapter II considers the simplest case, characterized by the following assumptions:

Assumption 4a: The shock u is a white-noise variable

Assumption 5a: The variables $\zeta^{(1)}, \ldots, \zeta^{(n)}$ are independent white-noise variables.

The model consisting of equations (1.1a, b, c) together with the set of assumptions 1, 2, 3, 4a and 5a will be referred to as Model I.

Chapter III considers more general stochastic assumptions for the shock process. In the first part of the chapter the shock follows a finite moving average process given by the equation

(1.1d) $u_t = S_s(L)\, a_t,$

where

$$S_s(L) = 1 + \theta_1 L + \theta_2 L^2 + \ldots + \theta_s L^s,$$

and in the second part of the chapter the shock follows an autoregressive, process, of the type:

(1.1e) $R_r(L)\, u_t = a_t,$

where

$$R_r(L) = 1 - \rho_1 L - \rho_2 L^2 - \ldots - \rho_r L^r.$$

Chapter IV combines the two different cases considered in Chapter III. In particular, the shock process is described by a mixed autoregressive-moving average equation, of the form:

(1.1f) $R_r(L)\, u_t = S_s(L)\, a_t,$

where $R_r(L)$ and $S_s(L)$ are the polynomials described above. The process given by (1.1d) or (1.1f) is assumed stationary. Also, the process given by (1.1e) or (1.1f) is assumed invertible. Thus the stochastic assumptions for the shock considered in Chapters III and IV can be summarized as follows:

Assumption 4b: The variable a is white-noise. The characteristic roots of the polynomials $R_r(L)$ and $S_s(L)$ lie outside the unit circle.

For easy reference, the model consisting of equations (1.1a, b, c, d), together with the set of assumptions 1, 2, 3, 4b and 5a, will be denoted Model II. Similarly, the set of equations (1.1a, b, c, e) and (1.1a, b, c, f), under the same assumptions, will be referred to as Models III and IV, respectively. Thus Chapter III deals with Models II and III, and Chapter IV analyses Model IV.

The next chapter considers the effect of introducing autocorrelation for the exogenous variables. To isolate this effect from the one due to an autocorrelated shock, the latter is assumed to be white-noise. The first part of the chapter considers exogenous variables that follow moving average processes of the form:

(1.1g) $\zeta_t^{(i)} = H_{h_i}^{(i)}(L)\, b_t^{(i)}$,

where

$$H_{h_i}^{(i)}(L) = 1 + \alpha_1^{(i)} L + \alpha_2^{(i)} L^2 + \ldots + \alpha_{h_i}^{(i)} L^{h_i},$$

while the second part of the chapter considers mixed autoregressive-moving average processes, given by

(1.1h) $M_{m_i}^{(i)}(L)\, \zeta_t^{(i)} = H_{h_i}^{(i)}(L)\, b_t^{(i)}$.

where

$$M_{m_i}^{(i)}(L) = 1 - \phi_1^{(i)} L - \phi_2^{(i)} L^2 - \ldots - \phi_{m_i}^{(i)} L^{m_i},$$

These processes are assumed stationary and invertible. Thus Chapter V considers models where assumption 5b below is substituted for assumption 5a.

Assumption 5b: The variables $b^{(1)}, \ldots, b^{(n)}$ are independent white-noise variables. The characteristic roots of the polynomials $H_{h_i}^{(i)}(L)$ and $M_{m_i}^{(i)}(L)$ lie outside the unit circle.

The set of equation (1.1a, b, c, g) together with the set of assumptions 1, 2, 3, 4a and 5b will be referred to as Model V. Similarly, equations (1.1a, b, c, h) under the same set of assumptions will be denoted Model VI.

Chapter VI considers models where the shock and the exogenous variables are autocorrelated. The models are described by equations (1.1a, b, c, f and h) and the set of assumptions 1, 2, 3, 4b and 5b. First, a particular case is considered, where each one of the exogenous variables is autocorrelated. This is referred to as Model VII. Finally, a model is analysed where any number of exogenous variables may or may not be autocorrelated. This is denoted by Model VIII, and Models I to VII can be derived as particular cases of it.

Chapter VII analyses the effects of relaxing some of the previous assumptions. In particular, assumptions 1, 3 and either 5a or 5b, are modified to allow for nonstationarity, autocorrelated errors and correlation between the exogenous variables. A final extension is considered, where further a priori information on the coefficients of equation (1.1a) is available.

Due to the fact that Models I to VII can be derived as particular cases of Model VIII, the rest of this chapter, which deals mostly with the methodology of our analysis, will refer to Model VIII.

2.2 Some Notation and Terminology

We shall adopt the following notational convention: the covariances of the unobserved variables (including the error terms) will be denoted by σ's, while the covariances of the observed variables will be denoted by ω's. This notation stresses the difference between the population covariances for which a sample analogue can be calculated (the ω's) and those that are not directly observable (the σ's).

With this notation, the τ-lag auto and crosscovariances will be denoted by:

$$\text{Cov}\,(x_t^{(i)},\, x_{t-\tau}^{(i)}) = \omega_{xx_{-\tau}}^{(i)}$$

$$\text{Cov}\,(y_t, y_{t-\tau}) = \omega_{yy_{-\tau}}$$

$$\text{Cov}\,(y_t, x_{t-\tau}^{(i)}) = \omega_{yx_{-\tau}}^{(i)}$$

$$\text{Cov}\,(\eta_t, \eta_{t-\tau}) = \sigma_{\eta\eta_{-\tau}}$$

$$\text{Cov}\,(\eta_t, \zeta_{t-\tau}^{(i)}) = \sigma_{\eta\zeta_{-\tau}}^{(i)}$$

$$\text{Cov}\,(\zeta_t^{(i)}, \zeta_{t-\tau}^{(i)}) = \sigma_{\zeta\zeta_{-\tau}}^{(i)}$$

$$\text{Cov}\,(\eta_t, u_{t-\tau}) = \sigma_{\eta u_{-\tau}}$$

$$\text{Cov}\,(u_t, u_{t-\tau}) = \sigma_{uu_{-\tau}}$$

where $\tau = 0, \pm 1, \pm 2, \ldots.$

The same convention will hold for the auto and crosscovariance generating functions. These will be denoted as follows:

(1.2a) $$\sigma_{\eta\eta}(L) = \sum_{\tau=-\infty}^{\infty} \sigma_{\eta\eta_{-\tau}} L^{\tau} \;;$$

$$(1.2b) \qquad \sigma^{(i)}_{\eta\zeta}(L) = \sum_{\tau=-\infty}^{\infty} \sigma^{(i)}_{\eta\zeta_{-\tau}} L^{\tau} ;$$

$$(1.2c) \qquad \sigma^{(i)}_{\zeta\zeta}(L) = \sum_{\tau=-\infty}^{\infty} \sigma^{(i)}_{\zeta\zeta_{-\tau}} L^{\tau} ;$$

$$\omega_{yy}(L) = \sum_{\tau=-\infty}^{\infty} \omega_{yy_{-\tau}} L^{\tau} ;$$

$$\omega^{(i)}_{yx}(L) = \sum_{\tau=-\infty}^{\infty} \omega^{(i)}_{yx_{-\tau}} L^{\tau} ;$$

$$\omega^{(i)}_{xx}(L) = \sum_{\tau=-\infty}^{\infty} \omega^{(i)}_{xx_{-\tau}} L^{\tau} ;$$

$$\sigma_{\eta u}(L) = \sum_{\tau=-\infty}^{\infty} \sigma_{\eta u_{-\tau}} L^{\tau} ;$$

$$\sigma_{uu}(L) = \sum_{\tau=-\infty}^{\infty} \sigma_{uu_{-\tau}} L^{\tau} .$$

2.3 Identification of the Model when no Errors are Present.

The stationarity requirements of assumptions 1, 4b and 5b are necessary for the validity of most of the analysis developed in the next chapters. The reason for imposing the invertibility requirements (i.e., the requirement that the roots of the polynomials S(L) and $H^{(i)}(L)$ lie outside the unit circle) is due to the following consideration.

As we shall be concerned with the identification effects of observation errors, we want to make sure that the model is uniquely identified when no observation errors are present. This implies the following: consider a given set of functions $\sigma_{\eta\eta}(L)$, $\sigma_{\eta\zeta}(L)$ and $\sigma_{\zeta\zeta}(L)$, which contain the observational information of the model (when no errors of measurement are present). These functions are generated by equations (1.1a, f and h). Each set of particular values of the parameters of these equations defines a structure of the model. If more than one structure (of the same model) can generate the given auto- and cross-covariance functions, the model is not identified. We shall see how the invertibility conditions of assumptions 4b and 5b (combined with the stationarity requirements) permit us to isolate a unique (admissible) structure for the model.

The stationarity conditions allow us to rewrite equations (1.1a, h) as:

$$(1.3a) \qquad \eta_t = \sum_{i=1}^{n} \psi^{(i)}(L) b_t^{(i)} + \psi^{(0)}(L) a_t$$

$$(1.3b) \qquad \zeta_t^{(i)} = \xi^{(i)}(L) b_t^{(i)},$$

where the polynomials $\psi^{(i)}(L)$, $\psi^{(0)}(L)$ and $\xi^{(i)}(L)$ are given by

$$(1.4a) \qquad \psi^{(i)}(L) = [G(L)M^{(i)}(L)]^{-1} B^{(i)}(L) H^{(i)}(L),$$

$$(1.4b) \qquad \psi^{(0)}(L) = [R(L)G(L)]^{-1} S(L),$$

$$(1.4c) \qquad \xi^{(i)}(L) = [M^{(i)}(L)]^{-1} H^{(i)}(L),$$

for i = 1, 2, ..., n (for notational simplicity, the subindexes of the polynomials have been deleted).

From equations (1.3a, b), the auto- and crosscovariance generating functions (1.2a, b, c) can be expressed as[10/]

10/ Expression (1.5a) is a straightforward application of the result in Box-Jenkins [1970, pp. 80-81]. Equation (1.5b) is derived as follows: From (1.3a),

$$\eta_{t+\tau} = \sum_{i=1}^{n} \psi^{(i)}(L)\, b_{t+\tau}^{(i)} + \psi^{(0)}(L)\, a_{t+\tau}$$

Multiplying the l.h.s. of this equation by the l.h.s. of (1.3a) and the r.h.s. by the r.h.s. of (1.3a), and taking expectations, yields:

$$\sigma_{\eta\eta_{-\tau}} = \sum_{i=1}^{n} \sigma_{bb}^{(i)} \sum_{j=0}^{\infty} \psi_j^{(i)} \psi_{\tau+j}^{(i)} + \sigma_{aa} \sum_{j=0}^{\infty} \psi_j^{(0)} \psi_{\tau+j}^{(0)} .$$

Substituting for $\sigma_{\eta\eta_{-\tau}}$ in (1.2a), the autocovariance generating function becomes

$$\sigma_{\eta\eta}(L) = \sum_{i=1}^{n} \sigma_{bb}^{(i)} \sum_{j=0}^{\infty} \sum_{h=0}^{\infty} \psi_j^{(i)} \psi_h^{(i)} L^{h-j} + \sigma_{aa} \sum_{j=0}^{\infty} \sum_{h=0}^{\infty} \psi_j^{(0)} \psi_h^{(0)} L^{h-j} ,$$

thus

$$\sigma_{\eta\eta}(L) = \sum_{i=1}^{n} \psi^{(i)}(L)\psi^{(i)}(L^{-1})\, \sigma_{bb}^{(i)} + \sigma_{aa}\psi^{(0)}(L)\psi^{(0)}(L^{-1})$$

which is expression (1.5b).

In order to derive expression (1.5c) we follow a similar procedure. First we multiply

$$\eta_{t+\tau} = \sum_{i=1}^{n} \sum_{j=0}^{\infty} \psi_j^{(i)} b_{t+\tau-j}^{(i)} + \sum_{j=0}^{\infty} \psi_j^{(0)} a_{t+\tau-j}$$

(1.5a) $\sigma^{(i)}_{\zeta\zeta}(L) = \xi^{(i)}(L)\ \xi^{(i)}(L^{-1})\ \sigma^{(i)}_{bb}$,

(1.5b) $\sigma^{(i)}_{\eta\eta}(L) = \sum_{j=1}^{n} \psi^{(i)}(L)\ \psi^{(i)}(L^{-1})\ \sigma^{(i)}_{bb} + \psi^{(0)}(L)\ \psi^{(0)}(L^{-1})\ \sigma_{aa}$

(1.5c) $\sigma^{(i)}_{\eta\zeta}(L) = \psi^{(i)}(L)\ \xi^{(i)}(L^{-1})\ \sigma^{(i)}_{bb}$

Since, for a constant k, the following identity holds:

$$(1-kL)(1-kL^{-1}) = k^2(1-k^{-1}L)(1-k^{-1}\ L^{-1}),$$

it is easily seen that:

a) If a root of the polynomial $\xi^{(i)}(L)$ is replaced by its inverse, the functions (1.5a, b, c) do not change;

b) the same is true for the polynomial $\psi^{(0)}(L)$;

c) if a root of the polynomial $\psi^{(i)}(L)$, for i=1, 2, ...,n, is replaced by its inverse, the functions (1.5a, b) do not change, but (1.5c) does change.

Thus in order to avoid a multiplicity of models with the same auto- and crosscovariance functions, restrictions on the roots of the polynomials $\xi^{(i)}(L)$ and $\psi^{(0)}(L)$ have to be introduced. According to (1.4a, b) this implies restrictions on the roots of the polynomials G(L), R(L), $M^{(i)}(L)$, S(L) and $H^{(i)}(L)$. The

---

10/ (continued)

by

$$\zeta^{(i)}_t = \sum_{j=0}^{\infty} \xi^{(i)}_j b^{(i)}_{t-j} ,$$

and, after taking expectations, we obtain

$$\sigma^{(i)}_{\eta\zeta_{-\tau}} = \sigma^{(i)}_{bb} \sum_{j=0}^{\infty} \psi^{(i)}_{\tau+j}\ \xi^{(i)}_j .$$

Substituting $\sigma^{(i)}_{\eta\zeta_{-\tau}}$ into $\sigma^{(i)}_{\eta\zeta}(L)$

$$\sigma^{(i)}_{\eta\zeta}(L) = \sum_{\tau=-\infty}^{\infty} \sigma^{(i)}_{\eta\zeta_{-\tau}} L^{\tau} = \sigma^{(i)}_{bb} \sum_{\tau=-\infty}^{\infty} \sum_{j=0}^{\infty} \psi^{(i)}_{\tau+j}\xi^{(i)}_j L^{\tau}$$

$$= \sigma^{(i)}_{bb} \sum_{j=0}^{\infty} \sum_{\tau=j}^{\infty} \psi^{(i)}_{\tau+j}\xi^{(i)}_j L^{\tau} = \sigma^{(i)}_{bb} \sum_{i=0}^{\infty} \sum_{h=0}^{\infty} \psi^{(i)}_h L^{h-j} = \psi^{(i)}(L)\xi^{(i)}(L^{-1})\sigma^{(i)}_{bb} .$$

which is expression (1.5c).

stationarity and invertibility requirements of assumption 1, 4b and 5b serve this purpose: by requiring that the roots of these five polynomials lie outside the unit circle, the inverses of the roots are not admissible, as they would have to lie inside the unit circle.[11/]

11/ Another source of underidentification in distributed lag and time series models is based on the following consideration: Consider for example, equation (1.1h')

(1.1h') $M_m(L)\ \zeta_t = H_h(L)\ b_t,$

where for notational simplicity, the subscript i has been deleted. Let $M_1, M_2, \ldots, M_m$ and $H_1, H_2, \ldots, H_h$ be the solutions of the equations:

$$M_m(L) = 0$$

$$H_h(L) = 0,$$

respectively. The polynomials $M_m(L)$ and $H_h(L)$ can be rewritten

$$\text{(f.1.1)}\quad \begin{aligned} M_m(L) &= (1-M_1L)(1-M_2L)\ \ldots\ (1-M_mL) \\ H_h(L) &= (1-H_1L)(1-H_2L)\ \ldots\ (1-H_hL). \end{aligned}$$

Let ζ_t be perfectly observable; the observational information corresponding to (1.1h') is contained in the autocovariance generating function $\sigma_{\zeta\zeta}(L)$, given by equation (1.5a), where $\xi(L)$ is defined in (1.4c). Thus,

$$\sigma_{\zeta\zeta}(L) = \frac{\prod_{i=1}^{h} (1-H_iL)(1-H_iL^{-1})}{\prod_{i=1}^{m} (1-M_iL)(1-M_iL^{-1})}$$

Therefore, if both sides of equation (1.1h') are multiplied by the factor (1-kL), the function $\sigma_{\zeta\zeta}(L)$ - the observational information - remains unchanged.

In order to avoid this problem, an assumption should be introduced, forcing the solutions of the equation $M_m(L) = 0$ to be different from the solutions of the equation $H_h(L) = 0$. But the constraints that this assumption implies for the parameters of the model are of the general form

$$f\ (\underline{\phi}, \underline{\alpha}) = 0,$$

where $\underline{\phi}$ and $\underline{\alpha}$ are the vectors of parameters in $M_m(L)$ and $H_h(L)$, respectively, and $f(\cdot)$ is an analytical function (not identically zero). As we prove in section 1.3, the set of points in the parameter space that are zeroes of an analytic function have zero Lebesgue measure. This implies that the constraint

$$f\ (\underline{\phi}, \underline{\alpha}) \neq 0$$

is satisfied almost everywhere in the admissible parameter space. Because of this reason, these types of constraints (and the kind of underidentification they avoid) will not be considered in the next chapters.

Identification of dynamic/time-series models along the lines discussed in this section and in this footnote, is considered in Quenouille [1957, pp. 22-25] Box-Jenkins [1970, pp. 195-199] and Hannan [1977].

3. THE PARAMETERS AND THE ADMISSIBLE PARAMETER SPACE

Assumption 3 and equations (1.1b, c) imply

$$\omega_{xx}^{(i)}(L) = \sigma_{\zeta\zeta}^{(i)}(L) + \sigma_{\delta\delta}^{(i)}$$

(1.6) $$\omega_{yx}^{(i)}(L) = \sigma_{\eta\zeta}^{(i)}(L)$$

$$\omega_{yy}(L) = \sigma_{\eta\eta}(L) + \sigma_{\varepsilon\varepsilon} \cdot$$

Also, assumptions 2 and equations (1.1a, f) yield

(1.7a) $$\sigma_{\eta u}(L) = [G(L)\ G(L^{-1})]\ \sigma_{uu}(L)$$

(1.7b) $$\sigma_{uu}(L) = [R(L)\ R(L^{-1})]^{-1}\ S(L)\ S(L^{-1})\ \sigma_{aa} \cdot$$

Therefore the unobservable auto- and crosscovariances between the variables η, ζ and u can be expressed as functions of the observable covariances and the parameters in G(L), R(L), S(L) together with $\sigma_{\delta\delta}^{(i)}$ and $\sigma_{\varepsilon\varepsilon}$.[12/] Thus identification of the model is achieved when the following parameters are identified:

$$\beta_0^{(i)},\ \beta_1^{(i)},\ \ldots,\ \beta_{q_i}^{(i)}$$

$$\gamma_1,\ \gamma_2,\ \ldots,\ \gamma_p$$

$$\phi_1^{(i)},\ \phi_2^{(i)},\ \ldots,\ \phi_{m_i}^{(i)}$$

$$\alpha_1^{(i)},\ \alpha_2^{(i)},\ \ldots,\ \alpha_{h_i}^{(i)}$$

$$\rho_1,\ \rho_2,\ \ldots,\ \rho_r$$

$$\theta_1,\ \theta_2,\ \ldots,\ \theta_s$$

$$\sigma_{aa},\ \sigma_{\varepsilon\varepsilon},\ \sigma_{\delta\delta}^{(i)}$$

for i=1, 2, ..., n. The total number of these parameters is equal to

(1.8) $$N = \sum_{i=1}^{n} (q_i + m_i + h_i) + p + r + s + 2(n+1).$$

12/ Notice that assumption 2 implies $\sigma_{\zeta u}^{(i)}(L) = 0$.

To see what constraints on the parameters are implied by assumptions 1, 3, 4b and 5b, define the vectors:

$$\underline{\gamma} = (\gamma_1, \ldots, \gamma_p)'$$

$$\underline{\beta}^{(i)} = (\beta_0^{(i)}, \ldots, \beta_{q_i}^{(i)})'$$

$$\underline{\beta} = (\underline{\beta}^{(1)'}, \ldots, \underline{\beta}^{(n)'})'$$

$$\underline{\emptyset}^{(i)} = (\emptyset_1^{(i)}, \ldots, \emptyset_{m_i}^{(i)})' \tag{1.9}$$

$$\underline{\emptyset} = (\underline{\emptyset}^{(1)'}, \ldots, \underline{\emptyset}^{(n)'})'$$

$$\underline{\alpha}^{(i)} = (\alpha_1^{(i)}, \ldots, \alpha_{h_i}^{(i)})'$$

$$\underline{\alpha} = (\underline{\alpha}^{(1)'}, \ldots, \underline{\alpha}^{(n)'})'$$

$$\underline{\rho} = (\rho_1, \ldots, \rho_r)'$$

$$\underline{\theta} = (\theta_1, \ldots, \theta_s)'$$

$$\underline{\sigma} = (\sigma_{aa}, \sigma_{\varepsilon\varepsilon}, \sigma_{\delta\delta}^{(1)}, \ldots, \sigma_{\delta\delta}^{(n)})$$

The requirement that the roots of the polynomials $G(L)$, $M^{(i)}(L)$, $H^{(i)}(L)$, $R(L)$ and $S(L)$ lie outside the unit circle can be translated into a set of constraints on the parameters, of the form:

$$f_1(\underline{\gamma}) > 0;\ f_2(\underline{\emptyset}) > 0;\ f_3(\underline{\alpha}) > 0;$$

(1.10a)

$$f_4(\underline{\rho}) > 0;\ f_5(\underline{\theta}) > 0.$$ [13/]

13/ To see some examples, consider the two polynomials

$$G_2(L) = 1 - \gamma_1 L - \gamma_2 L^2$$
$$S_1(L) = 1 + \theta_1 L.$$

Stationarity of $G_2(L)$ implies

$$\gamma_2 + \gamma_1 < 1$$
(f.1.2) $$\gamma_2 - \gamma_1 < 1$$
$$-1 < \gamma_2 < 1,$$

and $S_1(L)$ is invertible whenever $-1 < \theta_1 < 1$. (See Box-Jenkins [1970, p. 58-59 and 69]).

Also, the variances are constrained by the condition

(1.10b) $\underline{\sigma} > \underline{0}$,

where $\underline{0}$ is the (n+2)-dimensional zero vector.

Therefore the admissible parameter space is the subspace of the N- dimensional Eucledian space such that the inequalities given by (1.10a) and (1.10b) hold. The admissible parameter space will be denoted by Ω; a point in Ω (i.e., an N-dimensional vector of admissible parameter values) will be denoted by $\underline{\pi}$. We present a result that will be used frequently in the next chapters.

Consider the polynomial in L:

$$G_p(L) = 1 - \gamma_1 L - \gamma_2 L^2 - \dots - \gamma_p L^p,$$

and the vector $\underline{\gamma}$ of parameters. Define Lebesgue measures on the Borel sets of E^p, where E^p denotes the p-dimensional Eucledian space.[14/] Let $f_1(\underline{\gamma}) > 0$ represent the condition that the roots of $G_p(L)$ lie outside the unit circle. Clearly, the set

$$\Gamma = \{ \underline{\gamma} : \underline{\gamma} \in E^p, f_1 (\underline{\gamma}) > 0\}$$

has positive Lebesgue measure.

Consider now the cartesian product

$$E^N = E^p \times E^{\sum_{i=1}^{n} q_i + n} \times E^{\sum_{i=1}^{n} m_i} \times E^{\sum_{i=1}^{n} h_i} \times E^r \times E^s \times E^{n+2}$$

As the constraints in (1.10a, b) do not overlap over the vectors of parameters defined in (1.9), and the functions f_2, f_3, f_4 and f_5 are similar to f_1, it follows that the admissible parameter space Ω has positive Lebesgue measure.

Let $\underline{\pi}$ be the N-dimensional vector of all the parameters of the model:

(1.11) $\underline{\pi} = (\underline{\gamma}', \underline{\beta}', \underline{\emptyset}', \underline{\alpha}', \underline{\rho}', \underline{\theta}', \underline{\sigma}')'$,

and let $\bar{f}(\underline{\pi})$ denote an analytical function in the elements of $\underline{\pi}$, not identically zero. Then using Theorem 5.A.2 in Fisher [1966, p. 166], the set of points where

---

14/ See Williamson [1962].

this function vanishes, i.e., the set

$$\pi = \{ \underline{\pi} : \underline{\pi} \in E^N, \bar{f}(\underline{\pi}) = 0\}$$

has zero Lebesgue measure.15/

4. ANALYSIS OF IDENTIFICATION

4.1 The Identification Problem.

Following Rothenberg [1971], each structure of Model VIII can be characterized by a particular parameter point within the admissible parameter space. The model is identified if and only if no two different structures are observationally equivalent.

15/ As an example, consider the model:

$$\eta_t = \gamma_1 \eta_{t-1} + \gamma_2 \eta_{t-2} + \beta_0 \zeta_t + \beta_1 \zeta_{t-1} + u_t ,$$

$$y_t = \eta_t + \varepsilon_t$$

$$x_t = \zeta_t + \delta_t ,$$

where ε, δ, ζ and u are independent white-noise variables, the first two ones being independent of η also.
The vector $\underline{\pi}$ is given by:

$$\underline{\pi} = (\gamma_1, \gamma_2, \beta_0, \beta_1, \sigma_{uu}, \sigma_{\varepsilon\varepsilon} \sigma_{\delta\delta})'.$$

The prior constraints on the parameters are the stationarity conditions for γ_1 and γ_2, given by the inequalities (f.1.2) together with

(f.1.3) $\underline{\sigma} = (\sigma_{uu}, \sigma_{\varepsilon\varepsilon}, \sigma_{\delta\delta})' > \underline{0}$,

where $\underline{0} \in E^3$. The constraints in (f.1.2) define an admissible region for γ_1 and γ_2 given by the triangle:

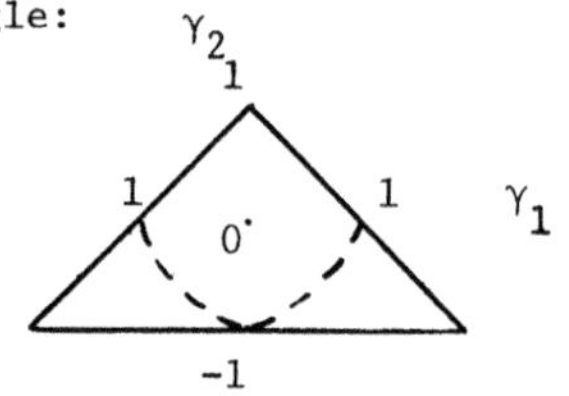

which has positive Lebesgue measure (the area of the triangle is equal to 4). The admissible parameter space is the cartesian product

$$\Omega = \Gamma \times E^2 \times E^3_+ ,$$

where Γ is the above triangle, E^2 corresponds to the parameters β_0 and β_1 (unconstrained) and E^3_+ is the positive orthant, corresponding to the variance parameters (constrained by (f.1.3)). Trivially, a polynomial such as for example: $\gamma_1^2 + \gamma_2^2 - 1 = 0$
(the dotted line in the figure), has zero Lebesgue measure.

Under the normality and zero-means conditions contained in assumptions 3, 4b and 6b, the observational information of Model VIII is given by the functions $\omega^{(i)}_{xx}(L)$, $\omega^{(i)}_{yx}(L)$ and $\omega_{yy}(L)$, since the joint distribution of the observable variables is fully characterized by the second moments. Therefore the identification problem can be reformulated as follows: the model is identified if and only if all the parameters can be uniquely determined from the elements of the functions $\omega^{(i)}_{xx}(L)$, $\omega^{(i)}_{yx}(L)$ and $\omega_{yy}(L)$.

4.2 The Covariance Equations.

The elements of the functions $\omega^{(i)}_{xx}(L)$, $\omega^{(i)}_{yx}(L)$ and $\omega_{yy}(L)$ are the τ-lag auto and crosscovariances: $\omega^{(i)}_{xx_{-\tau}}$, $\omega^{(i)}_{yx_{-\tau}}$, $\omega_{yy_{-\tau}}$, for $\tau = 0, \pm 1, \pm 2, \ldots$. These covariances can be expressed as follows: Consider equations (1.1a, h) with the unobservable variables η and $\zeta^{(i)}$ replaced by y and $x^{(i)}$, according to (1.1b, c). Write the equations in the following way:

(1.12a) $$y_t = \bar{G}_p(L)\,(y_{t-1} - \varepsilon_{t-1}) + \sum_{i=1}^{n} B^{(i)}_{q_i}(L)\,(x^{(i)}_t - \delta^{(i)}_t) + u_t + \varepsilon_t$$

(1.12b) $$x^{(i)}_t = \bar{M}^{(i)}_{m_i}(L)\,(x^{(i)}_{t-1} - \delta^{(i)}_{t-1}) + H^{(i)}_{h_i}(L)\,b^{(i)}_t + \delta^{(i)}_t ,$$

where

$$\bar{G}_p(L) = \gamma_1 + \gamma_2 L + \ldots + \gamma_p L^{p-1}$$

$$\bar{M}^{(i)}_{m_i}(L) = \emptyset^{(i)}_1 + \emptyset^{(i)}_2 L + \ldots + \emptyset^{(i)}_{m_i} L^{m_i-1} .$$

If both sides of equation (1.12a) are multiplied by $y_{t-\tau}$, and expectations are taken, an equation is obtained, which expresses $\omega_{yy_{-\tau}}$ as a function of the parameters and observable ω-covariances. This equation will be referred to as the τ-lag autocovariance equation (for the variable y).

Similarly, if equation (1.12a) is multiplied by $x^{(i)}_{t-\tau}$, and expectations are taken, an expression is obtained for $\omega^{(i)}_{yx_{-\tau}}$. This equation will be denoted the τ-lag crosscovariance equation corresponding to the variable $x^{(i)}$. Finally, if equation (1.12b) is multiplied by $x^{(i)}_{t-\tau}$ and expectations are taken, an equation for

$\omega^{(i)}_{xx_{-\tau}}$ is obtained, which will be called the τ-lag autocovariance equation (for $x^{(i)}$).

For $\tau = 0, \pm 1; \pm 2, \ldots$, the set of equations obtained in this way will be referred to as the system of covariance equations.16/ By construction, there is a 1-1 mapping between the elements of the functions $\omega^{(i)}_{xx}(L)$, $\omega^{(i)}_{yx}(L)$ and $\omega_{yy}(L)$, and the equations of this system. From the point of view of observational information, only "one side" of the autocovariance functions needs to be considered. This is due to the fact that $\omega_{yy_{-\tau}} = \omega_{yy_{\tau}}$, and $\omega^{(i)}_{xx_{-\tau}} = \omega^{(i)}_{xx_{\tau}}$. As a consequence, the τ-lag autocovariance equations for negative values of τ are identical to the ones corresponding to positive values of τ. Therefore, the system of covariance equations we shall consider will only contain τ-lag autocovariance equations for $\tau \geq 0$.

Going back to the question of identification, due to the 1-1 correspondence between the elements of the covariance functions and the equations of the system of covariance equations, the problem can be reformulated as follows:

If the system of covariance equations contains a subsystem that can be solved uniquely for the parameters of the model, if follows that these parameters can be uniquely expressed as functions of the ω-covariances, and the model is identified.

4.3 (Locally) Isolated Solutions of the Covariance Equations

Using a compact notation, let $\underline{\omega}$ be the (infinite dimensional) vector containing all the elements of the functions $\omega^{(i)}_{xx}(L)$, $\omega^{(i)}_{yx}(L)$ and $\omega_{yy}(L)$. The entire system of covariance equations can be written

(1.13) $\quad \underline{\omega} = \omega\,(\underline{\omega}, \underline{\pi})$,

where $\underline{\pi} \in E^N$. Consider the subsystem of (1.13) given by the N equations:

16/ The covariance equations can be given an instrumental variable interpretation, due to the fact that lagged variables may be used as instruments (see Goldberger [1964, p. 286]). Yet some qualifications should be made to account for the possible correlation of the lagged endogenous variables and the shock.

$$(1.14)\qquad \begin{aligned} \omega_1 &= \omega_1\,(\underline{\omega}\,,\,\underline{\pi}) \\ &\;\vdots \\ \omega_N &= \omega_N\,(\underline{\omega},\,\underline{\pi}). \end{aligned}$$

Let $\underline{\pi}_0$ be a point in the admissible parameter space, and denote by $J(\underline{\pi}_0)$ the Jacobian of the system (1.14) with respect to $\underline{\pi}$ evaluated at $\underline{\pi} = \underline{\pi}_0$. This Jacobian is an (N x N) matrix, and a necessary condition for $\underline{\pi}_0$ to be a solution of (1.14) is

$$\text{rank}\ \{\ J\ (\underline{\pi}_0)\ \} \leq N.$$

By the implicit function theorem, $\underline{\pi}_0$ is a locally isolated solution if

$$(1.15)\qquad \text{rank}\ \{\ J\ (\underline{\pi}_0)\ \} = N.$$

Following Fisher [1966, Theorem 5.A.1, p. 163], if $\underline{\pi}_0$ is a regular point, condition (1.15) is necessary and sufficient for $\underline{\pi}_0$ to be a locally isolated solution. Also, when the elements of $J(\pi)$ are analytic, the set of irregular points has zero Lebesgue measure (Fisher [1966, Corollary 5.A.1, p. 167]). Since for the model we shall be considering, the elements of $J(\pi)$ are analytic (if not zero), we shall accept that the necessary and sufficient condition for the system (1.14) to have an isolated solution $\underline{\pi}_0$ is given by (1.15).[17/]

4.4 Summary of the Methodology.

As we mentioned in the Introduction, in the next chapters we shall derive the necessary and sufficient conditions for identification of a sequence of models. For each model, we shall consider the entire system of covariance equations. Two situations can happen:

a) The system of covariance equations contains no subsystem that can provide a locally isolated solution for the parameters. If such is the case, the model is not identified.

17/ Strictly speaking, we shall only be concerned with local identification (i.e., the existence of locally isolated solutions for the parameters). A similar approach is used by Geraci [1977].

b) A subsystem of covariance equations provides a locally isolated solution for the parameters, and the model is identified (locally).[18/]

In this last case, the proof that the equations under consideration provide an isolated solution for the parameters is performed by proving that the Jacobian of the equations with respect to these parameters has full rank. In several instances, this is done by showing that the determinant of the Jacobian, expressed in terms of the parameters, is equal to an analytic function (generally, a ratio of finite polynomials). Using a result described at the end of Section 3, the set of parameters in the admissible parameter space for which such a function vanishes has zero Lebesgue measure. Thus in the next chapters, whenever identification of a model is proved by showing that the determinant of the relevant Jacobian is equal to a polynomial in the parameters, the qualification "almost everywhere" is implicitely being made.

In spite of the fact that it will not be mentioned explicitly in the chapters that follow, the reader should bear in mind that our results deal with local identification, and that in general our proofs are almost everywhere valid.

5. A REMARK ON ESTIMATION

Although we shall not be concerned with estimation, the following remark seems appropriate.

The procedure we follow to prove identification of a model (or the lack thereof) provides us with a method of obtaining consistent estimators of the parameters whenever the model is identified. This should not come as a surprise, since under out assumptions the model is identified if consistent estimators of the parameters can be found.[19/]

18/ Except for some examples (most of them in Chapter II), we shall not be concerned with partial identification of a subset of parameters.

19/ See Reiersøl [1950, p. 376].

More specifically, we shall prove that a model is identified by showing that a system of covariance equations can be solved for the parameters as functions of the observable ω-covariances. If, for a given time series on y, $x^{(1)}, \ldots, x^{(n)}$, the sample auto and crosscovariances are substituted for the ω-covariances, the solution expressed as a function of the sample covariances provides consistent estimators of the parameters.[20/] This is equivalent to the estimation procedure known as "method of moments", and it is well known that these estimators are not (asymptotically) efficient. In fact, the estimators obtained in such a way can be quite unsatisfactory; they are very sensitive to rounding errors, they are particularly inappropriate for the moving average processes, and they can oscillate wildly if the roots of the autoregressive polynomials are close to the boundary of the unit circle (i.e., if the processes approach nonstationarity). Still, they are relatively easy to compute and can be useful as starting values in an iterative, more efficient, maximum likelihood estimation procedure (see Box-Jenkins [1970] and Pandit [1973]).

6. AN EXAMPLE: DYNAMIC VS. CONTEMPORANEOUS MODELS

We shall discuss some examples that illustrate how identification of shock-error models differs according to whether the model is contemporaneous or dynamic. Through the discussion we shall illustrate also the metholology outlined in the previous sections.

First consider the standard contemporaneous model

(1.16a) $\quad \eta_t = \beta\zeta_t + u_t,$

where ζ and u are independent white-noise variables. The errors-in-variables equations

---

20/ A similar procedure is used by Telser [1974] to study identification and estimation of autoregressive models in the presence of systematic sampling or aggregation. Telser proves that the parameters of the disaggregate model can be expressed as functions of the covariances for which sample analogue exist. If the sample covariances are used, then consistent estimators are obtained.
Related types of estimators are considered in Hsiao [1976] and Karni and Weissman [1974].

(1.16b) $y_t = \eta_t + \varepsilon_t$

(1.16c) $x_t = \zeta_t + \delta_t$

are assumed to hold, and the errors ε and δ are white-noise variables, independent of each other, of u, ζ and η. The system of covariance equations is

$$\omega_{yy} = \beta\omega_{yx} + \sigma_{uu} + \sigma_{\varepsilon\varepsilon}$$

$$\omega_{yx} = \beta(\omega_{xx} - \sigma_{\delta\delta}) ,$$

with all lagged covariances equal to zero. The model is not identified, as these two equations cannot be solved for the four parameters β, $\sigma_{\varepsilon\varepsilon}$, $\sigma_{\delta\delta}$ and σ_{uu}. With minor variations, this is the basic result on errors-in-variables models that appears in standard econometrics textbooks.[21/]

Second, consider a similar model where the exogenous variable is replaced by a lagged endogenous variable. Equation (1.16a) is therefore replaced by the first order autoregression:

(1.16d) $\eta_t = \gamma\eta_{t-1} + u_t$,

where stationarity implies $-1 < \gamma < 1$. Corresponding to the two equations in (1.17), equation (1.16d) yields

(1.18a) $\omega_{yy} = \gamma\omega_{yy_{-1}} + \sigma_{uu} + \sigma_{\varepsilon\varepsilon}$

$$\omega_{yy_{-1}} = \gamma(\omega_{yy} - \sigma_{\varepsilon\varepsilon}) ,$$

We observe that, despite the fact that the number of parameters decreases (since $\sigma_{\delta\delta}$ disappears), these two equations still cannot be solved for γ, σ_{uu} and $\sigma_{\varepsilon\varepsilon}$. But the dynamic structure of the model, in this case reflected in the lagged value of η, implies the existence of additional information in the form of nonzero lagged covariances. For $\tau > 1$, the τ-lag autocovariance equation corresponding to equation (1.16d) yields:

(1.18c) $\omega_{yy_{-\tau}} = \gamma\omega_{yy_{-\tau+1}}$.

21/ A very similar analysis is contained in Zellner [1971, pp. 127-128].

Now, letting $\tau = 2$ in (1.18c), the system of covariance equations consisting of (1.18a, b, c) has a Jacobian, with respect to the parameters β, $\sigma_{\varepsilon\varepsilon}$, σ_{uu}, of the form:

$$J = \begin{pmatrix} \omega_{yy_{-1}} & 1 & 1 \\ \omega_{yy}-\sigma_{\varepsilon\varepsilon} & -\gamma & 0 \\ \omega_{yy_{-1}} & 0 & 0 \end{pmatrix}$$

Since $\det J = \gamma\, \omega_{yy_{-1}}$, and equations (1.18a, b) imply $\omega_{yy_{-1}} = \frac{\gamma\, \sigma_{uu}}{1-\gamma^2}$, the matrix will be singular if and only if $\gamma\,(1-\gamma^2)^{-1} = 0$. For values of γ between 1 and -1, this implies $\gamma = 0$, value that we can obviously discard.[22/] Thus the system of equations (1.18a, b, c) has a (locally) isolated solution for the parameters, and the model is therefore identified. In particular, the solution is given by:

$$\gamma = \frac{\omega_{yy_{-2}}}{\omega_{yy_{-1}}}$$

$$\sigma_{\varepsilon\varepsilon} = \frac{\omega_{yy}\,\omega_{yy_{-2}} - \omega^2_{yy_{-1}}}{\omega_{yy_{-2}}}$$

$$\sigma_{uu} = \frac{\omega^2_{yy_{-1}} - \omega^2_{yy_{-2}}}{\omega_{yy_{-2}}},$$

and if, for a particular time series, the ω-covariances are replaced by their sample estimates, these equations provide consistent estimators of the parameters.

The two examples considered show how drastically a dynamic feature affects

---

22/ The admissible parameter space is the cartesian product:

$$\Omega = \Gamma \times E^2_+ ,$$

where Γ is the region in E bounded by the inequalitites $-1 < \gamma < 1$, and E^2_+ is the positive orthant corresponding to $\sigma_{\varepsilon\varepsilon} > 0$, $\sigma_{uu} > 0$. Trivially, the subspace of Ω such that $\gamma = 0$ has zero Lebesgue measure.

identification of a model.[23/] To see the effects of other types of dynamic assumptions, consider a third example. The structural equation is again (1.16a), but the exogenous variable and the shock are now assumed to be autocorrelated. In particular, they follow the processes

(1.19a) $\zeta_t = \phi\zeta_{t-1} + b_t$

(1.19b) $u_t = \rho u_{t-1} + a_t$,

where a and b are white-noise variables independent of each other and of ε and δ and $-1 < \emptyset < 1$, $1 < \rho < 1$. Since equation (1.19a) is of the same form as (1.16d), we know that the system of τ-lag autocovariance equations (corresponding to the variable x) for $\tau = 0, 1, 2$, can be solved for the parameters $\emptyset$, σ_{bb} and $\sigma_{\delta\delta}$. Thus the model is identified if the rest of the covariance equations identify the parameters β, ρ, $\sigma_{\varepsilon\varepsilon}$ and σ_{aa}. Writing equation (1.19b) as

$$u_t = a_t + \rho a_{t-1} + \rho^2 a_{t-2} + \ldots$$

it follows that

$$\sigma_{uu_{-\tau}} = \frac{\rho^\tau}{1 - \rho^2} \sigma_{aa} .$$

Since for this model $\sigma_{uy_{-\tau}} = \sigma_{uu_{-\tau}}$, the system of τ-lag autocovariance equations (corresponding to the variable y) for $\tau = 0, 1, 2, 3$, is given by

---

23/ The fact that, under our assumptions, equation (1.16d) is identified, while (1.16a) is not, implies that lagged endogenous variables and "truly exogenous" variables have drastically different effects. Thus, from the point of view of errors-in-variables models, the econometric category of "predetermined variables" appears to be quite meaningless. Also, while the result corresponding to equation (1.16a) appears in most econometric textbooks, to my knowledge, the only published reference to the result corresponding to equation (1.16d) is contained in a footnote in Hurwicz [1950].

$$\omega_{yy} = \beta\omega_{yx} + \frac{1}{1-\rho^2}\sigma_{aa} + \sigma_{\varepsilon\varepsilon}$$

$$\omega_{yy_{-1}} = \beta\omega_{xy_{-1}} + \frac{\rho}{1-\rho^2}\sigma_{aa}$$

$$\omega_{yy_{-2}} = \beta\omega_{xy_{-2}} + \frac{\rho^2}{1-\rho^2}\sigma_{aa}$$

$$\omega_{yy_{-3}} = \beta\omega_{xy_{-3}} + \frac{\rho^3}{1-\rho^2}\sigma_{aa} .$$

The Jacobian of this system with respect to the parameters β, ρ, σ_{aa} and $\sigma_{\varepsilon\varepsilon}$ is found to be:

$$J = \begin{pmatrix} \omega_{yx} & \frac{2}{(1-\rho^2)^2}\sigma_{aa} & \frac{1}{1-\rho^2} & 1 \\ \omega_{xy_{-1}} & \frac{1+\rho^2}{(1-\rho^2)^2}\sigma_{aa} & \frac{\rho}{1-\rho^2} & 0 \\ \omega_{xy_{-2}} & \frac{2\rho}{(1-\rho^2)^2}\sigma_{aa} & \frac{\rho^2}{1-\rho^2} & 0 \\ \omega_{xy_{-3}} & \frac{3\rho^2-\rho^4}{(1-\rho^2)^2}\sigma_{aa} & \frac{\rho^3}{1-\rho^2} & 0 \end{pmatrix} ,$$

with determinant:

$$\det J = -\frac{\rho\sigma_{aa}}{(1-\rho^2)^3}\begin{vmatrix} \omega_{xy_{-1}} & 1+\rho^2 & 1 \\ \omega_{xy_{-2}} & 2\rho & \rho \\ \omega_{xy_{-3}} & 3\rho^2-\rho^4 & \rho^2 \end{vmatrix} ,$$

But, from (1.16a),

$$\omega_{xy_{-\tau}} = \beta\omega_{xx_{-\tau}} , \qquad \tau \geq 1$$

and, from (1.19a),

$$\omega_{xx_{-\tau}} = \frac{\phi^{\tau}}{1 - \phi^{\tau}} \sigma_{bb}, \qquad \tau > 1,$$

thus

$$\det J = - \frac{\rho\ \beta\ \phi\ \sigma_{aa}\ \sigma_{bb}}{(1 - \rho^2)^3 (1 - \phi^2)} \det \begin{vmatrix} 1 & 1 + \rho^2 & 1 \\ \phi & 2\rho & \rho \\ \phi^2 & 3\rho^2 - \rho^4 & \rho^2 \end{vmatrix}$$

$$= - \frac{\rho\ \beta\ \phi\ \sigma_{aa}\ \sigma_{bb}}{(1 - \rho^2)^3 (1 - \phi^2)} [\rho^4 - \rho^3\phi - \rho^2(1 - \phi^2) + 2\phi\rho - \phi^2],$$

which is different from zero. Thus the model is identified.

As a fourth and final example, let us go back to the structural equation (1.16d), the first order autoregression. Under the white-noise assumption for the shock, the model was identified. Consider, instead, a shock that follows a first order moving average:

$$(1.20) \qquad u_t = a_t + \theta a_{t-1}$$

Since equations (1.16d) and (1.20) imply

$$\sigma_{uy} = (1 + \theta^2 + \theta\gamma)\ \sigma_{aa}$$

$$\sigma_{uy_{-1}} = \theta\sigma_{aa}$$

$$\sigma_{uy_{-\tau}} = 0 \qquad \tau > 1,$$

the system of covariance equations is given by:

$$\omega_{yy} = \gamma\omega_{yy_{-1}} + (1 + \theta^2 + \theta\beta)\ \sigma_{aa} + \sigma_{\varepsilon\varepsilon}$$

$$\omega_{yy_{-1}} = \gamma(\omega_{yy} - \sigma_{\varepsilon\varepsilon}) + \theta\sigma_{aa}$$

$$\omega_{yy_{-\tau}} = \gamma\omega_{yy_{-\tau+1}}, \qquad \tau > 1,$$

It is seen that only the first two equations include the parameters θ, σ_{aa} and $\sigma_{\varepsilon\varepsilon}$; hence there is no subsystem that can be solved for these three parameters and the model is not identified.

At first sight it would seem that the main difference between the contemporaneous case and the dynamic models we have just seen lies in the fact that the latter include the existence of nonzero lagged covariances between the variables that bring additional information. Yet the effect of this information, as far as identification is concerned, deserves some further attention, for sometimes it seems to increase identification and sometimes it seems to have the opposite effect. The next chapters offer a more systematic treatment of these issues.

CHAPTER II

WHITE-NOISE SHOCK; WHITE-NOISE EXOGENOUS VARIABLES

This chapter develops the necessary and sufficient conditions for identification of a dynamic shock-error model under somewhat restrictive assumptions. In particular, the shock and the exogenous variables are assumed to be mutually independent white-noise variables. To illustrate the nature of the identification problem, Section 1 analyzes several models with one exogenous variable. In Section 2 the general model (Model I) is presented, and the necessary and sufficient conditions for identification are derived. The main result is presented as a theorem and, in order to facilitate understanding of the proof of the theorem, an Appendix illustrates the derivation for a particular model with two exogenous variables. Finally, in Section 3 the results are briefly discussed and interpreted.

1. THE CASE OF ONE EXOGENOUS VARIABLE

1.1 One Lag per Variable

Let the model be

$$\eta_t = \gamma_1 \eta_{t-1} + \beta_0 \zeta_t + \beta_1 \zeta_{t-1} + u_t , \tag{2.1}$$

or, substituting $y_t = \eta_t + \varepsilon_t$ and $x_t = \zeta_t + \delta_t$:

$$y_t = \gamma_1 (y_{t-1} - \varepsilon_{t-1}) + \beta_0 (x_t - \delta_t) + \beta_1 (x_{t-1} - \delta_{t-1}) + u_t + \varepsilon_t . \tag{2.2}$$

The variables ζ, u, ε, and δ are assumed to be mutually independent white-noise variables and η is independent of ε and δ. The stationarity assumption implies, for this particular model,

$$-1 < \gamma_1 < 1 , \tag{2.3}$$

This constraint, together with

$$\sigma_{\delta\delta}, \sigma_{\varepsilon\varepsilon}, \sigma_{\zeta\zeta}, \sigma_{uu} \geq 0 \tag{2.4}$$

represent all the a priori information on the parameters of the model. Multiplying both sides of equation (2.2) by x_t and taking expectations, the lag-zero cross covariance of y and x can be expressed as

(2.5.a) $\omega_{yx} = \beta_0(\omega_{xx}-\sigma_{\delta\delta})$.

Performing the same operations for $x_{t-\tau}$, $\tau = \pm 1, \pm 2, \pm 3, \ldots$, the cross covariances of y and x can be expressed as

(2.5.b) $\omega_{yx_{-1}} = \beta_1(\omega_{xx}-\sigma_{\delta\delta}) + \gamma_1\omega_{yx}$

(2.5.c) $\omega_{yx_{-\tau}} = \gamma_1\omega_{yx_{-\tau+1}}$, $\tau = 2, 3, 4, \ldots$

(2.5.d) $\omega_{yx_{\tau}} = 0$, $\tau = 1, 2, 3, \ldots$

Similarly, the autocovariances of y can be expressed as:

(2.5.e) $\omega_{yy} = \gamma_1\omega_{yy_{-1}} + \beta_0\omega_{yx} + \beta_1\omega_{yx_{-1}} + \sigma_{\varepsilon\varepsilon} + \sigma_{uu}$

(2.5.f) $\omega_{yy_{-1}} = \gamma_1(\omega_{yy}-\sigma_{\varepsilon\varepsilon}) + \beta_1\omega_{yx}$

(2.5.g) $\omega_{yy_{-\tau}} = \gamma_1\omega_{yy_{-\tau+1}}$, $\tau = 2, 3, 4, \ldots$

and, because of the stationarity assumption:

(2.5.h) $\omega_{yy_{\tau}} = \omega_{yy_{-\tau}}$, $\tau = 1, 2, 3, \ldots$

This system of equations represents the complete system of covariance equations. The model will be identified if and only if the Jacobian of this system with respect to the six parameters γ_1, β_0, β_1, $\sigma_{\delta\delta}$, $\sigma_{\varepsilon\varepsilon}$, and σ_{uu}, has rank equal to six. Obviously, this can never be the case for the system (2.5), since only four equations (a, b, e, and f) contain the five parameters, β_0, β_1, $\sigma_{\delta\delta}$, and σ_{uu}. We conclude that, under our assumptions, equation (2.1) is not identified. Notice that the parameter γ_1 is identified because (2.5c) with $\tau = 2$ yields

(2.6) $$\gamma_1 = \frac{\omega_{yx_{-2}}}{\omega_{yx_{-1}}}$$

where, from (2.5.a, b), the denominator is given by

$$\omega_{yx_{-1}} = (\beta_1 + \gamma_1\beta_0)(\omega_{xx}-\sigma_{\delta\delta}) = (\beta_1 + \gamma_1\beta_0)\ \sigma_{\zeta\zeta}$$

which is different from zero.

1.2. The Effect of Additional "a Priori" Information

We shall consider the effects of additional information in the form of "zero restrictions" on the parameters of the model.

Case a: The Exogenous Variable is measured without error.

Suppose $\sigma_{\delta\delta} = 0$. Then the equations (2.5.a, b, f, e) can be written as

$$\beta_0 = \frac{\omega_{yx}}{\omega_{xx}},$$

$$\beta_1 = \frac{\omega_{yx_{-1}} - \gamma_1 \omega_{yx}}{\omega_{xx}}$$

$$\sigma_{\varepsilon\varepsilon} = \omega_{yy} - \frac{\omega_{yy_{-1}} - \beta_1 \omega_{yx}}{\gamma_1}$$

$$\sigma_{uu} = \omega_{yy} - \gamma_1 \omega_{yy_{-1}} - \beta_0 \omega_{yx} - \beta_1 \omega_{yx_{-1}} - \sigma_{\varepsilon\varepsilon}$$

Substituting for γ_1 from (2.6), these last four equations can be solved recursively for the parameters as function of the observable covariances. Thus with the added restriction $\sigma_{\delta\delta} = 0$, the model becomes identified.

Case b: The endogenous variable is measured without error.

Suppose instead $\sigma_{\varepsilon\varepsilon} = 0$. Then, equations (2.5.f, b, a, e) can be written as

$$\beta_1 = \frac{\omega_{yy_{-1}} - \gamma_1 \omega_{yy}}{\omega_{yx}}$$

$$\sigma_{\delta\delta} = \omega_{xx} - \frac{\omega_{yx_{-1}} - \gamma_1 \omega_{yx}}{\beta_1}$$

$$\beta_0 = \frac{\omega_{yx}}{\omega_{xx} - \sigma_{\delta\delta}}$$

$$\sigma_{uu} = \omega_{yy} - \gamma_1 \omega_{yy_{-1}} - \beta_0 \omega_{yx} - \beta_1 \omega_{yx_{-1}} .$$

Since $\omega_{xx} - \sigma_{\delta\delta} = \sigma_{\zeta\zeta}$ and $\omega_{yx} = \beta_0 \sigma_{\zeta\zeta}$, upon substituting for γ_1 from (2.6), this last system of equations can be solved recursively for the parameters β_1, $\sigma_{\delta\delta}$, β_0, and σ_{uu}. Thus with the added restriction $\sigma_{\varepsilon\varepsilon} = 0$, the model becomes identified.

Case c: Lagged endogenous variable is absent.

Now suppose $\gamma_1 = 0$. The equations (2.5.f, b, a) can be rewritten as

$$\beta = \frac{\omega_{yy_{-1}}}{\omega_{yx}}$$

$$\sigma_{\delta\delta} = \omega_{xx} - \frac{\omega_{yx_{-1}}}{\beta_1}$$

$$\beta_0 = \frac{\omega_{yx}}{\omega_{xx} - \sigma_{\delta\delta}} .$$

This system can be solved recursively for β_1, $\sigma_{\delta\delta}$, and β_0, so those three parameters will be identified. But the parameters $\sigma_{\varepsilon\varepsilon}$ and σ_{uu} are included only in equation (2.5.e), so that only their sum $(\sigma_{\varepsilon\varepsilon} + \sigma_{uu})$ is identified.

Case d: Lagged exogenous variable is absent

Suppose instead $\beta_1 = 0$. Equation (2.6) still identifies γ_1 since $\omega_{yx_{-1}} = \gamma_1 \beta_0 \sigma_{\zeta\zeta}$. From equation (2.5.f),

$$\sigma_{\varepsilon\varepsilon} = \omega_{yy} - \frac{\omega_{yy_{-1}}}{\gamma_1}$$

so that the parameter $\sigma_{\varepsilon\varepsilon}$ is also identified. But the parameters β_0, $\sigma_{\delta\delta}$, and σ_{uu} only appear in the equations (2.5.a) and (2.5.e), therefore the model is not identified.

Case e: Shock is absent.

Let the additional constraint be $\sigma_{uu} = 0$. Then the Jacobian of the system of equations (2.5.a, b, e, and f) with respect to the parameters β_0, β_1, $\sigma_{\delta\delta}$, and $\sigma_{\varepsilon\varepsilon}$ is given by the matrix

$$J = \begin{pmatrix} \sigma_{\zeta\zeta} & 0 & -\beta_0 & 0 \\ 0 & \sigma_{\zeta\zeta} & -\beta_1 & 0 \\ \omega_{yx} & \omega_{yx_{-1}} & 0 & 1 \\ 0 & \omega_{yx} & 0 & -\gamma_1 \end{pmatrix},$$

where use has been made of the equality:

$$\omega_{xx} - \sigma_{\delta\delta} = \sigma_{\zeta\zeta}$$

The determinant of J is equal to

$$|J| = -\sigma_{\zeta\zeta}[\gamma_1\beta_1\omega_{yx_{-1}} + (\beta_1 + \beta_0\,\gamma_1)\omega_{yx}]$$

$$= -\sigma^2_{\zeta\zeta}[(\beta_1 + \gamma_1\beta_0)(\gamma_1\beta_1 + \beta_0)].$$

which is nonzero. We conclude that after substituting for γ_1 with the use of (2.6), if $\sigma_{uu} = 0$ the system of equations (2.5.a, b, e, and f) can be solved from the parameters β_0, β_1, $\sigma_{\delta\delta}$, and $\sigma_{\varepsilon\varepsilon}$ as functions of the observable covariances. Thus, the model becomes identified.

From the analysis of these cases, it is seen how the addition of a priori information concerning the parameters of the model can transform an under-identified model into an identified one. Until Chapter VII, the only a priori information that we shall consider is the one implied by the set of assumptions presented in Chapter I, which defines an admissible parameter space described in Section 1.3. Thus, up to Chapter VII, no a priori additional restrictions on the parameters of the model will be assumed.

1.3. Increasing the Number of Lags of the Variables.

Going back to the model discussed in subsection 2.1.1, we concluded that the model with one exogenous variable and one lag per variable is not identified (when no additional a priori information on the parameters is available). We shall see how this result changes when we consider an extra lag in one of the variables. In particular, let a second lagged value of the exogenous variable appear in the equation so that

(2.7) $\quad \eta_t = \gamma_1\eta_{t-1} + \beta_0\zeta_t + \beta_1\zeta_{t-1} + \beta_2\zeta_{t-2} + u_t,$

where, as before, $-1 < \gamma_1 < 1$. After substituting for η and ζ in terms of the observable variables, the covariances can be written as the system of covariance equations:

a) Crosscovariances:

(2.8.a) $\quad \omega_{yx} = \beta_0(\omega_{xx} - \sigma_{\delta\delta})$

(2.8.b) $\quad \omega_{yx_{-1}} = \gamma_1\omega_{yx} + \beta_1(\omega_{xx} - \sigma_{\delta\delta})$

(2.8.c) $\quad \omega_{yx_{-2}} = \gamma_1\omega_{yx_{-1}} + \beta_2(\omega_{xx} - \sigma_{\delta\delta})$

(2.8.d) $\quad \omega_{yx_{-\tau}} = \gamma_1\omega_{yx_{-\tau+1}}, \qquad \tau \geqq 3$

$\omega_{yx_\tau} = 0, \qquad \tau > 0$

b) Autocovariances:

(2.8.e) $\quad \omega_{yy} = \gamma_1\omega_{yy_{-1}} + \beta_0\omega_{yx} + \beta_1\omega_{yx_{-1}} + \beta_2\omega_{yx_{-2}} + \sigma_{uu} + \sigma_{\varepsilon\varepsilon}$

(2.8.f) $\quad \omega_{yy_{-1}} = \gamma_1(\omega_{yy} - \sigma_{\varepsilon\varepsilon}) + \beta_1\omega_{yx} + \beta_2\omega_{yx_{-1}}$

(2.8.g) $\quad \omega_{yy_{-2}} = \gamma_1\omega_{yy_{-1}} + \beta_2\omega_{yx}$

$\omega_{yy_{-\tau}} = \gamma_1\omega_{yy_{-\tau+1}}, \qquad \tau \geqq 3$

$\omega_{yy_\tau} = \omega_{yy_{-\tau}}, \qquad \tau > 0.$

Consider the system of equations (2.8 a to g); let $\tau = 3$ in (2.8.d), so that $\gamma_1 = \dfrac{\omega_{yx_{-3}}}{\omega_{yx_{-2}}}$. As the denominator, $\omega_{yx_{-2}}$, is equal to $\{\gamma_1[\gamma_1\beta_0 + \beta_1] + \beta_2\}(\omega_{xx} - \sigma_{\delta\delta})$, hence different from zero, the parameter γ_1 is identified. Noticing that the variance σ_{uu} only appears in equation (2.8.e), it follows that the model (2.7) will be identified if the Jacobian of the system of equations (2.7 a, b, c, f, and g) with respect to the five parameters β_0, β_1, β_2, $\sigma_{\delta\delta}$, and $\sigma_{\varepsilon\varepsilon}$ is nonsingular. This Jacobian is given by the matrix:

$$J = \begin{pmatrix} \sigma_{\zeta\zeta} & 0 & 0 & -\beta_0 & 0 \\ 0 & \sigma_{\zeta\zeta} & 0 & -\beta_1 & 0 \\ 0 & 0 & \sigma_{\zeta\zeta} & -\beta_2 & 0 \\ 0 & \omega_{yx} & \omega_{yx_{-1}} & 0 & -\gamma_1 \\ 0 & 0 & \omega_{yx} & 0 & 0 \end{pmatrix}$$

where $\sigma_{\zeta\zeta} = \omega_{xx} - \sigma_{\delta\delta}$. The determinant of this matrix is equal to (in absolute value)

$$|J| = \gamma_1 \beta_2 \omega_{yx} \sigma_{\zeta\zeta}^2 = \gamma_1 \beta_0 \beta_2 \sigma_{\zeta\zeta}^3 ,$$

thus different from zero, so that equation (2.7) is identified.

Comparing this result with the one obtained in subsection 2.1.1, we observe that identifiability increases when more lagged values of the exogenous variable appear in the structural equation of the model. As we shall see in the next section, for the general case of a model with several exogenous variables, identifiability increases when the polynomial lags appearing in the structural equation increase their size. In particular, we shall conclude that for large enough orders of the polynomial lags, the model is always identified.

2. THE GENERAL CASE (MODEL I).

In this section we shall derive the necessary and sufficient conditions for a dynamic regression model with n exogenous variables to be identified, when the variables are measured with error and when the shock and the exogenous variables are independent white-noise variables.

Let the model be described by the equation

$$(2.9) \qquad G(L)\eta_t = B_1^{(1)}(L)\zeta_t^{(1)} + \ldots + B_{q_n}^{(n)}(L)\zeta_t^{(n)} + u_t ,$$

$$y_t = \eta_t + \varepsilon_t$$

$$x_t^{(i)} = \zeta_t^{(i)} + \delta_t^{(i)} \qquad i = 1 \ldots, n$$

where the polynomial lags $G(L)$ and $B_{q_i}^{(i)}(L)$ were defined already in (1.2.b).[1/] Without loss of generality, we assume that $q_1 \leq q_2 \leq \ldots \leq q_n$. Equation (2.9) can be written also as:

$$\eta_t = \gamma_1\eta_{t-1} + \ldots + \gamma_p \eta_{t-p} + \sum_{i=1}^{n} (\beta_0^{(i)}\zeta_t^{(i)} + \beta_1^{(i)}\zeta_{t-1}^{(i)} + \ldots$$

$$+ \beta_{q_i}^{(i)}\zeta_{t-q_i}^{(i)}) + u_t ,$$

and it can be seen as an "errors-in-the-variables" univariate regression with n exogenous variable, where the endogenous and each one of the exogenous variables have a distributed lag structure. In accordance with assumption 1, the model is assumed to be stationary, so that the roots of $G(L) = 0$ lie outside the unit circle. Finally, assumptions 1, 2, 3, 4a and 5a represent the only a priori

---

1/ Unless otherwise specified, for all the models we consider the errors-in-the-variables equations:

$$x_t^{(i)} = \zeta_t^{(i)} + \delta_t^{(i)}, \ i = 1, \ldots, n$$

$$y_t = \eta_t + \varepsilon_t ,$$

(where $\delta_t^{(i)}$, $i = 1, \ldots, n$, and ε_t are independent white-noise variables) are assumed to hold. As specified in Chapter 1, also the following assumptions concerning the errors, $\delta_t^{(i)}$ and ε_t, are made:

$\delta_t^{(i)}$ and $\zeta_t^{(j)}$ are independent $(i, j = 1, \ldots, n)$

η_t and ε_t are independent

η_t and $\delta_t^{(i)}$ are independent $(i = 1, \ldots, n)$

$\delta_t^{(i)}$ and ε_t are independent of u_t $(i = 1, \ldots, n)$.

Bearing these equations and assumptions in mind, we shall avoid specifying them for each particular model.

constraints for the parameters of the model; and, as a consequence of this, all the parameters, γ_j, $\beta_k^{(i)}$ $(j = 1, \ldots, p;\ k = 0, 1, \ldots, q_i;\ i = 1, \ldots, n)$ will be different from zero (a.e.). We shall refer to this model as Model I.

We now establish:

Lemma 1. The autoregressive parameters, $\gamma_1, \ldots, \gamma_p$, are identified

Proof of the Lemma: For all $\tau > \max(p, q_n)$, consider the system of τ-lag autocovariance equations. The typical equation of this system is given by:

$$(2.10)\qquad \omega_{yy_{-\tau}} = \gamma_1\omega_{yy_{-\tau+1}} + \ldots + \gamma_p\omega_{yy_{-\tau+p}} \ .$$

As $\gamma_p \neq 0$, this equation represents a homogeneous linear difference equation of order p. It follows that equation (2.10) has one and only one solution, ω_{yy}, which depends on p initial consecutive values.2/ If, for all integers τ, $\tau > \max(p, q_n)$, the resulting system of equations has a Jacobian (with respect to the parameters $\gamma_1,\ldots,\gamma_p$) of full column rank, it is possible to find a subsystem of p equations that can be uniquely solved for the parameters $\gamma_1,\ldots,\gamma_p$, so that these parameters are identified. It follows that the γ-parameters will not be identified only if the Jacobian mentioned before has less than full column rank. In this case, a (non-trivial) linear combination of the columns of this Jacobian will vanish. Write this linear combination as

$$(2.11)\qquad \mu_0\omega_{yy_{-\tau+1}} + \mu_1\omega_{yy_{-\tau+2}} + \ldots + \mu_p\omega_{yy_{-\tau+p}} = 0,$$

where $\tau > \max(p, q_n)$, and $\mu_0, \mu_1,\ldots,\mu_p$ are constants. Equation (2.11) represents a homogeneous linear difference equation of order p-1 (at most), with a unique solution for $\omega_{yy_{-\tau}}$, $\tau \geqq \max(p, q_n)$, that depends on p-1 (at most) initial consecutive values. Thus the two equations, (2.10) and (2.11), contradict each other so that no linear combination such as (2.11) can exist. It follows that the Jacobian of the system of τ-lag autocovariance equations, for $\tau > \max(p, q_n)$, has full column rank, and the γ-parameters are identified. This proves the Lemma.

2/ See Anderson [1971], p. 248.

Identification of the remaining parameters, i.e., $\underline{\beta}^{(1)}, \ldots, \underline{\beta}^{(n)}$, $\sigma_{\delta\delta}^{(1)}$, $\ldots$, $\sigma_{\delta\delta}^{(n)}$, $\sigma_{\varepsilon\varepsilon}$, and σ_{uu}, is subject to certain conditions, as expressed in the following:

<u>Theorem 1</u>: If the (n+1) integers, $p, q_1, \ldots, q_n$, are arranged in increasing order (ties are immaterial) and q_j^* denotes the one occupying the $j^{\underline{th}}$ place in this new sequence, Model I is identified if and only if

$$q_j^* \geq j, \text{ for } j = 1, 2, \ldots, n+1 .$$

<u>Proof of the Theorem</u>:

<u>Necessity</u>: Suppose that the conditions of the Theorem do not hold and the smallest j for which $q_j^* < j$ is $j = j^0$. Consider two different cases:

a. $\underline{p \geqq j^0}$. Then, due to the fact that $q_{j+k} \geqq q_j$ for $k > 0$, it has to be that $q_j^* = q_j$ for $j \leqq j^0$. It follows that, for all $j \leq j^0$, the parameters in $\underline{\beta}^{(j)}$ and $\sigma_{\delta\delta}^{(j)}$ only appear in the following covariance equations:

i) the τ-lag crosscovariance equations corresponding to the $j^{\underline{th}}$ exogenous variable, for $\tau = 0, 1, \ldots, q_j^*$ and $j \leq j^0$, a total of $(q_1^* + \ldots + q_{j^0}^* + j^0)$ equations;

ii) The τ-lag autocovariance equations for $\tau = 0, 1, \ldots, q_{j^0}^*$, a total of $q_{j^0}^* + 1$ equations.

The parameter σ_{uu} only appears in the 0-lag autocovariance equation, already included in ii).

Thus, while the total number of equations available is $\sum_{j=1}^{j^0} q_j^* + q_{j^0}^* + j^0+1$, the number of parameters to be identified by these equations is $\sum_{j=1}^{j^0} q_j^* + 2j^0 + 1$, determined from:

parameters in $\underline{\beta}^{(1)}, \ldots, \underline{\beta}^{(j^0)}$: $\sum_{j=1}^{j^0} (q_j^* + 1)$

parameters $\sigma_{\delta\delta}^{(1)}, \ldots, \sigma_{\delta\delta}^{(j^0)}$: j^0

parameter σ_{uu} : 1

Thus, if $q^*_{j^0} < j^0$, the number of equations is smaller than the number of parameters, which proves necessity.

b. $\underline{p < j^0}$. Denote the set of exogenous variables for which $q^*_j < j^0$ by $\xi = \{\zeta^j | j \in J\}$. Notice that this set has to contain $(j^0 - 1)$ variables. Then, for $j \in J$, the parameters in $\underline{\beta}^{(j)}$ and $\sigma^{(j)}_{\delta\delta}$ only appear in the following covariance equations:

i) the τ-lag crosscovariance equations corresponding to the jth exogenous variable, for $\tau = 0, 1, \ldots, q^*_j$. The total number of these equations is $\sum_{j\varepsilon J} (q^*_j + 1)$;

ii) The τ-lag autocovariance equations for $\tau = 0, 1, \ldots, q^*_{j^0}$; a total of $(q^*_{j^0} + 1)$ equations.

For the model to be identified, these equations have to provide a solution for the parameters $\beta^{(j)}_k$, $j \in J$, $k = 0, 1, \ldots, q^*_j$, along with the variances $\sigma^{(j)}_{\delta\delta}$ of the variables in ξ, $\sigma_{\varepsilon\varepsilon}$, and σ_{uu}. The total number of these parameters is

(2.12) $$\sum_{j\varepsilon J} (q^*_j + 1) + (j^0 - 1) + 1 + 1 = \sum_{j\varepsilon J} (q^*_j + 1) + j^0 + 1,$$

where use has been made of the fact that ξ contains $(j^0 - 1)$ exogenous variables. The number of equations in i) and ii) comes out to be

(2.13) $$\sum_{j\varepsilon J} (q^*_j + 1) + q^*_{j^0} + 1.$$

Comparing (2.12) and (2.13), since $q^*_{j^0} < j^0$, there are more parameters than equations, which proves necessity.

Sufficiency: We shall prove that when the conditions of the Theorem are met, it is possible to find a system of covariance equations that can be solved for all the unknown parameters of the model. These parameters are the β and γ-coefficients, and the $\sigma_{\delta\delta}$, $\sigma_{\varepsilon\varepsilon}$, and σ_{uu} variances.

Consider the system of covariance equations consisting of:

i) The subsystem of τ-lag autocovariance equations for $\tau = \max(q_n, p) + 1, \ldots, \max(q_n, p) + p$.

ii) The subsystem of τ-lag autocovariance equations for $\tau = 0, 1, \ldots$ $n + 1$. (The condition $q_j^* \geq j$, $j = 1, 2 \ldots, n + 1$, guarantees that the subsystems in i) and ii) do not overlap).

iii) The τ-lag cross-covariance equations ($\tau = 0, 1, \ldots, q_j$) corresponding to each exogenous variable.

The Jacobian matrix for this system of equations with respect to the unknown parameters is of dimensions $(\sum_{i=1}^{n} q_i + 2n + p + 2) \times (\sum_{i=1}^{n} q_i + 2n + p + 2)$, and can be partitioned as indicated:

$$(2.14) \qquad J = \left(\begin{array}{c|c|c} 1 & \underline{J}_3' & \underline{J}_4' \\ \hline 0 & J_0 & 0 \\ \hline 0 & J_2 & J_I \\ \hline \end{array}\right) \begin{array}{l} \text{0-lag auto-covariance equation} \\ \text{subsystem in i) above} \\ \text{remaining covariance equations in ii) and ii)} \end{array}$$

$$\sigma_{uu} \qquad \underline{\gamma} \qquad \text{other parameters}$$

The matrix J_0 is nonsingular, as shown in Lemma 1. Therefore, $|J| \neq 0$ if and only if $|J_I| \neq 0$. The proof of sufficiency rests on showing that $|J_I| \neq 0$ if the conditions indicated in the theorem are met. The matrix J_I is square of order $(\sum_{i=1}^{n} q_i + 2n + 1)$, corresponding to the $\beta^{(i)}$'s, the $\sigma_{\delta\delta}^{(i)}$'s $(i = 1, \ldots, n)$ and $\sigma_{\varepsilon\varepsilon}$, respectively. Specifically, J_I has the form given by (2.15), where the first $\sum_{i=1}^{n} (q_i + 1)$ rows are derived from the subset of covariance equations in iii) above and the last $(n + 1)$ rows are derived from the subset of equations in ii) above, apart from the 0-lag autocovariance equation.

$$J_I = \begin{pmatrix} [\omega_{xx}^{(1)} - \sigma_{\delta\delta}^{(1)}]I_{(q_1+1)} & 0 & \cdots & 0 & -\underline{\beta}^{(1)} 0 \cdots\cdots 0 & 0 \\ 0 & [\omega_{xx}^{(2)} - \sigma_{\delta\delta}^{(2)}]I_{(q_2+1)} & \cdots & 0 & 0 \quad -\underline{\beta}^{(2)} \cdots 0 & 0 \\ 0 \vdots 0 & 0 \vdots 0 & \cdots & 0 \vdots 0 & \cdots & \vdots \\ 0 & 0 & \cdots & [\omega_{xx}^{(n)} - \sigma_{\delta\delta}]I_{(q_n+1)} & 0 \quad 0 \quad -\underline{\beta}^{(n)} & 0 \\ D_{yx}^{(1)} & D_{yx}^{(2)} & \cdots & D_{yx}^{(n)} & 0 \cdots\cdots\cdots 0 & -\underline{\gamma}^{*} \end{pmatrix} \tag{2.15}$$

(columns: $\underline{\beta}^{(1)}$, $\underline{\beta}^{(2)}$, …, $\underline{\beta}^{(n)}$, $\sigma_{\delta\delta}^{(1)} \cdots\cdots \sigma_{\delta\delta}^{(n)}$, $\sigma_{\varepsilon\varepsilon}$)

The $(n+1) \times (q_i+1)$ matrices $D_{yx}^{(i)}$ are defined as:

(2.16) $D_{yx}^{(i)} =$

$$\begin{pmatrix}
0 & \omega_{yx}^{(i)} & \omega_{yx_{-1}}^{(i)} & \omega_{yx_{-2}}^{(i)} & \cdots & \omega_{yx_{-q_i+1}}^{(i)} \\
\vdots & 0 & \omega_{yx}^{(i)} & \omega_{yx_{-1}}^{(i)} & \cdots & \omega_{yx_{-q_i+2}}^{(i)} \\
\vdots & \vdots & 0 & \omega_{yx}^{(i)} & \cdots & \omega_{yx_{-q_i+3}}^{(i)} \\
\vdots & \vdots & \vdots & 0 & \ddots & \vdots \\
\vdots & \vdots & \vdots & \vdots & \ddots & \omega_{yx}^{(i)} \\
\vdots & \vdots & \vdots & \vdots & & 0 \\
\vdots & \vdots & \vdots & \vdots & & \vdots \\
0 & 0 & 0 & 0 & \cdots & 0
\end{pmatrix}$$

If $q_i < n + 1$, or $D_{yx}^{(i)} =$

$$\begin{pmatrix}
0 & \omega_{yx}^{(i)} & \omega_{yx_{-1}}^{(i)} & \omega_{yx_{-2}}^{(i)} & \cdots & & \omega_{yx_{-q_i+1}}^{(i)} \\
\vdots & 0 & \omega_{yx}^{(i)} & \omega_{yx_{-1}} & \cdots & & \omega_{yx_{-q_i+2}}^{(i)} \\
\vdots & \vdots & 0 & \omega_{yx}^{(i)} & & & \vdots \\
\vdots & \vdots & \vdots & 0 & \ddots & & \vdots \\
\vdots & \vdots & \vdots & \vdots & & \ddots & \vdots \\
0 & 0 & 0 & 0 \; - - - \; 0 & & \omega_{yx}^{(i)} \; \cdots & \omega_{yx_{-q_i+n+1}}^{(i)}
\end{pmatrix}$$

If $q_i \geq n + 1$

The $(n+1) \times 1$ vector $\underline{\gamma}^*$ is defined by

$$\underline{\gamma}^* = \begin{cases} (-\gamma_1, -\gamma_2, \ldots, -\gamma_{n+1})' & \text{if } p \geq n + 1 \\ (-\gamma_1, \ldots, -\gamma_p, 0, \ldots, 0)' & \text{if } p < n + 1. \end{cases}$$

Write the $D_{yx}^{(i)}$ matrix given by (2.16) as:

(2.17) $D_{yx}^{(i)} = (\underline{0}, \underline{d}_1^{(i)}, \ldots, \underline{d}_{q_i}^{(i)})$, so that $\underline{d}_j^{(i)}$ denotes the (j + 1)th column of the matrix $D_{yx}^{(i)}$. Define the sets of positive integers:

$$I_1 = \{i_1: 1, 2, \ldots, q_1\}, \quad I_2 = \{i_2: 1, 2, \ldots, q_2\}, \ldots,$$

$$I_n = \{i_n: 1, 2, \ldots, q_n\},$$

where i_j designates an element of the set I_j (j=1, ..., n). By systematically expanding J_I and all subsequent cofactors by the elements of the first row, it is obtained that the determinant of J_I can be expressed (in absolute value) by

$$(2.18) \qquad |J_I| = \prod_{i=1}^{n} [\sigma_{\zeta\zeta}^{(i)}]^{q_i} [\sum_{i_1=1}^{q_1} \sum_{i_2=1}^{q_2} \ldots \sum_{i_n=1}^{q_n} \beta_{i_1}^{(1)} \beta_{i_2}^{(2)} \ldots \beta_{i_n}^{(n)} \det D_{i_1 i_2 \ldots i_n}]$$

where $\sigma_{\zeta\zeta}^{(i)} = \omega_{xx}^{(i)} - \sigma_{\delta\delta}^{(i)}$, and $D_{i_1 i_2 \ldots i_n}$ is the following (n + 1) x (n + 1) matrix:

$$(2.19) \qquad D_{i_1 i_2 \ldots i_n} = (\underline{d}_{i_1}^{(1)}, \underline{d}_{i_2}^{(2)}, \ldots, \underline{d}_{i_n}^{(n)}, -\underline{\gamma}^*). \text{ 3/}$$

In Appendix A it is proved that if the conditions $q_j^* \geq j$, j = 1, 2, ..., n + 1, are met, then $|J_I| \neq 0$. This implies that J of expression (2.14) is nonsingular. This proves sufficiency. (Appendix A also illustrates the proof for a model with two exogenous variables, when p = 2, q_1 = 2, and q_2 = 3.)

3. SOME EXAMPLES AND CONCLUSIONS

The theorem states that, under our assumptions, when no additional constraints on the coefficients are imposed, identification of the model

$$G_p(L)\eta_t = \sum_{i=1}^{n} \beta_{q_i}^{(i)}(L)\zeta_t^{(i)} + u_t$$

depends only on the values taken by the subindices p, $q_1, \ldots, q_n$. The conditions stated in the theorem can be rewritten as follows: Let the exogenous variables appear according to increasing order of $q_1, \ldots, q_n$. Then, for the model to be identified, it has to be that

(1) when $p > q_n$, then $q_1 \geq 1, \ldots, q_n \geq n$

(2) when $q_1 \leq \cdots \leq q_{i_0-1} \leq p \leq q_{i_0} \leq \cdots q_n$ (for $i_0 = 2, \ldots, n$),

3/ An example is provided in Section 2, Appendix A.

then $q_1 \geq 1, \ldots, q_{i_0 - 1} \geq i_0 - 1$, $p \geq i_0$, $q_{i_0} \geq i_0 + 1, \ldots, q_n \geq n + 1$

(3) when $p < q_1$, then $p \geq 1$, $q_1 \geq 2, \ldots, q_n \geq n + 1$.

These conditions are simply "order conditions," yet they happen to be necessary and sufficient almost everywhere. The computation needed to check whether they are satisfied for any given model is trivial. Heuristically speaking, what Theorem 1 states is that the lag polynomials appearing in the structural equation have to have a minimum length in order for the model to be identified.

To illustrate the theorem, we shall discuss some particular applications. If we consider a univariate time series with no exogenous variables, identification of the model (a "pure autoregressive" equation), requires that $p \geq 1$.4/ If the equation contains an exogenous variable:

$$G_p(L)\eta_t = B_q(L)\zeta_t + u_t ,$$

then the necessary and sufficient conditions for identification are $q_j^* \geq j$, $j=1, 2$, which implies:

$$\min (p, q) \geq 1, \max (p, q) \geq 2.$$

To see another example, consider the three-exogenous variables equation:

$$\eta_t = \sum_{j=1}^{3} \gamma_j \eta_{t-j} + \sum_{j=0}^{2} \beta_j^{(1)} \zeta_{t-j}^{(1)} + \sum_{j=0}^{2} \beta_j^{(2)} \zeta_{t-j}^{(2)} + \sum_{j=0}^{3} \beta_j^{(3)} \zeta_{t-j}^{(3)} + u_t \qquad (2.20)$$

Here $p = 3$, $q_1 = q_2 = 2$, and $q_3 = 3$. Identification of the model requires that one of the q's has to be greater than or equal to $n + 1 = 4$, thus the model is not identified. Now, if a term, $\beta_4^{(3)}\zeta_{t-4}^{(3)}$, is added to the equation, so that $q_3 = 4$, we notice that

$$q_1 = q_1^* = 2 \geq 1; \; q_2 = q_2^* = 2 \geq 2; \; p = q_3^* = 3 \geq 3; \; q_3 = q_4^* = 4 \geq 4 ,$$

and the model is identified.

4/ The "pure autoregressive" model is given by the equation:

$$G_p(L)\eta_t = u_t ,$$

where u_t is white-noise.

For the special case in which all exogenous variables have the same set of lags:

$$G_q(L)\eta_t = \sum_{i=1}^{n} B_q^{(i)}(L)\, \zeta_t^{(i)} + u_t ,$$

so that $p = q_1 = \dots = q_k = q$. The necessary and sufficient condition for identification simply becomes

$$q \geq n + 1 .$$

We have been considering models where all the variable were measured with error. To relax this assumption, consider the general model given by (2.9) with only n_1 ($\leq n + 1$) of the variables being measured with error. To simplify notation, denote p by q_0. It is straightforward to verify that the theorem can be extended as follows:

Consider only the q_i's of the lag polynomials of the n_1 variables that are measured with error. Arrange these q_i's in increasing order, and let q_j^* denote the one occupying the jth place in this sequence. Then the model is identified if and only if $q_j^* \geq j$, $j = 1, \dots, n_1$.

To see an example, if in equation (2.20) one of the variables is measured without error, then the model becomes identified.

This concludes the analysis of the dynamic shock-error model when the shock and the exogenous variables are independent white-noise variables. The following chapters will extend the analysis to models under more general assumptions.

CHAPTER III

AUTOCORRELATED SHOCK; WHITE NOISE EXOGENOUS VARIABLES I

In the previous chapter we analyzed a dynamic shock-error model where the exogenous variables and the shock were assumed to be independent white-noise variables. We shall gradually relax these assumptions and, in this chapter, we start considering how the identification results of Chapter II, are affected when the shock is allowed to be autocorrelated. We shall see that different patterns of autocorrelation may have drastically different effects as far as identification of the model is concerned. In particular, we consider two cases:

a) the shock follows a (finite) Moving Average process (Model II)

b) the shock follows a (finite) Autoregressive process (Model III)

In the next chapter a more general model will be considered, where the shock follows an Autoregressive-Moving Average process.

1. MOVING AVERAGE PROCESS (MODEL II)

1.1 An Example

Let us go back to the one-exogenous-variable model analyzed in subsection 2.1.3, where the structural equation contains one lag on η and two lags on ζ. Under the assumption that the exogenous variable, ζ_t, and the shock, u_t, were independent white-noise variables, we concluded that the model was identified. In particular, we proved that the system of covariance equations contained a subsystem that could be solved for all unknown parameters of the model.

Let us maintain the white-noise assumption for ζ_t, but assume instead that u_t follows a first-order Moving Average process (MA(1)). Accordingly, we have

(2.7) $$\eta_t = \gamma_1\eta_{t-1} + \beta_0\zeta_t + \beta_1\zeta_{t-1} + \beta_2\zeta_{t-2} + u_t ,$$

(3.1) $$u_t = a_t + \theta_1 a_{t-1}$$

where a_t is white-noise, independent of $\zeta_{t-\tau}$ (for any value of τ). The complete system of covariance equations for (2.7) is the system of equations (2.8a to g), except for the fact that equations (2.8.e) and (2.8.f) are replaced by

(3.2.a) $\omega_{yy} = \gamma_1 \omega_{yy_{-1}} + \beta_0 \omega_{yx} + \beta_1 \omega_{yx_{-1}} + \beta_2 \omega_{yx_{-2}} + \sigma_{\varepsilon\varepsilon} + \sigma_{ya} + \theta_1 \sigma_{ya_{-1}}$

(3.2.b) $\omega_{yy_{-1}} = \gamma_1 (\omega_{yy}-\sigma_{\varepsilon\varepsilon}) + \beta_1 \omega_{yx} + \beta_2 \omega_{yx_{-1}} + \theta_1 \sigma_{ya}.$

Multiplying (3.1) by a_t and a_{t-1} in turn and taking expectations, noticing that, under our assumptions, $\sigma_{\eta a} = \sigma_{ya}$ and $\sigma_{\eta a_{-1}} = \sigma_{ya_{-1}}$, we find that

$$\sigma_{ya} = \sigma_{aa}$$

$$\sigma_{ya_{-1}} = (\gamma_1 + \theta_1)\, \sigma_{aa} \;.$$

Therefore, the covariance equations (3.2.a) and (3.2.b) can be rewritten:

(3.2.a´) $\omega_{yy} = \gamma_1 \omega_{yy_{-1}} + \beta_0 \omega_{yx} + \beta_1 \omega_{yx_{-1}} + \beta_2 \omega_{yx_{-2}} + \sigma_{\varepsilon\varepsilon} + (1+\theta_1 \gamma_1+\theta_1^2)\, \sigma_{aa}$

(3.2.b´) $\omega_{yy_{-1}} = \gamma_1 (\omega_{yy}-\sigma_{\varepsilon\varepsilon}) + \beta_1 \omega_{yx} + \beta_2 \omega_{yx_{-1}} + \theta_1 \sigma_{aa} \;.$

Now it is apparent that the system of covariance equations does not contain a subsystem that can be solved for all the parameters, as seven of the parameters (β_0, β_1, β_2, θ_1, σ_{aa}, $\sigma_{\delta\delta}$, and $\sigma_{\varepsilon\varepsilon}$) are contained in only six of the covariance equations (2.8.a, b, c, g; 3.2.a´, b´). Thus, a model that was identified when u_t was assumed to be white-noise becomes underidentified when u_t is assumed to follow an MA(1) process.

We shall see how the analysis can be extended to a model with n exogenous variables, when the shock u_t follows a Moving Average process of order s.

1.2. The General Case

Consider now Model II, where the structural equation is given by expression (2.9), and the shock, u_t, follows a Moving Average process of order s, [MA(s)]. The structural equation can be written as

(3.3.a) $G_p(L)\,\eta_t = \sum_{i=1}^{n} B_{q_i}^{(i)}(L)\,\zeta_t^{(i)} + u_t$

(3.3.b) $u_t = S_s(L)\,a_t$,

where $S_s(L) = 1 + \theta_1 L + \ldots + \theta_s L^s$, and , according to assumptions 1 and 4b, the characteristic roots of the polynomials G(L) and S(L) lie outside the unit circle. Let us analyze the system of covariance equations. Due to the fact that u_t follows an MA(s) process, the τ-lag autocovariance of u_t, for $\tau > s$, will be equal to zero. It follows that the τ-lag autocovariance equations for $\tau > s$, will not include the parameters $\theta_1, \ldots, \theta_s$, and σ_{aa}. Nor will these parameters appear in any τ-lag crosscovariance equation. Hence for the model to be identified it has to be that the system of τ-lag autocovariance equations for $\tau = 0, 1, \ldots, s$ (a system of s + 1 equations) can be solved for the (s + 1) parameters $\theta_1, \ldots, \theta_s$ and σ_{aa} in terms of the other parameters. Then, if the rest of the covariance equations can be solved for these other parameters as functions of the observable covariances, the model is identified. We shall prove (Lemma 2) that it is always true that the system of τ-lag autocovariance for $\tau = 0, 1, \ldots, s$, can be solved for the parameters $\theta_1, \ldots, \theta_s$ and σ_{aa} in terms of the other parameters of the model. The condition under which these other parameters are identified with the use of the rest of the covariance equations is stated in Theorem 2.

Lemma 2: The system of τ-lag autocovariance equations for $\tau = 0, 1, \ldots, s$ has a locally isolated solution for the parameters $\theta_1, \ldots, \theta_s$ and σ_{aa} (in terms of other parameters and observable covariances).

Proof: For $\tau = 0, 1, \ldots, s$, the system of τ-lag autocovariance equations can be written as follows:

$$\omega_{yy} = k_0 + \sigma_{\eta a} + \theta_1\,\sigma_{\eta a_{-1}} + \theta_2\,\sigma_{\eta a_{-2}} + \ldots + \theta_s\,\sigma_{\eta a} + \sigma_{\varepsilon\varepsilon}$$

$$\omega_{yy_{-1}} = k_1 + \theta_1\,\sigma_{\eta a} + \theta_2\,\sigma_{\eta a_{-1}} + \theta_3\,\sigma_{\eta a_{-2}} + \ldots + \theta_s\,\sigma_{\eta a_{-s+1}}$$

$$(3.4) \qquad \omega_{yy_{-2}} = k_2 + \qquad + \theta_2 \sigma_{\eta a} + \theta_3 \sigma_{\eta a_{-1}} + \dots + \theta_s \sigma_{\eta a_{-s+2}}$$

$$\text{---}$$

$$\omega_{yy_{-s}} = k_s + \qquad\qquad + \theta_s \sigma_{\eta a} \quad ,$$

where

$$k_\tau = \sum_{j=1}^{p} \gamma_j (\omega_{yy_{-j+\tau}} - d_{j\tau} \sigma_{\varepsilon\varepsilon}) + \sum_{i=1}^{n} \sum_{j=0}^{q_i} \beta_j^{(i)} \omega_{yx_{-j+\tau}}^{(i)} , \quad \tau = 0, \dots, s$$

and

$$d_{j\tau} = \begin{cases} 1 \text{ if } j = \tau \\ 0 \text{ otherwise.} \end{cases}$$

(Notice that, under our assumptions, $\sigma_{\eta a_{-\tau}} = \sigma_{ya_{-\tau}}$, $\tau = 0, 1, \dots, s$). This system can be written:

$$(3.5) \qquad \underline{\omega}_{yy} = \underline{k} + \Theta \underline{\sigma}_{\eta a} ,$$

where: $\underline{\omega}_{yy} = (\omega_{yy}, \dots, \omega_{yy_{-s}})'$, $\underline{k} = (k_0, \dots, k_s)'$, $\underline{\sigma}_{\eta a} = (\sigma_{\eta a}, \sigma_{\eta a_{-1}}, \dots, \sigma_{\eta a_{-s}})'$, and Θ is the $(s + 1) \times (s + 1)$ triangular matrix:

$$(3.6) \qquad \Theta = \begin{pmatrix} 1 & \theta_1 & \theta_2 & \dots & \theta_{s-1} & \theta_s \\ \theta_1 & \theta_2 & \theta_3 & \dots & \theta_s & 0 \\ \theta_2 & \theta_3 & & \dots & 0 & 0 \\ \text{--} & \text{--} & \text{--} & \text{--} & \text{--} & \text{--} \\ \theta_{s-1} & \theta_s & 0 & \dots & 0 & 0 \\ \theta_s & 0 & 0 & \dots & 0 & 0 \end{pmatrix}$$

The vector $\underline{\sigma}_{\eta a}$ itself is a function of the θ-parameters and σ_{aa}. This function can be obtained as follows: multiply both sides of equation (3.3) by $a_{t-\tau}$ and take expectations for $\tau = 0, 1, 2, \dots, s$. The following system of equations is obtained:

$$
\begin{aligned}
\sigma_{\eta a} &= && && && && \sigma_{aa} \\
\sigma_{\eta a_{-1}} &= \gamma_1\, \sigma_{\eta a} && && && && +\, \theta_1\, \sigma_{aa} \\
\sigma_{\eta a_{-2}} &= \gamma_1\, \sigma_{\eta a_{-1}} && +\, \gamma_2\, \sigma_{\eta a} && && && +\, \theta_2\, \sigma_{aa} \\
&\cdots \\
\sigma_{\eta a_{-s}} &= \gamma_1\, \sigma_{\eta a_{-s+1}} && +\, \gamma_2\, \sigma_{\eta a_{-s+2}} && +\, \ldots && +\, \gamma_s\, \sigma_{\eta a} && +\, \theta_s\, \sigma_{aa}
\end{aligned}
$$

or:

(3.7) $$\Gamma\, \underline{\sigma}_{\eta a} = \underline{\theta}^{*}\, \sigma_{aa},$$

where $\underline{\theta}^{*} = (1, \theta_1, \ldots, \theta_s)'$, and Γ is the matrix

(3.8) $$\Gamma = \begin{pmatrix} 1 & 0 & 0 & \cdots & 0 \\ -\gamma_1 & 1 & 0 & \cdots & 0 \\ -\gamma_2 & -\gamma_1 & 1 & \cdots & 0 \\ \vdots & & & & \vdots \\ -\gamma_s & -\gamma_{s-1} & -\gamma_{s-2} & \cdots & 1 \end{pmatrix}$$

(Notice that $\gamma_s = 0$ if $p < s$). Since Γ is nonsingular, from (3.7),

$$\sigma_{\underline{\eta} a} = \Gamma^{-1}\, \underline{\theta}^{*}\, \sigma_{aa} \,.$$

Substituting for $\sigma_{\underline{\eta} a}$ in (3.5), the system of τ-lag autocovariance equations can be rewritten:

(3.9) $$\underline{\omega}_{yy} = \underline{A} + \sigma_{aa}\, \Gamma^{-1}\, \underline{\theta}^{*} \,.$$

Lemma 2 would be proved if we prove that the Jacobian of this system of equations with respect to the parameters σ_{aa} and $\theta_1, \ldots, \theta_s$ is nonsingular. Denote this Jacobian by J_θ, and define the vectors $\underline{\theta} = (\theta_1, \ldots, \theta_s)'$ and $\underline{\ell} = \Theta^{-1}\, \underline{\theta}^{*}$. As $\underline{A}$ does not include $\underline{\theta}$ or σ_{aa}, we have that

(3.10) $$J_\theta = \left(\frac{\partial(\underline{\ell}\, \sigma_{aa})}{\partial\, \sigma_{aa}} \;\vdots\; \frac{\partial(\underline{\ell}\, \sigma_{aa})}{\partial\, \underline{\theta}} \right) = \left(\underline{\ell} \;\vdots\; \sigma_{aa} \frac{\partial \underline{\ell}}{\partial \underline{\theta}} \right)$$

To express $\underline{\ell}$ and $\frac{\partial \underline{\ell}}{\partial \underline{\theta}}$ as functions of the parameters of the model, we notice that the matrix Γ^{-1} can be written as

$$\Gamma^{-1} = \begin{pmatrix} 1 & 0 & 0 & \cdots & 0 \\ g_{21} & 1 & 0 & \cdots & 0 \\ g_{31} & g_{32} & 1 & \cdots & 0 \\ - & - & - & - & - \\ g_{s+1,1} & g_{s+1,2} & g_{s+1,3} & & 1 \end{pmatrix}$$

where g_{ij} ($j = 1, 2, \ldots, i-1$; $i=2, 3, \ldots, s+1$) denotes a polynomial in the γ-parameters with no constant term.[1/] It follows that the vector $\underline{\ell}$ will be equal

---

1/ Lemma: Denote by g_{ij} the $(i, j)^{th}$ element of the matrix Γ^{-1}. Then:

$$g_{ij} = \begin{cases} 0 \text{ for } i > j; \\ 1 \text{ for } i = j; \\ \text{a polynomial in the } \gamma\text{-parameters, with no constant term, for } i < j. \end{cases}$$

Proof: Since the matrix Γ is lower triangular, its inverse will be also lower triangular, thus $g_{ij} = 0$ for $i < j$. As the elements of the main diagonal of Γ are ones, the cofactor of the (i,i) element will be the determinant of a lower triangular matrix with ones in the main diagonal, thus $g_{ij} = 1$ for $i = j$. Finally, the $(i, j)^{th}$ element of Γ^{-1} for $i > j$ will be the cofactor of the $(j, i)^{th}$ element of Γ (since det. $\Gamma = 1$). These cofactors will be determinants of matrices with all elements below the main diagonal being γ-parameters (or zero), and at least one element of the main diagonal being also a γ-parameter. It follows that g_{ij} will be a polynomial in $\gamma_1, \ldots, \gamma_p$, with no constant term.

To see an example, for the case s=3, p=2, the matrix:

$$\Gamma = \begin{pmatrix} 1 & 0 & 0 & 0 \\ -\gamma_1 & 1 & 0 & 0 \\ -\gamma_2 & -\gamma_1 & 1 & 0 \\ 0 & -\gamma_2 & -\gamma_1 & 1 \end{pmatrix}$$

to:

$$(3.11)\qquad \underline{\ell} = \Theta\Gamma^{-1}\,\underline{\theta}^* = \begin{pmatrix} 1 + \sum_{k=2}^{s+1} \underline{g}_k'\,\underline{\theta}^*\,\theta_{k-1} \\ \theta_1 + \sum_{k=2}^{s} \underline{g}_k'\,\underline{\theta}^*\,\theta_k \\ \vdots \\ \theta_i + \sum_{k=2}^{s-i+1} \underline{g}_k'\,\underline{\theta}^*\,\theta_{k+i-1} \\ \vdots \\ \theta_s \end{pmatrix}$$

where g_i' denotes the ith row of Γ^{-1}, and

$$(3.12)\qquad \underline{g}_i'\,\underline{\theta}^* = g_{i1} + g_{i2}\,\theta_1 + \ldots + g_{i,i-1}\,\theta_{i-2} + \theta_{i-1}$$

for i = 2, 3, ..., s+1.

According to the last equality in (3.11), $\underline{\ell}$ can be expressed as:

1/ (continued)

has the inverse:

$$\Gamma^{-1} = \begin{pmatrix} 1 & 0 & 0 & 0 \\ \gamma_1 & 1 & 0 & 0 \\ \gamma_1^2 + \gamma_2 & \gamma_1 & 1 & 0 \\ \gamma_1^3 + 2\gamma_1\gamma_2 & \gamma_1^2 + \gamma_2 & \gamma_1 & 1 \end{pmatrix}$$

$$(3.13) \qquad \underline{\ell} = \begin{pmatrix} 1 + m_{10} \\ m_{20} \\ \vdots \\ m_{s+1,0} \end{pmatrix} ,$$

where $m_{10}, \ldots, m_{s+1,0}$ are polynomials in the γ and θ-parameters not involving a constant term. Let ℓ_i denote the ith element of the vector $\underline{\ell}$. From (3.11) and (3.12),

$$\frac{\partial \ell_i}{\partial \theta_j} = \underline{g}'_{j-i+2}\, \underline{\theta}^* + \sum_{k=j+1}^{s} g_{k,j+1}\, \theta_{k+i-2} \quad .$$

Thus, all elements $\frac{\partial \ell_i}{\partial \theta_j}$ will be polynomials in the γ and θ-parameters that do not involve a constant term, except for the case when $\underline{g}'_{j-i+2}\, \underline{\theta}^* = \underline{g}'_1\, \underline{\theta}^* = 1$. In this last case, it has to be that $j-i+2 = 1$, or $j = i-1$. Thus we can write

$$(3.14) \qquad \frac{\partial \ell_i}{\partial \theta_j} = \begin{cases} m_{ij} & \text{if } j \neq i-1 \\ 1 + m_{i,j} & \text{if } j = i-1, \end{cases}$$

where m_{ij} $(i = 1, \ldots, s+1;\ j = 1, \ldots, s)$ is, again, a polynomial in the γ and θ-parameters, not involving a constant term.

Define

$$(3.15) \qquad m^*_{i,j+1} = m_{i,j} , \quad \begin{cases} i = 1, 2, \ldots, s+1 \\ j = 0, 1, \ldots, s \quad . \end{cases}$$

Considering (3.13), (3.14), and (3.15), the matrix given by (3.10) will have a determinant equal to:

$$\det J_\theta = \sigma^s_{aa} \det \begin{pmatrix} 1 + m^*_{11} & m^*_{12} & \cdots & m^*_{1,s+1} \\ m^*_{21} & 1 + m^*_{22} & \cdots & m^*_{2,s+1} \\ \hdashline m^*_{s+1,1} & m^*_{s+1,2} & \cdots & 1+m^*_{s+1,s+1} \end{pmatrix}$$

hence

$$\det J_\theta = \sigma^s_{aa}\, [1 + m(\underline{\gamma}, \underline{\theta})],$$

where $m(\underline{\gamma}, \underline{\theta})$ is a polynomial in the γ and θ-parameters not involving a constant term. As $m(\underline{\gamma}, \underline{\theta}) + 1 = 0$ represents a set of zero measure in the admissible parameter space, det J_θ will be different from zero almost everywhere and Lemma 2 is proved.

Thus, as we mentioned previously, Lemma 2 implies that the first $(s + 1)$ autocovariance equations can be used to identify $\underline{\theta}$ and σ_{aa} if the rest of the covariance equations can identify the rest of the parameters. Before we proceed to analyse the conditions under which these last parameters are identified, we state a result on partial identification.

Lemma 3: In model II, the autoregressive parameters $\gamma_1, \gamma_2, \ldots, \gamma_p$ are identified.

Proof: For $\tau > \max(p, q_n, s)$, the τ-lag autocovariance equations follows the difference equation given by (2.10), and the rest of the proof parallels the proof of Lemma 1.

The analysis of the complete identification of model II is a straightforward extension of the analysis in Chapter II, that takes into consideration the fact that the τ-lag autocovariance equations for $\tau = 0, 1, \ldots, s$ now include the Moving Average parameters, $\theta_1, \ldots, \theta_s$ and σ_{aa}. Except for these autocovariance equations, the system of covariance equations is identical to the corresponding one for Model I. Consequently, the necessary and sufficient conditions for identification of the complete model are presented in the following Theorem.

Theorem 2: Let q_j^* $(j = 1, 2, \ldots, n + 1)$ be defined as in Theorem 1. Then Model II is identified if and only if

$$q_j^* \geqq j + s, \qquad j = 1, 2, \ldots, n + 1 .$$

Proof of the Theorem:

Necessity: Suppose that the condition of Theorem 2 does not hold, and let j^0 be the smallest j such that $q_j^* < j + s$. The proof is analogous to the corresponding one for Model I except that now we have to allow for the fact that the θ-coefficients and σ_{aa} appear in the τ-lag autocovariance equations for $\tau = 0, 1, \ldots, s$. We illustrate the proof for the case $p \geq j^0$; for the case $p < j^0$, similar modifications have to be performed.

Let $p \geqq j^0$. Then it has to be that $q_j^* = q_j$ for $j \leqq j^0$. The parameters in $\underline{\beta}^{(j)}$, along with $\sigma_{\delta\delta}^{(j)}$, $j \leq j^0$, only appear in the following covariance equations:

i) the τ-lag crosscovariance equation corresponding to the jth exogenous variable, for $\tau = 0, 1, \ldots, q_j^*$ and $j \leq j^0$, (a total of $\sum_{j=1}^{j^0} q_j^* + j^0$ equations);

ii) the τ-lag autocovariance equations for $\tau = 0, 1, \ldots, q_{j^0}^*$, (a total of $q_{j^0}^* + 1$ equations).

The parameters $\theta_1, \ldots, \theta_s$ and σ_{aa} only appear in the τ-lag autocovariance equations for $\tau = 0, 1, \ldots, s$. (Notice that this set of equations overlaps with the second set discussed above).

Thus, the total number of equations is $\{\sum_{j=1}^{j^0} q_j^* + j^0 + \max(s, q_{j^0}^*) + 1\}$, while the total number of parameters to be identified by these equations is:

parameters in $\underline{\beta}^{(j)}$, for $j \leq j^0$: $\sum_{j=1}^{j^0} q_1^* + j^0$;

parameters $\sigma_{\delta\delta}^{(1)}, \ldots, \sigma_{\delta\delta}^{(j^0)}$: j^0;

parameters $\theta_1, \ldots, \theta_s$ and σ_{aa}: $s + 1$

Hence, the total number of parameters is $\{\sum_{j=1}^{j^0} q_j^* + 2j^0 + s + 1\}$. Clearly if $q_{j^0}^* < j^0 + s$, it has to be that $\max(s, q_{j^0}^*) < j^0 + s$, and the number of parameters exceeds the number of equations. Then Model II is not identified.

<u>Sufficiency</u>: Consider the following system of covariance equations:

i) τ-lag autocovariance equations for $\tau > \max(p, q_n, s)$;

ii) τ-lag autocovariance equations for $\tau = 0, 1, \ldots, s$;

iii) τ-lag crosscovariance equations for $\tau = 0, 1, \ldots, q_i$ $(i = 1, 2, \ldots, n)$, and τ-lag autocovariance equations for $\tau = s + 1, s + 2, \ldots, s + n + 1$.

The Jacobian of this system with respect to the parameters of Model II can be partitioned as follows:

$$J_{II} = \left(\begin{array}{c|c|c} \gamma\text{-parameters} & \theta\text{-parameters plus } \sigma_{aa} & \text{Other parameters} \\ J_{11} & 0 & 0 \\ \hline J_{21} & J_{22} & J_{23} \\ \hline J_{31} & 0 & J_{33} \end{array}\right) \begin{array}{l} \text{covariance equations in i)} \\ \text{covariance equations in ii)} \\ \text{covariance equations in iii)} \end{array}$$

Lemma 3 implies that the matrix J_{11} is nonsingular. Also, J_{22} is the Jacobian J_θ which was proved nonsingular in Lemma 2. It follows that J_{II} will have full column rank (and the model will be identified) if and only if the matrix J_{33} has full rank. We shall prove that $q_j^* \geq j + s$ ($j = 1, 2, \ldots, n + 1$) is a sufficient condition for that to happen.

The matrix J_{33} is the Jacobian of the system of equations in iii with respect to the parameters in $\underline{\beta}^{(1)}, \ldots, \underline{\beta}^{(n)}, \sigma_{\delta\delta}^{(1)}, \ldots, \sigma_{\delta\delta}^{(n)}$ and $\sigma_{\varepsilon\varepsilon}$. In particular, J_{33} is a $(\sum_{i=1}^{n} q_i + 2n + 1) \times (\sum_{i=1}^{n} q_i + 2n + 1)$ matrix, which can be written in the form of J_I of (2.15) except for the fact that $D_{yx}^{(i)}$ is now the $(n + 1) \times (q_i + 1)$ matrix:

$$(3.16) \qquad D_{yx}^{(i)} = \begin{pmatrix} 0 & \ldots & 0 & \omega_{yx}^{(i)} & \omega_{yx_{-1}}^{(i)} & \ldots\ldots & \omega_{yx_{-q_i+s+1}}^{(i)} \\ \vdots & & \vdots & 0 & \omega_{yx}^{(i)} & \ldots\ldots & \omega_{yx_{-q_i+s+2}}^{(i)} \\ \vdots & & \vdots & \vdots & 0 & & \vdots \\ \vdots & & \vdots & \vdots & \vdots & & \vdots \\ 0 & \ldots & 0 & 0 & 0 & \ldots\ldots & \omega_{yx_{-q_i+s+n-1}}^{(i)} \end{pmatrix}$$

(s+1) columns

$i = 1, \ldots, n$, and the vector $\underline{\gamma}^*$ becomes the $(n + 1)$-dimensional vector:

$$\underline{\gamma}^* = \begin{cases} (\gamma_{s+1}, \ldots, \gamma_{s+n+1})' & \text{if } p \geq s + n + 1 , \\ (\gamma_{s+1}, \ldots, \gamma_p, 0, \ldots, 0)' & \text{if } p < s + n + 1 . \end{cases}$$

(Notice that $\omega_{yx_{-q_i+\tau}} = 0$ whenever $\tau > q_i$).

The rest of the proof is analogous to the proof that the Jacobian J_I given by (2.15) is nonsingular (Appendix A), except for the following modifications:

Expression (A.1) changes to:

$$\sum_{i_1=s+1}^{q_1} \sum_{i_2=s+1}^{q_2} \cdots \sum_{i_n=s+1}^{q_n} \beta_{i_1}^{(i)} \beta_{i_2}^{(i)} \cdots \beta_{i_n}^{(n)} \det D_{i_1 i_2 \ldots i_n} = 0. \tag{3.17}$$

Assume $p > n + s$. The proof in Appendix A (case $p > n$) has to be modified as follows: Let $i_1 = s + 1$, $i_2 = s + 2, \ldots, i_n = s + n$, the matrix $D_{s+1,\, s+2,\, \ldots,\, s+n}$ has a determinant given by (A.2). The summation term (A.3) becomes

$$-\gamma_{s+n+1} \prod_{i=1}^{n} \beta_{i+s}^{(i)} \beta_0^{(i)} \sigma_{\zeta\zeta}^{(i)} \quad . \tag{3.18}$$

If $q_i = i + s$ $(i = 1, \ldots, n)$, no vector $d_\ell^{(i)}$ with $\ell > i + s$ appears in the $D_{yx}^{(i)}$-matrices. If, for some i, $q_i > i + s$, then the $D_{i_1 i_2 \ldots i_n}$ matrices of expression (3.17) that have nonzero determinant (different from (A.2)) contain a column of the form $\underline{d}_\ell^{(i)}$ with $\ell > i + s$. Thus, considering (3.17), any nonzero summation term different from (3.18) has to contain a coefficient $\beta_\ell^{(i)}$ $(\ell > i + s)$ that never appears in (3.18). Thus, the equation (3.17) will only hold on a zero measure set on the parameter space. It follows that J_{33} has full column rank, and the model is identified.

The proof for the second case $(p \leq n + s)$ is a similar extension of the proof that J_I is nonsingular when $p \leq n$, contained in Appendix A.

1.3 Some Examples and Conclusions

Going back to the example analysed at the beginning of the chapter (equations (2.7) and (3.1)), for this model $q_1^* = 1$, $q_2^* = 2$, $s = 1$. According to Theorem 2, the conditions for identification for a one-exogenous-variable model with $s = 1$ are $q_1^* \geqq 2$, $q_2^* \geqq 3$, thus the model is not identified. If, for example, the structural equation of the model is given by

$$\eta_t = \gamma_1 \eta_{t-1} + \gamma_2 \eta_{t-2} + \beta_0 \zeta_t + \beta_1 \zeta_{t-1} + \beta_2 \zeta_{t-2} + \beta_3 \zeta_{t-3} + u_t \ ,$$

and the shock follows the MA(1) process of equation (3.1), then Theorem 2 implies that the model is identified.

An interesting particular case of Model II is when $n = 0$. Then, the structural equation becomes a univariate "Autoregressive-Moving Average" process:

$$G_p(L)\eta_t = S_s(L)a_t,$$

This is the ARMA (p, s) process considered in Box-Jenkins [1970]. Using Theorem 2, we find that an ARMA (p, s) process, where the variable is observed with error, is identified if and only if

$$p \geq s + 1.$$

It seems worthwhile to compare this result with two other properties of ARMA models:

a) In Pandit [1973; p. 288] it is proved that a continous stationary stochastic process can be approximated by an ARMA (p, s) process for which $s = p - 1$.

b) Brewer [1973; p. 141] has proved that an ARMA (p, s) series of which only every kth term is observed ("systematic sampling") is appropriately estimated as an ARMA (p, p - 1), if k is large and $q \leqq p$.

Thus, if an ARMA (p, s) model is used as an approximation to a continuous process or as the process obtained by sampling an underlying ARMA process at equally spaced (relatively large) intervals, then it has to be that $p = s + 1$. Therefore, if for this ARMA process the variable is measured with error, the model is identified.

Going back to the general case, if we compare the result in Theorem 2 with the one in Theorem 1, it is seen that the introduction of a Moving Average assumption for the shock may destroy the identification of a model with white-noise shock. In fact, the necessary and sufficient conditions for Model II to be identified are more restrictive than the corresponding ones for Model I; in this sense, we can say that the Moving Average assumption decreases identification.

As we mentioned in subsection 2.1.2, this effect is, in some way, a consequence of the fact that for moving average processes, only a finite number of autocorrelations are nonzero. The question of what are the effects of processes with different patterns of autocorrelation is analyzed in the next sections.

2. AUTOREGRESSIVE PROCESS

2.1. The General Case (Model III)

We shall assume now that the shock u_t is generated by a process with an autocorrelation function that does not vanish after a finite number of lags. In particular, let u_t in the equation

$$G_p(L)\eta_t = \sum_{i=1}^{n} B_{q_i}^{(i)}(L)\,\zeta_t^{(i)} + u_t \tag{3.19}$$

follow a stationary Autoregressive process of order r, [AR(r)], given by the equation:

$$u_t = \rho_1 u_{t-1} + \ldots + \rho_r u_{t-r} + a_t\ , \tag{3.20.a}$$

where a_t is white-noise, independent of $\zeta^{(i)}$, $\delta^{(i)}$ $(i = 1, \ldots, n)$ and ε. Equation (3.20a) can be rewritten as

$$R_r(L)\, u_t = a_t\ , \tag{3.20b}$$

where $R_r(L) = 1 - \rho_1 L - \rho_2 L^2 - \ldots - \rho_r L^r$, and according to assumptions 1 and 4b, the roots of the polynomials G(L) and R(L) lie outside the unit circle.

As in the previous cases, in order to analyze identification of Model III we shall consider the system of covariance equations. Due to the fact that the variables u and $\zeta^{(i)}$, $i = 1, \ldots, n$, are independent, the cross covariance equations for Model III are the same as for Model I. On the other hand, due to the nonzero lagged autocorrelations of u, the autocovariance equations for Model III will include the new terms, $\sigma_{uy_{-\tau}}$ $(= E(u_t\, y_{t-\tau}))$, which will be nonzero for all $\tau \geq 0$. We establish first a result on partial identification.

Lemma 4: The autoregressive parameters $\gamma_1, \ldots, \gamma_p, \rho_1, \ldots, \rho_r$ and the variance σ_{aa} are identified.

Proof of Lemma 4: For $\tau > \max(p, q_i)$ the τ-lag crosscovariance equations between y and $x^{(i)}$ follows the pth-order linear homogenous difference equation:

$$\omega_{yx_{-\tau}}^{(i)} = \gamma_1 \omega_{yx_{-\tau+1}} + \ldots + \gamma_p \omega_{yx_{-\tau+p}}^{(i)}\ . \tag{3.21.a}$$

From this, applying the same reasoning as for the case of Lemma 1, it follows that the coefficients $\gamma_1, \ldots, \gamma_p$ are identified. We shall prove that the τ-lag autocovariance equations for $\tau > \max(p, q_n)$ identify the parameters $\rho_1, \ldots, \rho_r$ and σ_{aa}.

Consider the τ-lag autocovariance equation for $\tau > \max(p, q_n)$:

$$(3.21.b) \quad \omega_{yy_{-\tau}} = \sum_{i=1}^{p} \gamma_i \omega_{yy_{-\tau+i}} + \sigma_\tau$$

where, in order to simplify notation, $\sigma_\tau = \sigma_{uy_{-\tau}}$. Since the γ-parameters are identified, equation (3.21b) implies that the covariance σ_τ is identified also, for $\tau > \max(p, q_n)$.

Multiplying (3.20a) by $y_{t-\tau}$ and taking expectations, the following system of equations is obtained:

$$(3.22) \quad \begin{array}{lcl} \sigma_\tau & = & \rho_1\sigma_{\tau-1} + \ldots + \rho_r\sigma_{\tau-r} \\ \vdots & & \vdots \qquad\qquad\quad \vdots \\ \sigma_{\tau+r-1} & = & \rho_1\sigma_{\tau+r-2} + \ldots + \rho_r\sigma_\tau \end{array}$$

Letting $\tau-r > \max(p, q_n)$, it follows that all the σ-covariances of this system of equations are identified. Thus the system (3.22) can be solved for the parameters $\rho_1, \ldots, \rho_r$, so that these parameters are identified.

Once the γ and ρ-parameters are identified, it is easily seen that the variance σ_{aa} is identified also.

Define the autocovariance generating function for u:

$$\sigma_{uu}(L) = \sum_{\tau=-\infty}^{\infty} \sigma_{uu_{-\tau}} L^\tau ,$$

and the crosscovariance generating function between the variables u and y:

$$\sigma_{uy}(L) = \sum_{\tau=-\infty}^{\infty} \sigma_\tau L^\tau ,$$

Equation (3.20b) implies:[2/]

$$(3.23) \quad \sigma_{uu}(L) = [R_r(L)\, R_r(L^{-1})]^{-1} \sigma_{aa} ,$$

2/ See Box-Jenkins [1970, p. 49], equation (3.1.11).

and equation (3.19) implies[3/]

(3.24) $\sigma_{uy}(L) = G_p(L)^{-1}\,\sigma_{uu}(L)$,

where use has been made of the fact that u and $\zeta^{(i)}$ are independent for i = 1, 2, ..., n. Substituting for $\sigma_{uu}(L)$ in (3.24) with (3.23) and equating the coefficients of L^τ in both sides of the resulting equation, we obtain

(3.25) $\sigma_\tau = \bar{\rho}_\tau\,\sigma_{aa}$

where $\bar{\rho}_\tau$ is a function of the γ and ρ-parameters (i.e., the coefficient of L^τ in the polynomial $[G_p(L)R_r(L)R_r(L^{-1})]^{-1}$). Thus letting $\tau > \max(p, q_n)$, the parameter σ_{aa} is identified through equation (3.25). This completes the proof of Lemma 4. In the next section an example will illustrate the proof.

Corollary 1: The autocovariances of the shock u are identified.

Proof: From equation (3.23) it follows that the autocovariance generating function for u is a function of the ρ-parameter and of σ_{aa}. As these parameters are identified, the Corollary is proved.

This Corollary represents the main difference with respect to the analysis of Model I: when u_t was white-noise, the only covariance equation that included the parameter σ_{uu} was the 0-lag autocovariance equation. For the case of Model III, σ_{uu} can be identified through a τ-lag autocovariance equation with $\tau > \max(p, q_n)$, which for the case of Model I, could only be used to identify the γ-parameters. Also, in Model I, only the 0-lag autocovariance equation included σ_{uu}. Therefore, in Model III, this 0-lag autocovariance equation is not anymore needed to identify σ_{uu} and can be incorporated to the system of covariance equations that has to provide a solution for the β-parameters plus the variances $\sigma_{\delta\delta}$ and $\sigma_{\varepsilon\varepsilon}$.

We can state now the necessary and sufficient conditions for identification of Model III.

3/ See Box-Jenkins [1970, p. 414], equation (A.11.1.3).

Theorem 3: Let q_j^* $(j = 1, 2, \ldots, n + 1)$ be defined as in Theorem 1. Then Model III is identified if and only if

$$q_j^* \geqq j - 1 , \qquad j = 1, \ldots, n + 1.$$

Proof of Theorem 3: From Lemma 4 we know that the γ, ρ and σ_{aa} parameters are identified. Thus, Theorem 3 will be proved if we prove that the condition $q_j^* \geqq j - 1$, $j = 1, \ldots, n + 1$, is necessary and sufficient for a system of covariance equations, not overlapping with the ones used in Lemma 4, to have a Jacobian with respect to the parameters in $\underline{\beta}^{(1)}, \ldots, \underline{\beta}^{(n)}$, $\underline{\sigma}_{\delta\delta}$, and $\sigma_{\varepsilon\varepsilon}$ of full column rank. The following two results are direct implications of our assumptions:

a) The crosscovariance equations for Model III are exactly the same as the corresponding ones for Model I.

b) The autocovariance equations for Model III differ from the corresponding ones for Model I only be the term, $\sigma_{uy_{-\tau}}$. This term does not depend on the β, $\sigma_{\delta\delta}$, and $\sigma_{\varepsilon\varepsilon}$-parameters.

Thus, the proof of Theorem 3 is analogous to the proof of Theorem 1, except for the fact that in the present case, the 0-lag autocovariance equation can be included in the system of covariance equations that can be solved for the β, $\sigma_{\delta\delta}$, and $\sigma_{\varepsilon\varepsilon}$-parameters. We proceed to illustrate how the proof of Theorem 1 has to be modified in order to prove Theorem 3.

Necessity: We consider only the case $p \geqq j^0$; the case $p < j^0$ can be extended in a parallel way. The subindex j^0 denotes now the smallest j for which $q_j^* < j - 1$. The parameter σ_{uu} does not have to be considered.

Thus, the number of parameters becomes

$$\sum_{j=1}^{j^0} q_j^* + 2j^0,$$

and the number of equations remains the same: $\sum_{j=1}^{j^0} q_j^* + q_{j^0}^* + j^0 + 1$. Thus, if $q_{j^0}^* + 1 < j^0$, not enough equations contain a set of the unknown parameters, and Model III cannot be identified.

<u>Sufficiency</u>: The format of the Jacobian of (2.15) remains unchanged, but the matrix $D_{yx}^{(i)}$ and the vector $\underline{\gamma}^*$ are given now by the expressions:

(3.26) $D_{yx}^{(i)} =$

$$\begin{pmatrix} \omega_{yx}^{(i)} & \omega_{yx_{-1}}^{(i)} & \omega_{yx_{-2}}^{(i)} & \cdots & \omega_{yx_{-q_i+1}}^{(i)} \\ 0 & \omega_{yx}^{(i)} & \omega_{yx_{-1}}^{(i)} & \cdots & \omega_{yx_{-q_i+2}}^{(i)} \\ \vdots & 0 & \omega_{yx}^{(i)} & \cdots & \omega_{yx_{-q_i+3}}^{(i)} \\ \vdots & \vdots & 0 & \ddots & \vdots \\ \vdots & \vdots & \vdots & & \omega_{yx}^{(i)} \\ \vdots & \vdots & \vdots & & 0 \\ \vdots & \vdots & \vdots & & \vdots \\ 0 & 0 & 0 & \cdots & 0 \end{pmatrix}$$

if $q_i < n$, or $D_{yx}^{(i)} =$

$$\begin{pmatrix} \omega_{yx}^{(i)} & \omega_{yx_{-1}}^{(i)} & \omega_{yx_{-2}}^{(i)} & \cdots & \cdots & \omega_{yx_{-q_i+1}}^{(i)} \\ 0 & \omega_{yx}^{(i)} & \omega_{yx_{-1}}^{(i)} & \cdots & \cdots & \omega_{yx_{-q_i+2}}^{(i)} \\ \vdots & 0 & \omega_{yx}^{(i)} & & & \vdots \\ \vdots & \vdots & 0 & \ddots & & \vdots \\ \vdots & \vdots & \vdots & & \ddots & \vdots \\ 0 & 0 & 0 - - 0 & & \omega_{yx}^{(i)} & \cdots \omega_{yx_{-q_i+n+1}}^{(i)} \end{pmatrix}$$

if $q_i \geq n$,

$$(3.27) \qquad -\underline{\gamma}^* = \begin{cases} (1, -\gamma_1, \gamma_2, \ldots, -\gamma_n)', & \text{if } p \geq n \\ (1, -\gamma_1, \ldots, -\gamma_p, 0, \ldots, 0)' & \text{if } p < n . \end{cases}$$

Notice that these modifications correspond to the fact that the 0-lag autocovariance equation can be used to identify the β, $\sigma_{\delta\delta}$, and $\sigma_{\varepsilon\varepsilon}$-parameters. In particular, the elements of the first row of $D_{yx}^{(i)}$ in (3.26) and of $\underline{\gamma}^*$ in (3.27) are the derivatives of the 0-lag autocovariance equation with respect to the coefficients

$\beta_0^{(i)}, \ldots, \beta_{q_i}^{(i)}$, and with respect to the parameter $\sigma_{\varepsilon\varepsilon}$, respectively.

The matrix $D_{yx}^{(i)}$ can be written as:

$$D_{yx}^{(i)} = (\underline{d}_0^{(i)}, \underline{d}_1^{(i)}, \ldots, \underline{d}_{q_i}^{(i)}) ,$$

and expression (2.18) becomes:

$$(3.28) \qquad |J_{III}| = \prod_{i=1}^{n} [\sigma_{\zeta\zeta}^{(i)}]^{q_i} [\sum_{i_1=0}^{q_1} \sum_{i_2=0}^{q_2} \cdots \sum_{i_n=0}^{q_n} \beta_{i_1}^{(1)} \beta_{i_2}^{(2)} \cdots \beta_{i_n}^{(n)} \det D_{i_1 i_2 \ldots i_n}]$$

where $D_{i_1 i_2 \ldots i_n}$ was defined in expression (2.19). Consider the case $p > n-1$. Set $i_1 = 0$, $i_2 = 1$, ..., $i_n = n-1$ so that the matrix

$$(3.29) \qquad D_{0,1,\ldots,n-1} = (\underline{d}_0^{(1)}, \underline{d}_1^{(2)}, \ldots, \underline{d}_{n-1}^{(n)}, -\underline{\gamma}_*)$$

is a nonsingular upper triangular matrix with determinant equal to $-\gamma_n \prod_{i=1}^{n} (\beta_0^{(i)} \sigma_{\zeta\zeta}^{(i)})$. If $q_i = i-1$, $i=1, \ldots, n$, then all the determinants of the matrices $D_{i_1, i_2, \ldots, i_n}$ of expression (3.28) are zero except for the one given by (3.29). Thus, J_{III} is nonsingular and the Theorem is proved. On the other hand, if for some $i(< n+1)$ we have $q_i > j-1$, then any nonzero determinant in expression (3.28), different from $\det D_{0,1,\ldots,n-1}$, is the determinant of a matrix that includes a column of the form $\underline{d}_\ell^{(i)}$, for $\ell > i-1$. Therefore, such a determinant has to include a parameter $\beta_\ell^{(i)}$, $\ell > i-1$. Now the summation term of (3.28) corresponding to $\det D_{0,1,\ldots,n-1}$ is given by the expression:

$$-\gamma_n \prod_{i=1}^{n} (\beta_{i-1}^{(i)} \beta_0^{(i)} \sigma_{\zeta\zeta}^{(i)}),$$

which can never include a parameter $\beta_\ell^{(i)}$ for $\ell > i-1$. Thus, $|J_{III}| \neq 0$ almost everywhere. The proof for the case $p \leq n-1$ is a similar extension of the proof of Theorem 1 for the case $p \leq n$.

2.2. An Example

Consider the model with structural equation:

$$(3.30) \qquad \eta_t = \gamma\eta_{t-1} + \beta\zeta_t + u_t .$$

As $q_1^* = 0$, $q_2^* = 1$, according to Theorem 1, when ζ_t and u_t are independent white-noise variables, the model is not identified. Indeed the system of covariance equations is given by

$$\omega_{yx} = \beta(\omega_{xx} - \sigma_{\delta\delta})$$

$$\left.\begin{aligned} \omega_{yx_{-\tau}} &= \gamma\omega_{yx_{-\tau+1}} \\ \omega_{yx_{\tau}} &= 0 \end{aligned}\right\} \quad \tau \geqq 1$$

$$\omega_{yy} = \gamma\omega_{yy_{-1}} + \beta\omega_{yx} + \sigma_{\varepsilon\varepsilon}$$

$$\omega_{yy_{-1}} = \gamma(\omega_{yy} - \sigma_{\varepsilon\varepsilon})$$

$$\omega_{yy_{-\tau}} = \gamma\omega_{yy_{-\tau+1}} , \quad \tau \geqq 2$$

$$\omega_{yy_{\tau}} = \omega_{yy_{-\tau}} , \quad \tau \geqq 1 .$$

Inspection of the system shows that the three parameters, β, $\sigma_{\delta\delta}$, and σ_{uu}, are only contained in two equations, so that no subsystem of covariance equations can be solved for all parameters.

If we assume, instead, that u_t follows the AR(1) process:

(3.31) $$u_t = \rho u_{t-1} + a_t ,$$

according to Theorem 3, the model should be identified.

First we shall prove that the parameters γ, ρ and σ_{aa} are identified. For $\tau = 1$, the τ-lag crosscovariance equation

$$\omega_{yx_{-1}} = \gamma\omega_{yx}$$

identifies the parameter γ (notice that ω_{yx} is nonzero, since $\omega_{yx} = \beta(\omega_{xx} - \sigma_{\delta\delta})$).

Next consider the τ-lag autocovariance equations for $\tau = 2, 3$

$$\omega_{yy_{-2}} = \gamma\omega_{yy_{-1}} + \sigma_2$$

$$\omega_{yy_{-3}} = \gamma\omega_{yy_{-2}} + \sigma_3$$

As γ is identified, so are the covariance σ_2 and σ_3. Since equation

(3.31) implies

(3.32) $\sigma_3 = \rho\sigma_2$,

the parameter ρ is also identified.

Equations (3.23) and (3.24) yield, for our example:

$$\sigma_{uy}(L) = [(1-\gamma L)\ (1-\rho L)\ (1-\rho L^{-1})]^{-1}\ \sigma_{aa}\ ,$$

from which it is found that

(3.33) $$\sigma_3 = \frac{\rho^3\ \sigma_{aa}}{(1-\rho\gamma)\ (1-\rho^2)}$$

so that σ_{aa} is identified.[4/]

Consider now the system of τ-lag crosscovariance equations for $\tau = 0$, and τ-lag autocovariance equations for $\tau = 0, 1$:

$$\omega_{yx} = \beta\ (\omega_{xx} - \sigma_{\delta\delta})$$

$$\omega_{yy} = \gamma\ \omega_{yy_{-1}} + \beta\ \omega_{yy} + \sigma_{\varepsilon\varepsilon} + \sigma_0$$

$$\omega_{yy_{-1}} = \gamma\ (\omega_{yy} - \sigma_{\varepsilon\varepsilon}) + \sigma_1$$

Since the covariance σ_0 and σ_1 do not depend on β, $\sigma_{\delta\delta}$ and $\sigma_{\varepsilon\varepsilon}$, the Jacobian of the above system with respect to these last three parameters is given by the matrix:

4/ Equation (3.33) can be derived also as follows: From (3.30),

$$\sigma_0 = \gamma\sigma_1 + \sigma_{uu}$$

and, from (3.31),

$$\sigma_1 = \rho\sigma_0\ .$$

Thus solving these two equations for σ_1,

$$\sigma_1 = \frac{\rho\sigma_{uu}}{1-\rho^2}\ .$$

Since equation (3.31) implies

$$\sigma_{uu} = \frac{\sigma_{aa}}{1-\rho^2}$$

and $\sigma_3 = \rho^2\ \sigma_1$, We obtain equation (3.33).

$$\begin{pmatrix} \omega_{xx} - \sigma_{\delta\delta} & -\beta & 0 \\ \omega_{yx} & 0 & 1 \\ 0 & 0 & -\gamma \end{pmatrix}$$

with determinant equal to (in absolute value)

$$\gamma\beta\omega_{yx} = \gamma\beta^2\sigma_{\zeta\zeta} \ .$$

Therefore, the complete model is identified.

2.3 A Remark on the Identification of the Autoregressive Process for the Shock

In Lemma 4 we proved that the parameters $\rho_1, \ldots, \rho_r$ and σ_{aa} were identified. The covariance equations used in the proof were τ-lag autocovariance equations for $\tau > \max(p, q_n)$:

$$\text{(3.21b)} \qquad \omega_{yy_{-\tau}} = \sum_{i=1}^{p} \gamma_i \, \omega_{yy_{-\tau+i}} + \sigma_\tau \ .$$

The fact that σ_τ is identified through this equation, together with the relationships between these covariances and the ρ-parameters implied by the shock process (i.e., system (3.22)), was enough to identify the ρ-parameters. Then, any of these σ_τ-covariances, expressed as a function of the γ and ρ-parameters and of σ_{aa}, can identify this last parameter.

It can be seen directly that the ρ and σ_{aa}-parameters can be identified by a system of (r+1) covariance equations of the form (3.21b). In fact, the Jacobian of such a system with respect to the parameters $\rho_1, \ldots, \rho_r$ and σ_{aa}:

$$\text{(3.34)} \qquad J_\rho = \begin{pmatrix} \frac{\partial\sigma_\tau}{\partial\rho_1} & \cdots & \frac{\partial\sigma_\tau}{\partial\rho_r} & \frac{\partial\sigma_\tau}{\partial\sigma_{aa}} \\ \frac{\partial\sigma_{\tau+1}}{\partial\rho_1} & \cdots & \frac{\partial\sigma_{\tau+1}}{\partial\rho_r} & \frac{\partial\sigma_{\tau+1}}{\partial\sigma_{aa}} \\ \vdots & & \vdots & \vdots \\ \frac{\partial\sigma_{\tau+r}}{\partial\rho_1} & \cdots & \frac{\partial\sigma_{\tau+r}}{\partial\rho_r} & \frac{\partial\sigma_{\tau+r}}{\partial\sigma_{aa}} \end{pmatrix}$$

for $\tau > \max(p, q_n)$, is nonsingular when u_t follows an AR(r) process, and (3.22) holds.

In the example we have analyzed, this Jacobian is the matrix

$$\begin{pmatrix} \frac{\partial \sigma_2}{\partial \rho} & \frac{\partial \sigma_2}{\partial \sigma_{aa}} \\ \frac{\partial \sigma_3}{\partial \rho} & \frac{\partial \sigma_3}{\partial \sigma_{aa}} \end{pmatrix}$$

As equation (3.32) implies

$$\frac{\partial \sigma_3}{\partial \rho} = \rho \frac{\partial \sigma_2}{\partial \rho} + \sigma_2$$

$$\frac{\partial \sigma_3}{\partial \sigma_{aa}} = \rho \frac{\partial \sigma_2}{\partial \sigma_{aa}} ,$$

the Jacobian becomes:

$$\begin{pmatrix} \frac{\partial \sigma_2}{\partial \rho} & \frac{\partial \sigma_2}{\partial \sigma_{aa}} \\ \rho \frac{\partial \sigma_2}{\partial \rho} + \sigma_2 & \rho \frac{\partial \sigma_2}{\partial \sigma_{aa}} \end{pmatrix} ,$$

which is nonsingular, since its determinant is equal to:

$$\sigma_2 \frac{\partial \sigma_2}{\partial \sigma_{aa}} = \left[\frac{\rho^2}{(1-\rho\gamma)(1-\rho^2)}\right]^2 \sigma_{aa} .$$

2.4 Some Final Remarks

If we compare the necessary and sufficient conditions for identification of the Models I, II, and III, as expressed in Theorems 1, 2, and 3, we observe that different patterns of autocorrelation for the shock may have opposite effects as far as identification is concerned. When the autocorrelation function vanishes after a finite number of lags (MA process) identification of the model can be said to decrease. When the autocorrelation function follows the pattern of an Autoregressive process, identification of the model increases in the sense that models with the same structural equation, that are not identified under the white-noise assumption, may be identified under the Autoregressive one. In a way, this may be another situation where AR and MA processes have dual properties, yet it is somewhat surprising that the opposite effects of the two assumptions are not symmetric.[5/] By this we mean that while the decrease in identification induced by an MA assumption is proportional to the order of the MA process (as specified by the condition $q_j^* \geq j + s$ of Theorem 2), for the case of an AR process, the increase in identification is constant (as specified by the condition $q_j^* \geqq j - 1$ of Theorem 3, which does not involve r, the order of the process itself).

In the next chapter, we proceed to analyse how the two effects combine when the shock u_t follows a mixed autoregressive-moving average process.

5/ Some of the dual properties of finite Autoregressive and Moving Average processes are summarized in Box-Jenkins [1970, p. 79].

CHAPTER IV

AUTOCORRELATED SHOCK: WHITE NOISE EXOGENOUS VARIABLES. II.

1. AUTOREGRESSIVE-MOVING AVERAGE PROCESS

Let the shock u_t be the outcome of a stochastic process with an autocorrelation function that combines the two previous cases. We shall assume that u_t follows in general an Autoregressive-Moving Average process of orders r and s, respectively [ARMA(r, s)], given by

$$(4.1) \qquad R_r(L)u_t = S_s(L)a_t.$$

The polynomials $R_r(L)$ and $S_s(L)$ were defined in the previous chapter and a is a white-noise variable, independent of $\zeta^{(i)}$, $\delta^{(i)}$ $(i = 1, \ldots, n)$ and ε. The process is assumed to be stationary and invertible, according to Assumption 4b of Chapter I.

1.1 The General Case

We shall analyze identification of Model IV, with structural equation:

$$(4.2) \qquad G_p(L)\eta_t = \sum_{i=1}^{n} B_{q_i}^{(i)}(L)\, \zeta_t^{(i)} + u_t,$$

where u_t follows the process given by (4.1) and the variables η_t and $\zeta_t^{(i)}$ are measured with error (according to equations (1.1b) and (1.1c) of Chaper I).

Lemma 5: The autoregressive parameters $\gamma_1, \ldots, \gamma_p, \rho_1, \ldots, \rho_r$ are always identified.

Proof: Combine equations (4.1) and (4.2) into:

$$(4.3) \qquad \Lambda_{p+r}^{(0)}(L)\eta_t = \sum_{i=1}^{n} \Lambda_{q_i+r}(L)\, \zeta_t^{(i)} + S_s(L)\, a_t ,$$

where

$$\Lambda_{p+r}^{(0)}(L) = R_r(L)\, G_p(L)$$

$$\Lambda_{q_i+r}^{(i)}(L) = R_r(L)\, B_{q_i}^{(i)}(L), \; i = 1, 2, \ldots, n.$$

Equation (4.3) can be seen as a particular case of equation (3.3), when the shock is pure moving average process. For $\tau > \max(p, q_n)+r$, the τ-lag autocovariance equations corresponding to (4.3) is of the form:

$$\omega_{yy_{-\tau}} = \lambda_1^{(0)} \omega_{yy_{-\tau+1}} + \lambda_2^{(0)} \omega_{yy_{-\tau+2}} + \ldots + \lambda_{p+r}^{(0)} \omega_{yy_{-\tau+p+r}} ,$$

where $\lambda_i^{(0)}$ is the coefficient of L^i in the polynomial $-\Lambda_{p+r}^{(0)}(L)$. Letting $\tau_0 = \max(p, q_n)+r$, the system of τ-lag autocovariance equations for $\tau = \tau_0 + 1, \ldots, \tau_0 + p+r$ can be solved for the parameters $\lambda_1^{(0)}, \lambda_2^{(0)}, \ldots, \lambda_{p+r}^{(0)}$.1/ Now the $\lambda^{(0)}$-parameters can be expressed as functions of the ρ and γ-parameters as follows:

$$\begin{aligned}
\lambda_1^{(0)} &= \gamma_1 + \rho_1 \\
\lambda_2^{(0)} &= \gamma_2 - \rho_1 \gamma_1 + \rho_2 \\
&- - - - - - - - - - - - - - - - - \\
\lambda_i^{(0)} &= \gamma_i + \rho_i - \sum_{j=1}^{i-1} \rho_j \gamma_{i-j} \qquad (4.4) \\
&- - - - - - - - - - - - - - - - - \\
\lambda_{p+r-1}^{(0)} &= -\rho_{r-1}\gamma_p - \rho_r \gamma_{p-1} \\
\lambda_{p+r}^{(0)} &= -\rho_r \gamma_p ,
\end{aligned}$$

The Jacobian of the system (4.4) with respect to the γ and ρ-parameters is given by the $(p+r) \times (p+r)$ matrix:

$$J_\lambda = \begin{pmatrix}
1 & 0 & 0 & \cdots & 0 & 1 & 0 & 0 & & 0 \\
-\rho_1 & 1 & 0 & \cdots & 0 & -\gamma_1 & 1 & 0 & & 0 \\
-\rho_2 & -\rho_1 & 1 & \cdots & 0 & -\gamma_2 & \gamma_1 & 1 & \cdots & 0 \\
\vdots & & & \ddots & \vdots & \vdots & & & & \\
 & & & & 1 & & & & & 1 \\
-\rho_r & & & & -\rho_1 & -\gamma_p & & & & -\gamma_1 \\
0 & & & & -\rho_2 & 0 & & & & -\gamma_2 \\
\vdots & & & & \vdots & \vdots & & & & \vdots \\
0 & \cdots & \cdots & 0 & -\rho_r & 0 & \cdots & \cdots & 0 & -\gamma_p
\end{pmatrix}$$

1/ This statement was proved in the first part of the proof Lemma 4.

Direct inspection of the matrix J_λ shows that its determinant can be expressed as $\det J_\lambda = (-1)^r \gamma_p^r + c$, where $(-1)^r \gamma_p^r$ represents the term corresponding to the elements of the main diagonal and c is not a function of γ_p^r. (Notice that γ_p does not appear below the main diagonal).[2/] It follows that J_λ will be nonsingular, which implies that the system (4.4) can be solved for the ρ and γ-parameters as functions of the $\lambda^{(0)}$-parameters. As the $\lambda^{(0)}$-parameters are identified, Lemma 5 is proved.

Notice that the γ-parameters can be also identified through the cross-covariance equations corresponding to (4.2). In particular, for $\tau > q_i$, the τ-lag crosscovariance equation for the ith exogenous variable has the form:

(4.5a) $$\omega^{(i)}_{yx_{-\tau}} = \gamma_1 \, \omega^{(i)}_{yx_{-\tau+1}} + \ldots + \gamma_p \, \omega^{(i)}_{yx_{-\tau+p}}$$

The necessary and sufficient conditions for Model IV to be identified are given by the following Theorem (which includes Theorems 1, 2, and 3 as particular cases).

<u>Theorem 4</u>: Let q_j^* (j = 1, 2, ..., n+1) be defined as in Theorem 1. Then Model IV is identified if and only if

---

2/ For the case r=2, p=2, the system (4.4) becomes

$$\lambda_1 = \rho_1 + \gamma_1$$
$$\lambda_2 = \gamma_2 - \rho_1\gamma_1 + \rho_2$$
$$\lambda_3 = -\rho_1\gamma_2 - \rho_2\gamma_1$$
$$\lambda_4 = -\rho_2\gamma_2 \ ,$$

and the matrix J_λ is given by

$$J_\lambda = \begin{pmatrix} 1 & 0 & 1 & 0 \\ -\rho_1 & 1 & -\gamma_1 & 1 \\ -\rho_2 & -\rho_1 & -\gamma_2 & -\gamma_1 \\ 0 & -\rho_2 & 0 & -\gamma_2 \end{pmatrix}$$

so that

$$\det J_\lambda = \gamma_2^2 + c \ ,$$

and $$c = \rho_2^2 - \rho_1^2 \gamma_2 - \gamma_1^2 \rho_2 - 2\gamma_2\rho_2 + 2\rho_1\gamma_1\gamma_2$$

a) when $r > s$,

$$q_j^* \geqq j-1,$$

b) when $r \leqq s$,

$$q_j^* \geqq j+s-r,$$

for $j = 1, 2, \ldots, n+1$.

Proof of Theorem 4.

Necessity. When $r \geq s$ the proof of the necessity of condition $q_j^* \geqq j - 1$ is identical to the proof of necessity in Theorem 3. (Notice that the covariance $\sigma_{uy_{-\tau}}$ are functions of the γ, ρ, θ and σ_{aa} parameters only).

When $r \leqq s$, consider equation (4.3), where the shock follows a pure moving average process. Substituting q_j^* by $q_j^* + r$, the proof of the necessity of condition $q_j^* + r \geqq j + s$ can be performed in exactly the same way as the necessity part of Theorem 2.

(Notice that when $r > s$, the condition $q_j^* \geqq j-1$ implies $q_j^* \geqq j + s - r$; similarly, when $r \leqq s$, the condition $q_j^* \geqq j + s - r$ implies $q_j^* \geqq j - 1$).

The proof of the sufficiency part of Theorem 4 will be simplified if we make use of the following result:

Lemma 6: Let the model consisting of equations (4.1) and (4.2) with $p = p^0$, $q_i = q_i^0$ $(i = 1, \ldots, n)$ be identified. Then the model consisting of equation (4.1) and (4.2) with $p \geqq p^0$, $q_i \geqq q_i^0$ is identified also (for the same values of r and s).

Proof of Lemma 6: Denote by Model A the model with maximum lags $p^0, q_1^0, \ldots, q_n^0$, and by Model B the one with larger maximum lags. Model B contains all the parameters of Model A plus some additional parameters $\beta_\tau^{(i)}$ $(\tau > q_i^0)$ and γ_τ $(\tau > p^0)$. Corresponding to these $\beta_\tau^{(i)}$, the τ-lag crosscovariance equation for Model B is given by

$$\omega_{yx_{-\tau}}^{(i)} = \sum_{j=1}^{n} \gamma_j \, \omega_{yx_{-\tau+j}}^{(i)} + \beta_\tau^{(i)} \left(\omega_{xx}^{(i)} - \sigma_{\delta\delta}^{(i)}\right) . \tag{4.5b}$$

Since $\sigma_{\delta\delta}^{(i)}$ in Model A is identified, the same will be true for Model B. Thus equation (4.5b) identifies $\beta_\tau^{(i)}$. As the γ-parameters are always identified the Lemma is proved.

Sufficiency (Theorem 4)

a) Consider first the case $r > s$. By using the previous Lemma, we need to prove only that Model IV is identified when $q_1^* = 0$, $q_2^* = 1$, ..., $q_{n+1}^* = n$. Consider the following system of covariance equations:

(S1): τ-lag crosscovariance equations (corresponding to the ith exogenous variable) for $\tau = q_i + 1, \ldots, q_i + p$;

(S2): τ-lag crosscovariance equations for $\tau = 0, 1, \ldots, q_i$; $1 = 1, 2, \ldots, n$

(S3): τ-lag autocovariance equations for $\tau = 0, 1, \ldots, n$;

(S4): τ-lag autocovariance equations for $\tau = n + 1, n + 2, \ldots, n + s + r + 1$.

The Jacobian of this entire system with respect to the parameters, $\gamma_1, \ldots, \gamma_p$; $\beta_0^{(i)}, \ldots, \beta_{q_i}^{(i)}$ $(i = 1, 2, \ldots, n)$; $\sigma_{\delta\delta}^{(i)}, \ldots, \sigma_{\delta\delta}^{(n)}, \sigma_{\varepsilon\varepsilon}$; $\theta_1, \ldots, \theta_s, \sigma_{aa}, \rho_1, \ldots, \rho_r$ can be partitioned as follows

$$J_{IV} = \begin{pmatrix} J_{11} & 0 & 0 & 0 \\ J_{21} & J_{22} & J_{23} & 0 \\ J_{31} & J_{32} & J_{33} & J_{34} \\ J_{41} & 0 & 0 & J_{44} \end{pmatrix},$$

where the first row corresponds to the subsystem (S1), the second row to the subsystem (S2) and so on. The order of the columns is as follows:

first column: parameters $\gamma_1, \ldots, \gamma_p$;

second column: parameters $\beta_0^{(i)}, \ldots, \beta_{q_i}^{(i)}$ $(i = 1, 2, \ldots, n)$

third column: parameters $\sigma_{\delta\delta}^{(1)}, \ldots, \sigma_{\delta\delta}^{(n)}, \sigma_{\varepsilon\varepsilon}$

fourth column: parameters $\theta_1, \ldots, \theta_s, \sigma_{aa}, \rho_1, \ldots, \rho_r$.

As the matrices J_{11}, J_{22}, J_{33} and J_{44} are square, applying the Laplace Expansion Theorem, first expanding around the matrices in the first row and then expanding around the matrices in the last row, it follows that J_{IV} will be nonsingular if the matrices

$$(4.6)\qquad J_{11},\quad \begin{pmatrix} J_{22} & J_{23} \\ J_{32} & J_{33} \end{pmatrix},\quad J_{44}$$

are nonsingular. It is easily seen that the matrix J_{11} is the Jacobian of a system of equations of the form (4.5a) with respect to the parameters $\gamma_1,\ldots,\gamma_p$, which is nonsingular. Also, the second matrix of (4.6) is identical to the Jacobian J_{III} of Theorem 3, which was also proved nonsingular. Thus J_{IV} will be nonsingular if det $J_{44} = 0$. The matrix J_{44} is the Jacobian of the τ-lag autocovariance equations for $\tau = n+1, n+2, \ldots, n+s+r+1$, with respect to the parameters $\theta_1, \ldots, \theta_s, \sigma_{aa}, \rho_1, \ldots, \rho_r$. As these autocovariance equations are of the form:

$$\omega_{yy_{-\tau}} = \gamma_1 \omega_{yy_{-\tau+1}} + \ldots + \gamma_p \omega_{yy_{-\tau+p}} + \sigma_\tau ,$$

where $\sigma_\tau = E(u_t\, y_{t-\tau})$, the matrix J_{44} can be expressed as:

$$J_{44} = \begin{pmatrix} \frac{\partial\sigma_{n+1}}{\partial\theta_1} & \cdots & \frac{\partial\sigma_{n+1}}{\partial\theta_s} & \frac{\partial\sigma_{n+1}}{\partial\sigma_{aa}} & \frac{\partial\sigma_{n+1}}{\partial\rho_1} & \cdots & \frac{\partial\sigma_{n+1}}{\partial\rho_r} \\ \text{---} & & \text{---} & \text{---} & \text{---} & & \text{---} \\ \frac{\partial\sigma_{n+s+r+1}}{\partial\theta_1} & \cdots & \frac{\partial\sigma_{n+s+r+1}}{\partial\theta_s} & \frac{\partial\sigma_{n+s+r+1}}{\partial\sigma_{aa}} & \frac{\partial\sigma_{n+s+r+1}}{\partial\rho_1} & \cdots & \frac{\partial\sigma_{n+s+r+1}}{\partial\rho_r} \end{pmatrix}$$

Partition J_{44} in the following way:

$$J_{44} = (A \mid B),$$

where A contains the first (s + 1) columns and B the last r columns.

Since equation (4.1) implies:

$$(4.7a)\qquad \sigma_\tau = \rho_1\,\sigma_{\tau-1} + \rho_2\,\sigma_{\tau-2} + \ldots + \rho_r\,\sigma_{\tau-r} + f(\tau, \theta, \sigma_{aa}),$$

where $f(\tau, \theta, \sigma_{aa}) = 0$ for $\tau > s$, it follows that

$$(4.7b)\qquad \frac{\partial\sigma}{\partial\rho_i} = \sum_{j=1}^{r} \rho_j \frac{\partial\sigma_{\tau-j}}{\partial\rho_i} + \sigma_{\tau-i} ,$$

Thus each row of B is a linear combination of the previous r rows plus a term, $\sigma_{\tau-i}$, that does not appear in any of the previous rows. Consider again equation (4.7a), from which:

$$(4.8a)\quad \frac{\partial\sigma_\tau}{\partial\theta_i} = \sum_{j=1}^{r} \rho_j \frac{\partial\sigma_{\tau-j}}{\partial\theta_i}$$

$$(4.8b)\quad \frac{\partial\sigma_\tau}{\partial\sigma_{aa}} = \sum_{j=1}^{r} \rho_j \frac{\partial\sigma_{\tau-j}}{\partial\sigma_{aa}},$$

for $\tau > s$. As the linear combinations of equations (4.8a) and (4.8b) require, in each case, $(r + 1)$ consecutive terms, the condition $r > s$ implies that all minors of order $(s + 1) \times (s + 1)$ will have $(s + 1)$ linearly independent rows (unless $\rho_{s+1} = \rho_{s+2} = \ldots = \rho_r = 0$). Combining (4.7b), (4.8a) and (4.8b), it can be seen that the $(s + r + 1)$ rows of J_{44} are linearly independent, hence J_{44} is nonsingular.

b) For the case $r \leqq s$, we shall prove that Model IV is identified when $q_1^* = 1+s-r$, $q_2^* = 2+s-r$, ..., $q_{n+1}^* = n+1+s-r$. Consider the following system of covariance equations:

(S1'): τ-lag crosscovariance equations (corresponding to the ith exogenous variable), for $\tau = q_i + 1, \ldots, q_i + p$;

(S2'): τ-lag crosscovariance equations for $\tau = 0, 1, \ldots, q_i$; $i = 1, 2, \ldots, n$;

(S3'): τ-lag autocovariance equations for $\tau = 0, 1, \ldots, n + 1 + s - r$;

(S4'): τ-lag autocovariance equations for $\tau = n + 1 + s - r + 1, \ldots, n + 1 + s + r$.

The Jacobian of this system with respect to the parameters

$\gamma_1, \ldots, \gamma_p; \beta_0^{(i)}, \ldots, \beta_{q_i}^{(i)}, \sigma_{\delta\delta}^{(i)}$ $(i = 1, \ldots, n)$, $\sigma_{\varepsilon\varepsilon}; \theta_1, \ldots, \theta_s, \sigma_{aa}, \rho_1, \ldots \rho_r$

can be partitioned as indicated:

$$(4.9a)\quad \begin{pmatrix} J_{11} & 0 \\ J_{21} & J_{22} \end{pmatrix}$$

where J_{11} denotes the Jacobian of the system (S1') with respect to the γ-parameters, and J_{22} denotes the Jacobian of the system composed of (S2'), (S3') and (S4') with respect to the rest of the parameters. Since J_{11} in nonsingular, the model will be identified if $\det J_{22} \neq 0$. Partition J_{22} in the following way:

$$(4.9b) \qquad J_{22} = \left(\begin{array}{c|c} J_c & J_D \\ \hline J_A & J_u \end{array} \right)$$

where J_c is the $(\sum_{i=1}^{n} q_i + 2n + s - r + 2) \times (\sum_{i=1}^{n} q_i + 2n + 1)$ Jacobian of the system composed of (S2') and (S3') with respect to the β, $\sigma_{\delta\delta}$ and $\sigma_{\varepsilon\varepsilon}$-parameters, and J_u denotes the $(n + s + r + 2) \times (s + r + 1)$ Jacobian of the system consisting of (S3') and (S4') with respect to the θ, ρ and σ_{aa}-parameters. Due to the fact that the covariance equations do not contain the θ, ρ, and σ_{aa}-parameters, J_D is a zero matrix. Similarly, due to the fact that the τ-lag autocovariance equations for $\tau \geq n + 1 + s - r$ do not contain the β, $\sigma_{\delta\delta}$ and $\sigma_{\varepsilon\varepsilon}$-parameters, J_A is also a zero matrix.

Consider the Laplace expansion of det J_{22} around the last $(r + s + 1)$ columns. We shall prove that one and only one of the elements in this expansion is different from zero.

Each one of the elements in this expansion is the product of two determinants, say A_i and E_i, where A_i is a minor consisting of $(\sum_{i=1}^{n} q_i + 2n + 1)$ rows of the matrix $\left(\frac{J_c}{J_A}\right)$, and E_i is the corresponding complementary minor of A_i (consisting of $(s + r + 1)$ rows of the matrix $\left(\frac{J_D}{J_u}\right)$). As $J_D = 0$ and J_u is given by the matrix:

$$(4.9c) \qquad J_u = \begin{pmatrix} \frac{\partial\sigma_0}{\partial\theta_1} & --- & \frac{\partial\sigma_0}{\partial\theta_s} & \frac{\partial\sigma_0}{\partial\sigma_{aa}} & \frac{\partial\sigma_0}{\partial\rho_1} & --- & \frac{\partial\sigma_0}{\partial\rho_r} \\ \vdots & & & & & & \vdots \\ \frac{\partial\sigma_{n+1+s+r}}{\partial\theta_1} & & & ------ & & & \frac{\partial\sigma_{n+1+s+r}}{\partial\rho_r} \end{pmatrix} ,$$

the minors E_i are the determinants of the matrices formed by selecting $(s + r + 1)$ of the rows of J_u.

From the fact that $J_A = 0$, it follows that any complementary minor E_i corresponding to a minor A_i different from zero has to include the last 2r rows of the matrix J_u (notice that the matrix J_A has 2r rows). Thus all the minors E_i for which $A_i \neq 0$ contain the last 2r rows of J_u plus combinations of the rest of the rows of J_u, taken $(1 + s - r)$ at a time. To see which ones of these E_i minors are nonzero, we shall use an additional result:

Lemma 7: Any set of $(r + 1)$ covariances σ_τ, with $\tau > s - r$, is linearly dependent.

Proof of Lemma 7: Equation (4.1) implies

(4.10a) $$\sigma_\tau = \rho_1 \sigma_{\tau-1} + \rho_2 \sigma_{\tau-2} + \dots + \rho_r \sigma_{\tau-r} ,$$

for $\tau > s$. Thus by applying (4.10a) repeatedly, any covariance σ_τ (for $\tau > s - r$) can be written as

(4.10b) $$\sigma_\tau = \rho_1^\tau \sigma_s + \rho_2^\tau \sigma_{s-1} + \dots + \rho_r^\tau \sigma_{s-r+1}$$

where ρ_i^τ is a function of $\rho_1, \dots, \rho_r$ different for every τ (notice that when $s - r < \tau \leq s$, $\rho_{s-\tau+1}^\tau = 1$ and $\rho_i^\tau = 0$ for $i \neq s-\tau+1$). Therefore, any covariance σ_τ $(\tau > s-r)$ is a linear combination of the r covariances $\sigma_s, \sigma_{s-1}, \dots, \sigma_{s-r+1}$. It follows that any set of $(r + 1)$ covariances σ_τ $(\tau > s - r)$ has to be linearly dependent.[3/]

3/ The statement is implied by the following consideration: In the linear system of $(r + 1)$ equations

$$\sigma_{\tau_1} = \rho_1^{\tau_1} \sigma_s + \dots + \rho_r^{\tau_1} \sigma_{s-r+1}$$

$$\sigma_{\tau_2} = \rho_1^{\tau_2} \sigma_s + \dots + \rho_r^{\tau_2} \sigma_{s-r+1}$$

$$\sigma_{\tau_{r+1}} = \rho_1^{\tau_{r+1}} \sigma_s \dots + \rho_r^{\tau_{r+1}} \sigma_{s-r+1} ,$$

the r terms $\sigma_s, \sigma_{s-1}, \dots, \sigma_{s-r+1}$ can be eliminated, to yield:

$$\sigma_{\tau_1} = \rho_1^* \sigma_{\tau_2} + \dots + \rho_r^* \sigma_{\tau_{r+1}} .$$

Notice that the parameters $\rho_1^*, \dots, \rho_r^*$ are such that

$$\sum_{i=1}^{r} \rho_1^* \rho_j^{\tau_{i+1}} = \rho_j^{\tau_1}, \quad j = 1, \dots, r.$$

For an example, see footnote 6 of the present chapter.

Thus we can write:

$$(4.11) \qquad \sigma_{\tau_1} = \rho_1^* \sigma_{\tau_2} + \ldots + \rho_r^* \sigma_{\tau_{r+1}}$$

for $\tau_i > s - r$, $i = 1, 2, \ldots, r + 1$, and the coefficients ρ_i^* are functions of the ρ-parameters. Equation (4.11) implies:

$$(4.12) \qquad \sum_{i=2}^{r+1} \rho_{i-1}^* \frac{\partial \sigma_{\tau_i}}{\partial \theta_j} = \frac{\partial \sigma_{\tau_1}}{\partial \theta_j} \; ; \qquad \sum_{i=2}^{r+1} \rho_{i-1}^* \frac{\partial \sigma_{\tau_i}}{\partial \sigma_{aa}} = \frac{\partial \sigma_{\tau_1}}{\partial \sigma_{aa}}$$

for $\tau_i > s - r$.

Now, any minor E_i for which the complementary minor is nonzero is a determinant formed with the last 2r rows of J_u, plus (s - r + 1) of the other rows of J_u. Of these E_i minors, only the one for which the first (s - r + 1) rows are the partial derivatives of $\sigma_0, \sigma_1, \ldots, \sigma_{s-r}$ is nonzero. The fact that any other E_i-minor is zero is implied by the following consideration: expanding around the last r columns, the resulting minors have (r + 1) rows that are linear combinations, according to Lemma 7 (notice that (r + 1) rows have to be the partial derivatives of covariances σ_τ for $\tau > s - r$).

Now consider the E_i minor for which the first (s - r + 1) rows are the partial derivative of $\sigma_0, \sigma_1, \ldots, \sigma_{s-r}$. By substituting for the elements of the last r rows using (4.10a), the minor can be rewritten as [4/]:

$$(4.13) \qquad \begin{vmatrix} E_{i0} & E_{i1} \\ 0 & E_{i2} \end{vmatrix} ,$$

4/ Use has been made of a well known property of determinants. Let E^0 represent the first (k - 1) rows of the (k x k) determinant:

$$E = \begin{vmatrix} E^0 \\ a_{k1} + b_{k1} \; \ldots\ldots \; a_{kk} + b_{kk} \end{vmatrix} .$$

Then:

$$E = \begin{vmatrix} E^0 \\ a_{k1} \; \ldots\ldots \; a_{kk} \end{vmatrix} + \begin{vmatrix} E^0 \\ b_{k1} \; \ldots\ldots \; b_{kk} \end{vmatrix} .$$

where

$$E_{i0} = \begin{vmatrix} \frac{\partial\sigma_0}{\partial\theta_1} & \cdots & \frac{\partial\sigma_0}{\partial\theta_s} & \frac{\partial\sigma_0}{\partial\sigma_{aa}} \\ \vdots & & \vdots & \vdots \\ \frac{\partial\sigma_{s-r}}{\partial\theta_1} & \cdots & \frac{\partial\sigma_{s-r}}{\partial\theta_s} & \frac{\partial\sigma_{s-r}}{\partial\sigma_{aa}} \\ \vdots & & \vdots & \vdots \\ \frac{\partial\sigma_{s-r+n+2}}{\partial\theta_1} & \cdots & \frac{\partial\sigma_{s-r+n+2}}{\partial\theta_s} & \frac{\partial\sigma_{s-r+n+2}}{\partial\sigma_{aa}} \\ \vdots & & \vdots & \vdots \\ \frac{\partial\sigma_{s+n+1}}{\partial\theta_1} & \cdots & \frac{\partial\sigma_{s+n+1}}{\partial\theta_s} & \frac{\partial\sigma_{s+n+1}}{\partial\sigma_{aa}} \end{vmatrix},$$

$$E_{i1} = \begin{vmatrix} \frac{\partial\sigma_0}{\partial\rho_1} & \cdots & \frac{\partial\sigma_0}{\partial\rho_r} \\ \vdots & & \vdots \\ \frac{\partial\sigma_{s-r}}{\partial\rho_1} & \cdots & \frac{\partial\sigma_{s-r}}{\partial\rho_r} \\ \vdots & & \vdots \\ \frac{\partial\sigma_{s-r+n+2}}{\partial\rho_1} & \cdots & \frac{\partial\sigma_{s-r+n+2}}{\partial\rho_r} \\ \vdots & & \vdots \\ \frac{\partial\sigma_{s+n+1}}{\partial\rho_1} & \cdots & \frac{\partial\sigma_{s+n+1}}{\partial\rho_r} \end{vmatrix}, \qquad E_{i2} = \begin{vmatrix} \frac{\partial\sigma_{s+n+2}}{\partial\rho_1} & \cdots & \frac{\partial\sigma_{s+n+2}}{\partial\rho_r} \\ \vdots & & \vdots \\ \frac{\partial\sigma_{s+n+r+1}}{\partial\rho_1} & \cdots & \frac{\partial\sigma_{s+n+r+1}}{\partial\rho_r} \end{vmatrix}$$

where the minors E_{i0}, E_{i1} and E_{i2} have dimensions (s + 1) x (s + 1), (s + 1) x r, and (r x r), respectively. The determinant E_{i2} is similar to det J_ρ of expression (3.34); also, equations (4.7) and (4.12) imply that the (s + 1) rows of E_{i0} are linearly independent.

Thus the determinant of the Jacobian J_{22} of expression (4.9b) is equal the product of E_{i0}, E_{i2} and the complementary minor of the determinant (4.13). This complementary minor can be proved to be equal (in absolute value) to the expression:

$$\gamma_p \pi_{i=1}^{n} (\omega_{xx}^{(i)} - \sigma_{\delta\delta}^{(i)})^{q_i} \beta_{q_i}^{(i)} \omega_{yx}^{(i)} = \gamma_p \pi_{i=1}^{n} \beta_0^{(i)} \beta_{q_i}^{(i)} (\omega_{xx}^{(i)} - \sigma_{\delta\delta}^{(i)})^{q_i+1}$$

which is also different from zero (a.e.). This finishes the proof that, when $r \leqq s$, Model IV with $q_j^* = j + s - r$ is identified. Considering Lemma 6, Theorem 4 is proved.

1.2 Some Remarks

It is easily seen that Theorem 4 becomes Theorem 1 when $r = s = 0$. Similarly, Theorem 4 becomes Theorem 2 and 3 when $r = 0$, $s > 0$, and when $r > 0$, $s = 0$, respectively.

Theorem 4 indicates a somewhat asymmetric behavior of the autoregressive and moving average polynomials of the shock process, as far as identification is concerned. When the order of the moving average is at least as large as the order of the autoregressive, the combined effect is "additive" ($q_j^* \geq j + s - r$), and the increase in identification due to the autoregression is similar to the decrease in identification due to the moving average. Thus for example, a model with an ARMA (1, 2) process for the shock needs, in order to be identified, larger lag-polynomials in the structural equation than a model with an ARMA (2, 2) process for the shock. On the other hand, when the order of the autoregressive polynomial is larger than the order of the moving average polynomial the combined effect is constant, since the condition ($q_j^* \geq j - 1$) is independent of the relative size of the two polynomials. Thus, for example, ARMA (2, 1) ARMA (3, 1) and ARMA (3, 2) processes for the shock will have the same effects on the identification of the model.

This difference between the identification effects of autoregressive and moving average terms according to whether $r > s$ or $r \leqq s$ originates from the following consideration:

When $r > s$, any set of $(r + s + 1)$ independent autocovariance equations can be solved for the θ, ρ and σ_{aa}-parameters. On the other hand, when $r \leqq s$ this is not anymore true, because the constraints given by (4.12) force the

Jacobian of any set of (s + r + 1) autocovariance equations (except the sets containing the first (s - r + 1) of these equations) to be singular.

This point--and, in general, the proof of Theorem 4--is illustrated with the use of some examples in the next section.

1.3 Some Examples

The first two example illustrate the case r > s while the last two illustrate the case $r \leqq s$. In all the models considered the the error-in-variable equations (1.1b) and (1.1c) are assumed to hold as well as the stationarity and invertibility constraints for the parameters of the shock process.

First Example

Consider the model given by the equations:

(4.14a) $\eta_t = \beta\zeta_t + u_t$

(4.14b) $u_t = \rho_1 u_{t-1} + \rho_2 u_{t-2} + a_t + \theta a_{t-1}$,

where assumption 4b implies:

$$\rho_2 + \rho_1 < 1, \quad \rho_2 - \rho_1 < 1, \quad -1 < \rho_2 < 1, \quad -1 < \theta < 1 .$$

As r = 2, s = 1 (so that r > s), according to Theorem 4, necessary conditions for identification are $q_i^* \geqq i-1$, i = 1, 2, which imply $q_1^* = 0$, $q_2^* = 1$. Thus the model is not identified. To check this result consider the system of covariance equations. The complete system is given by:

$$\omega_{yx} = \beta(\omega_{xx} - \sigma_{\delta\delta})$$

$$\omega_{yx_{-\tau}} = 0, \ \tau > 0$$

$$\omega_{yy} = \beta\omega_{yx} + \sigma_0 + \sigma_{\varepsilon\varepsilon}$$

$$\omega_{yy_{-\tau}} = \sigma_\tau, \ \tau > 0 ,$$

where $\sigma_\tau = E(u_t y_{t-\tau})$ is a function of ρ_1, ρ_2, θ and σ_{aa}. As the three parameters β, $\sigma_{\delta\delta}$ and $\sigma_{\varepsilon\varepsilon}$ are only included in two equations, the model is not identified.

Notice that, if equation (4.14b) is substituted by any other ARMA (r, s) process for the shock, but equation (4.14a) remains unchanged, for the resulting model it would still be true that the parameters β, $\sigma_{\delta\delta}$ and $\sigma_{\varepsilon\varepsilon}$ only appear in two covariance equations. Thus the model is not identified no matter how large the order of the autoregressive polynomial for the shock becomes.[5/]

5/ One could think of transforming the model into "pure moving average" shock model by combining the structural equation and the equation for the shock (i.e., equation (4.3)). But this transformation implies certain restrictions for the parameters as shown in the following example. Consider equation (4.14a) and let the shock follow the process:

$$u_t = \rho_1 u_{t-1} + \rho_2 u_{t-2} + a_t$$

Combining the two equations yields:

$$\eta_t = \rho_1 \eta_{t-1} + \rho_2 \eta_{t-2} + \beta\zeta_t - \rho_1 \beta\zeta_{t-1} - \rho_2 \beta\zeta_{t-2} + a_t \,.$$

If Theorem 1 were directly applicable, as $q_1^* = q_2^* = 2$ the model would satisfy the conditions for identification. But it is seen that the relationship between the coefficients of the transformed equation imply a singular Jacobian of the system of covariance equations. Consider, for example, the system:

$$\omega_{yx} = \beta(\omega_{xx} - \sigma_{\delta\delta})$$

$$\omega_{yy} = \rho_1 \omega_{yy_{-1}} + \rho_2 \omega_{yy_{-2}} + \beta\omega_{yx} + \sigma_{aa} + \sigma_{\varepsilon\varepsilon}$$

$$\omega_{yy_{-1}} = \rho_1 (\omega_{yy} - \sigma_{\varepsilon\varepsilon}) + \rho_2 \omega_{yy_{-1}} - \rho_1 \beta\omega_{yx}$$

$$\omega_{yy_{-2}} = \rho_1 \omega_{yy_{-1}} + \rho_2 (\omega_{yy} - \sigma_{\varepsilon\varepsilon}) - \rho_2 \beta\omega_{yx}$$

$$\omega_{yy_{-3}} = \rho_1 \omega_{yy_{-2}} + \rho_2 \omega_{yy_{-1}}$$

$$\omega_{yy_{-4}} = \rho_1 \omega_{yy_{-3}} + \rho_2 \omega_{yy_{-2}}$$

(Notice the $\omega_{yx_{-\tau}} = 0$ for $\tau \neq 0$.) The Jacobian of this system with respect to the parameters β, $\sigma_{\delta\delta}$, $\sigma_{\varepsilon\varepsilon}$, ρ_1, ρ_2 and σ_{aa} is given by the matrix:

Second Example

Consider the model given by the equation

(4.14c) $\eta_t = \beta_0 \zeta_t + \beta_1 \zeta_{t-1} + u_t$

together with equation (4.14b) for the shock. Now $q_1^* = 0$ and $q_2^* = 1$, thus according to Theorem 4 the model should be identified. To check the result consider the following system of covariance equations:

$$\omega_{yx} = \beta_0 (\omega_{xx} - \sigma_{\delta\delta})$$

$$\omega_{yx_{-1}} = \beta_1 (\omega_{xx} - \sigma_{\delta\delta})$$

$$\omega_{yy} = \beta_0 \omega_{yx} + \beta_1 \omega_{yx_{-1}} + \sigma_{\varepsilon\varepsilon} + \sigma_0$$

$$\omega_{yy_{-1}} = \beta_1 \omega_{yx} + \sigma_1$$

$$\omega_{yy_{-\tau}} = \sigma_\tau, \ \tau = 2, 3, 4, 5 .$$

5/ (Continued)

$$J = \begin{pmatrix} \omega_{xx} - \sigma_{\delta\delta} & -\beta & 0 & 0 & 0 & 0 \\ \omega_{yx} & 0 & 1 & \omega_{yy_{-1}} & \omega_{yy_{-2}} & 1 \\ -\rho_1 \omega_{yx} & 0 & -\rho_1 & \omega_{yy} - \sigma_{\varepsilon\varepsilon} - \beta\omega_{yx} & \omega_{yy_{-1}} & 0 \\ -\rho_2 \omega_{yx} & 0 & -\rho_2 & \omega_{yy_{-1}} & \omega_{yy} - \sigma_{\varepsilon\varepsilon} - \beta\omega_{yx} & 0 \\ 0 & 0 & 0 & \omega_{yy_{-2}} & \omega_{yy_{-1}} & 0 \\ 0 & 0 & 0 & \omega_{yy_{-3}} & \omega_{yy_{-2}} & 0 \end{pmatrix}$$

And

$$\det J = \det \begin{pmatrix} \omega_{yy_{-2}} & \omega_{yy_{-1}} \\ \omega_{yy_{-3}} & \omega_{yy_{-2}} \end{pmatrix} \det \begin{pmatrix} -\rho_1 \omega_{yx} & -\rho_1 \\ -\rho_2 \omega_{yx} & -\rho_2 \end{pmatrix} = 0,$$

because the last matrix is singular.

As σ_τ is a function of the parameters ρ_1, ρ_2, θ and σ_{aa} only, the Jacobian of this system with respect to the parameters β_0, β_1, $\sigma_{\delta\delta}$, $\sigma_{\varepsilon\varepsilon}$ θ, σ_{aa}, ρ_1 and ρ_2 is given by the matrix:

$$J = \left(\begin{array}{cccc|cccc}
\omega_{xx} - \sigma_{\delta\delta} & 0 & -\beta_0 & 0 & 0 & 0 & 0 & 0 \\
0 & \omega_{xx} - \sigma_{\delta\delta} & -\beta_1 & 0 & 0 & 0 & 0 & 0 \\
\omega_{yx} & \omega_{yx_{-1}} & 0 & 1 & \frac{\partial\sigma_0}{\partial\theta} & \frac{\partial\sigma_0}{\partial\sigma_{aa}} & \frac{\partial\sigma_0}{\partial\rho_1} & \frac{\partial\sigma_0}{\partial\rho_2} \\
0 & \omega_{yx} & 0 & 0 & \frac{\partial\sigma_1}{\partial\theta} & \cdots & \cdots & \frac{\partial\sigma_1}{\partial\rho_2} \\
\hline
0 & 0 & 0 & 0 & \frac{\partial\sigma_2}{\partial\theta} & \cdots & \cdots & \frac{\partial\sigma_2}{\partial\rho_2} \\
0 & 0 & 0 & 0 & \frac{\partial\sigma_3}{\partial\theta} & \cdots & \cdots & \frac{\partial\sigma_3}{\partial\rho 2} \\
0 & 0 & 0 & 0 & \frac{\partial\sigma_4}{\partial\theta} & \cdots & \cdots & \frac{\partial\sigma_4}{\partial\rho_2} \\
0 & 0 & 0 & 0 & \frac{\partial\sigma_5}{\partial\theta} & \cdots & \cdots & \frac{\partial\sigma_5}{\partial\rho_2}
\end{array}\right)$$

Denote by J_1 and J_2 the (4 x 4) matrices of the upper left and lower right corner of J. It follows that det J = 0 if and only if one of the two matrices J_1 and J_2 is singular. It is easily seen that

$$\det J_1 = -\beta_1\omega_{yx} (\omega_{xx} - \sigma_{\delta\delta}) = \beta_0 \beta_1 (\omega_{xx} - \sigma_{\delta\delta})^2 ,$$

which is different from zero (a.e.). Consider now the matrix:

$$J_2 = \begin{pmatrix}
\frac{\partial\sigma_2}{\partial\theta} & \frac{\partial\sigma_2}{\partial\sigma_{aa}} & \frac{\partial\sigma_2}{\partial\rho_1} & \frac{\partial\sigma_2}{\partial\rho_2} \\
\frac{\partial\sigma_3}{\partial\theta} & \frac{\partial\sigma_3}{\partial\sigma_{aa}} & \frac{\partial\sigma_3}{\partial\rho_1} & \frac{\partial\sigma_3}{\partial\rho_2} \\
\frac{\partial\sigma_4}{\partial\theta} & \frac{\partial\sigma_4}{\partial\sigma_{aa}} & \frac{\partial\sigma_4}{\partial\rho_1} & \frac{\partial\sigma_4}{\partial\rho_2} \\
\frac{\partial\sigma_5}{\partial\theta} & \frac{\partial\sigma_5}{\partial\sigma_{aa}} & \frac{\partial\sigma_5}{\partial\rho_1} & \frac{\partial\sigma_5}{\partial\rho_2}
\end{pmatrix} .$$

Expanding J_2 around the last two columns, since

$$\text{(4.15)} \qquad \frac{\partial \sigma_\tau}{\partial \rho_i} = \rho_1 \frac{\partial \sigma_{\tau-1}}{\partial \rho_i} + \rho_2 \frac{\partial \sigma_{\tau-2}}{\partial \rho_i} + \sigma_{\tau-i}, \quad i = 1, 2,$$

it follows that the rows of the (2 x 2) minors obtained from the last two columns are linearly independent. Equations (4.14a) and (4.14c) imply also:

$$\sigma_\tau = E(u_t\, u_{t-\tau}) \ ,$$

thus:

$$\text{(4.16a)} \qquad \sigma_0 = \rho_1\sigma_1 + \rho_2\sigma_2 + [1 + \theta(\rho_1 + \theta)]\, \sigma_{aa}$$

$$\text{(4.16b)} \qquad \sigma_1 = \rho_1\sigma_0 + \rho_2\sigma_1 + \theta\, \sigma_{aa}$$

$$\text{(4.16c)} \qquad \sigma_\tau = \rho_1\sigma_{\tau-1} + \rho_2\sigma_{\tau-2}, \quad \tau > 1.$$

From which it follows that:

$$\text{(4.16d)} \qquad \frac{\partial \sigma_\tau}{\partial \theta} = \rho_1 \frac{\partial \sigma_{\tau-1}}{\partial \theta} + \rho_2 \frac{\partial \sigma_{\tau-2}}{\partial \theta} \ , \quad \tau > 1 \ ,$$

$$\text{(4.16e)} \qquad \frac{\partial \sigma_\tau}{\partial \sigma_{aa}} = \rho_1 \frac{\partial \sigma_{\tau-1}}{\partial \sigma_{aa}} + \rho_2 \frac{\partial \sigma_{\tau-2}}{\partial \sigma_{aa}} \ , \quad \tau > 1 \ .$$

Using equations (4.15) and (4.16d and e), for $\tau = 5$, in the last row of J_2, after some simplifications it is obtained that:

$$\det J_2 = \det \begin{pmatrix} \frac{\partial \sigma_2}{\partial \theta} & \frac{\partial \sigma_2}{\partial \sigma_{aa}} & \frac{\partial \sigma_2}{\partial \rho_1} & \frac{\partial \sigma_2}{\partial \rho_2} \\ \frac{\partial \sigma_3}{\partial \theta} & \frac{\partial \sigma_3}{\partial \sigma_{aa}} & \frac{\partial \sigma_3}{\partial \rho_1} & \frac{\partial \sigma_3}{\partial \rho_2} \\ \frac{\partial \sigma_4}{\partial \theta} & \frac{\partial \sigma_4}{\partial \sigma_{aa}} & \frac{\partial \sigma_4}{\partial \rho_1} & \frac{\partial \sigma_4}{\partial \rho_1} \\ 0 & 0 & \sigma_4 & \sigma_3 \end{pmatrix}$$

Performing the same substitutions for the third row, we obtain:

$$\det J_2 = \det \begin{pmatrix} \frac{\partial\sigma_2}{\partial\theta} & \frac{\partial\sigma_2}{\partial\sigma_{aa}} & \frac{\partial\sigma_2}{\partial\rho_1} & \frac{\partial\sigma_2}{\partial\rho_2} \\ \frac{\partial\sigma_3}{\partial\theta} & \frac{\partial\sigma_3}{\partial\sigma_{aa}} & \frac{\partial\sigma_3}{\partial\rho_1} & \frac{\partial\sigma_3}{\partial\rho_2} \\ 0 & 0 & \sigma_3 & \sigma_2 \\ 0 & 0 & \sigma_4 & \sigma_3 \end{pmatrix}$$

from which it follows that J_2 is nonsingular if the matrices:

$$J_{21} = \begin{pmatrix} \frac{\partial\sigma_2}{\partial\theta} & \frac{\partial\sigma_2}{\partial\sigma_{aa}} \\ \frac{\partial\sigma_3}{\partial\theta} & \frac{\partial\sigma_3}{\partial\sigma_{aaa}} \end{pmatrix} \qquad J_{22} = \begin{pmatrix} \sigma_3 & \sigma_2 \\ \sigma_4 & \sigma_3 \end{pmatrix}$$

are nonsingular. Using (4.16d and e) for $\tau = 2$ and 3 in the elements of J_{21}:

$$(4.17) \quad \det J_{21} = \rho_2^2 \det \begin{pmatrix} \frac{\partial\sigma_0}{\partial\theta} & \frac{\partial\sigma_0}{\partial\sigma_{aa}} \\ \frac{\partial\sigma_1}{\partial\theta} & \frac{\partial\sigma_1}{\partial\sigma_{aa}} \end{pmatrix} .$$

From (4.16b):

$$\sigma_1 = \frac{1}{1-\rho_2} (\rho_1\sigma_0 + \theta\sigma_{aa}) ,$$

and substituting in (4.17), it is found that:

$$\det J_{21} = \frac{\rho_2^2}{1-\rho_2} \det \begin{pmatrix} \frac{\partial\sigma_0}{\partial\theta} & \frac{\partial\sigma_0}{\partial\sigma_{aa}} \\ \sigma_{aa} & \theta \end{pmatrix}$$

As equations (4.16a, b and c) imply:

$$(4.18) \qquad \sigma_0 = \frac{2\rho_1\theta + (\theta^2+1)(1-\rho_2)}{(1+\rho_2)[(1-\rho_2)^2-\rho_1^2]} \sigma_{aa} ,$$

we obtain finally:

$$\det J_{21} = \frac{\rho_2^2\,(\theta^2-1)}{(1+\rho_2)[(1-\rho_2)^2-\rho_1^2]}\;\sigma_{aa}$$

so that J_{21} is nonsingular (a.e.).

Now, using equation (4.16c) for $\tau = 4, 3, 2$, in the matrix J_{22}, it is obtained that

$$\det J_{22} = \rho_2^2 \det \begin{pmatrix} \sigma_1 & \sigma_0 \\ \sigma_2 & \sigma_1 \end{pmatrix},$$

and considering (4.10b) and (4.18), it is straightforward to verify that $\det J_{22} \neq 0$ (a.e.).

Third Example

Consider now a model with the same structural equation as in the previous example (i.e., (4.14c)), but assume that the shock process is an ARMA (2,2). That is:

(4.19) $$u_t = \rho_1 u_{t-1} + \rho_2 u_{t-2} + a_t + \theta_1 a_{t-1} + \theta_2 a_{t-2} ,$$

where the stationarity conditions for the ρ-parameters are as in the previous example, and the invertibility conditions imply

$$\theta_2 + \theta_1 > -1,\ \theta_1 - \theta_2 < 1,\ -1 < \theta_2 < 1.$$

As $r = 2$, $s = 2$ (so that $r \leqq s$), the conditions for identification of the model are $q_j^* \geqq j+s-r$, or $q_1^* \geqq 1$, $q_2^* \geqq 2$. It follows that the model is not identified.

The system of covariance equations is identical to the one corresponding to the second example, thus the model will be identified only if the system of autocovariance equations:

(4.20) $$\omega_{yy_{-\tau}} = \sigma_\tau, \quad \tau \geq 1$$

provides a subsystem that can be solved for the parameters θ_1, θ_2, σ_{aa}, ρ_1, ρ_2. Consider the equations for $\tau = 2, 3, 4, 5, 6$, and the Jacobian:

$$J = \begin{pmatrix} \frac{\partial \sigma_2}{\partial \theta_1} & \frac{\partial \sigma_2}{\partial \theta_2} & \frac{\partial \sigma_2}{\partial \sigma_{aa}} & \frac{\partial \sigma_2}{\partial \rho_1} & \frac{\partial \sigma_2}{\partial \rho_2} \\ \frac{\partial \sigma_3}{\partial \theta_1} & \frac{\partial \sigma_3}{\partial \theta_2} & \frac{\partial \sigma_3}{\partial \sigma_{aa}} & \frac{\partial \sigma_3}{\partial \rho_1} & \frac{\partial \sigma_3}{\partial \rho_2} \\ \frac{\partial \sigma_4}{\partial \theta_1} & \frac{\partial \sigma_4}{\partial \theta_2} & \frac{\partial \sigma_4}{\partial \sigma_{aa}} & \frac{\partial \sigma_4}{\partial \rho_1} & \frac{\partial \sigma_4}{\partial \rho_2} \\ \frac{\partial \sigma_5}{\partial \theta_1} & \frac{\partial \sigma_5}{\partial \theta_2} & \frac{\partial \sigma_5}{\partial \sigma_{aa}} & \frac{\partial \sigma_5}{\partial \rho_1} & \frac{\partial \sigma_5}{\partial \rho_2} \\ \frac{\partial \sigma_6}{\partial \theta_1} & \frac{\partial \sigma_6}{\partial \theta_2} & \frac{\partial \sigma_6}{\partial \sigma_{aa}} & \frac{\partial \sigma_6}{\partial \rho_1} & \frac{\partial \sigma_6}{\partial \rho_2} \end{pmatrix}$$

Due to the fact that equation (4.19) implies

$$\sigma_\tau = \rho_1 \sigma_{\tau-1} + \rho_2 \sigma_{\tau-2}, \qquad \tau > 2 ,$$

the above Jacobian is singular. This is easily seen by considering the Laplace expansion of det J around the last two columns: any (3 x 3) complementary minor formed with the first three columns has a row which is a linear combination of the other two rows, since

$$\frac{\partial \sigma_\tau}{\partial \theta} = \rho_1 \frac{\partial \sigma_{\tau-1}}{\partial \theta_i} + \rho_2 \frac{\partial \sigma_{\tau-2}}{\partial \theta_i}, \qquad i = 1, 2$$

$$\frac{\partial \sigma_\tau}{\partial \sigma_{aa}} = \rho_1 \frac{\partial \sigma_{\tau-1}}{\partial \sigma_{aa}} + \rho_2 \frac{\partial \sigma_{\tau-2}}{\partial \sigma_{aa}},$$

for $\tau \geq 2$.

It can be verified that any other combination of five autocovariance equations of the form (4.20) will have a Jacobian with respect to the five parameters θ_1, θ_2, σ_{aa}, ρ_1 and ρ_2 that is singular also. Thus the model is not identified.[6/]

6/ To see an example of Lemma 7, consider the minor

Fourth Example

Finally we shall illustrate the case of an identified model when $r \leqq s$.

Let the structural equation be given by

$$(4.21a) \quad \eta_t = \gamma_1\eta_{t-1} + \gamma_2\eta_{t-2} + \gamma_3\eta_{t-3} + \beta_0^{(1)}\zeta_t^{(1)} + \beta_1^{(1)}\zeta_{t-1}^{(1)} + \beta_2^{(1)}\zeta_{t-2}^{(1)}$$

$$+ \beta_0^{(2)}\zeta_t^{(2)} + \beta_1^{(2)}\zeta_{t-1}^{(2)} + \beta_2^{(2)}\zeta_{t-2}^{(2)} + \beta_3^{(2)}\zeta_{t-3}^{(2)} + \beta_4^{(2)}\zeta_{t-4}^{(2)} + u_t ,$$

and the shock be the outcome of the ARMA (1, 2) process:

6/ (Continued)

$$\begin{pmatrix} \frac{\partial\sigma_2}{\partial\theta_1} & \frac{\partial\sigma_2}{\partial\theta_2} & \frac{\partial\sigma_2}{\partial\sigma_{aa}} \\ \frac{\partial\sigma_4}{\partial\theta_1} & \frac{\partial\sigma_4}{\partial\theta_2} & \frac{\partial\sigma_4}{\partial\sigma_{aa}} \\ \frac{\partial\sigma_5}{\partial\theta_1} & \frac{\partial\sigma_5}{\partial\theta_2} & \frac{\partial\sigma_5}{\partial\sigma_{aa}} \end{pmatrix}$$

We shall prove that σ_2, σ_4 and σ_5 are related by an equation of the form:

$$(f.4.1) \quad \sigma_5 = \rho_1^* \sigma_4 + \rho_2^* \sigma_2$$

where ρ_1^* and ρ_2^* are functions of ρ_1 and ρ_2. From (4.19)

$$(f.4.2) \quad \sigma_5 = \rho_1\sigma_4 + \rho_2\sigma_3 = (\rho_1^2 + \rho_2)\sigma_3 + \rho_1\rho_2\sigma_2 .$$

Also, equation (f.4.1) implies:

$$(f.4.3) \quad \sigma_5 = \rho_1^*(\rho_1\sigma_3 + \rho_2\sigma_2) + \rho_2^*\sigma_2 = \rho_1^*\rho_1\sigma_3 + (\rho_1^*\rho_1 + \rho_2^*)\sigma_2$$

Equation (f.4.2) and (f.43) yield:

$$\rho_1^* = \frac{\rho_1^2 + \rho_2}{\rho_1} \quad ; \quad \rho_2^* = \frac{-\rho_2^2}{\rho_1} ,$$

thus

$$\sigma_5 = \frac{\rho_1^2 + \rho_2}{\rho_1}\sigma_4 - \frac{\rho_2^2}{\rho_1}\sigma_2 .$$

It follows that:

$$\frac{\partial\sigma_5}{\partial\theta_i} = \rho_1^*\frac{\partial\sigma_4}{\partial\theta_i} + \rho_2^*\frac{\partial\sigma_2}{\partial\theta_i} , \quad i = 1, 2$$

$$\frac{\partial\sigma_5}{\partial\theta_{aa}} = \rho_1^*\frac{\partial\sigma_4}{\partial\sigma_{aa}} + \rho_2^*\frac{\partial\sigma_2}{\partial\sigma_{aa}} ,$$

and the above minor is equal to zero.

(4.21b) $u_t = \rho\, u_{t-1} + a_t + \theta_1\, a_{t-1} + \theta_2\, a_{t-2}$,

where the γ, ρ and θ-parameters satisfy the appropriate stationarity and invertiibility conditions

As $r = 1$, $s = 2$, the conditions for identification of the model are $q_j^* \geqq j + 1 \quad j = 1, 2, 3$. As $q_1^* = 2$, $q_2^* = 3$ and $q_3^* = 4$, the conditions are met and the model should be identified.

The parameters γ_1, γ_2 and γ_3 are identified through the crosscovariance equations:

$$\omega_{yx_{-\tau}}^{(1)} = \gamma_1\, \omega_{yx_{-\tau+1}}^{(1)} + \gamma_2\, \omega_{yx_{-\tau+2}}^{(1)} + \gamma_3\, \omega_{yx_{-\tau+3}}^{(1)} , \quad \tau = 3, 4, 5.$$

Consider the following system of covariance equations:

$$\omega_{yx}^{(1)} = \beta_0^{(1)} (\omega_{xx}^{(1)} - \sigma_{\delta\delta}^{(1)})$$

$$\omega_{yx_{-1}}^{(1)} = \gamma_1 \omega_{yx}^{(1)} + \beta_1^{(1)} (\omega_{xx}^{(1)} - \sigma_{\delta\delta}^{(1)})$$

$$\omega_{yx_{-2}}^{(1)} = \gamma_1 \omega_{yx_{-1}}^{(1)} + \gamma_2 \omega_{yx}^{(1)} + \beta_2^{(1)} (\omega_{xx}^{(1)} - \sigma_{\delta\delta}^{(1)})$$

$$\omega_{yx}^{(2)} = \beta_0^{(2)} (\omega_{xx}^{(2)} - \sigma_{\delta\delta}^{(2)})$$

$$\omega_{yx_{-1}}^{(2)} = \gamma_1 \omega_{yx}^{(2)} + \beta_1^{(2)} (\omega_{xx}^{(2)} - \sigma_{\delta\delta}^{(2)})$$

$$\omega_{yx_{-2}}^{(2)} = \gamma_1 \omega_{yx_{-1}}^{(2)} + \gamma_2 \omega_{yx}^{(2)} + \beta_2^{(2)} (\omega_{xx}^{(2)} - \sigma_{\delta\delta}^{(2)})$$

$$\omega_{yx_{-3}}^{(2)} = \gamma_1 \omega_{yx_{-2}}^{(2)} + \gamma_2 \omega_{yx_{-1}}^{(2)} + \gamma_3 \omega_{yx}^{(2)} + \beta_3^{(2)} (\omega_{xx}^{(2)} - \sigma_{\delta\delta}^{(2)})$$

$$\omega_{yx_{-4}}^{(2)} = \gamma_1 \omega_{yx_{-3}}^{(2)} + \gamma_2 \omega_{yx_{-2}}^{(2)} + \gamma_3 \omega_{yx_{-1}}^{(2)} + \beta_4^{(2)} (\omega_{xx}^{(2)} - \sigma_{\delta\delta}^{(2)})$$

$$\omega_{yy} = \gamma_1 \omega_{yy_{-1}} + \gamma_2 \omega_{yy_{-2}} + \gamma_3 \omega_{yy_{-3}} + \beta_0^{(1)} \omega_{yx}^{(1)} + \beta_1^{(1)} \omega_{yx_{-1}}^{(1)} + \beta_2^{(1)} \omega_{yx_{-2}}^{(1)} + \beta_0^{(2)} \omega_{yx}^{(2)} + \beta_1^{(2)} \omega_{yx_{-1}}^{(2)} + \beta_2^{(2)} \omega_{yx_{-2}}^{(2)} + \beta_3^{(2)} \omega_{yx_{-3}}^{(2)} + \beta_4^{(2)} \omega_{yx_{-4}}^{(2)} + \sigma_{\varepsilon\varepsilon} + \sigma_0$$

$$\omega_{yy_{-1}} = \gamma_1 (\omega_{yy} - \sigma_{\varepsilon\varepsilon}) + \gamma_2 \omega_{yy_{-1}} + \gamma_3 \omega_{yy_{-2}} + \beta_1^{(1)} \omega_{yx}^{(1)} + \beta_2^{(1)} \omega_{yx_{-1}}^{(1)} + \beta_1^{(2)} \omega_{yx}^{(2)} + \beta_2^{(2)} \omega_{yx_{-1}}^{(2)} + \beta_3^{(2)} \omega_{yx_{-2}}^{(2)} + \beta_4^{(2)} \omega_{yx_{-3}}^{(2)} + \sigma_1$$

$$\omega_{yy_{-2}} = \gamma_1\omega_{yy_{-1}} + \gamma_2\,(\omega_{yy} - \sigma_{\varepsilon\varepsilon}) + \gamma_3\omega_{yy_{-1}} + \beta_2^{(1)}\,\omega_{yx}^{(1)} + \beta_2^{(2)}\,\omega_{yx}^{(2)} + \beta_3^{(2)}\,\omega_{yx_{-1}}^{(2)} + \beta_4^{(2)}\,\omega_{yx_{-2}}^{(2)} + \sigma_2$$

$$\omega_{yy_{-3}} = \gamma_1\omega_{yy_{-2}} + \gamma_2\omega_{yy_{-1}} + \gamma_3\,(\omega_{yy} - \sigma_{\varepsilon\varepsilon}) + \beta_3^{(2)}\,\omega_{yx}^{(2)} + \beta_4^{(2)}\,\omega_{yx_{-1}}^{(2)} + \sigma_3$$

$$\omega_{yy_{-4}} = \gamma_1\omega_{yy_{-3}} + \gamma_2\omega_{yy_{-2}} + \gamma_3\omega_{yy_{-1}} + \beta_4^{(2)}\,\omega_{yx}^{(2)} + \sigma_4$$

$$\omega_{yy_{-5}} = \gamma_1\omega_{yy_{-4}} + \gamma_2\omega_{yy_{-3}} + \gamma_3\omega_{yy_{-2}} + \sigma_5$$

$$\omega_{yy_{-6}} = \gamma_1\omega_{yy_{-5}} + \gamma_2\omega_{yy_{-4}} + \gamma_3\omega_{yy_{-3}} + \sigma_6$$

The model is identified if the Jacobian of this system of fifteen equations with respect to the parameters $\beta_0^{(1)}$, $\beta_1^{(1)}$, $\beta_2^{(1)}$, $\beta_0^{(2)}$, $\beta_1^{(2)}$, $\beta_2^{(2)}$, $\beta_3^{(2)}$, $\beta_4^{(2)}$, $\sigma_{\delta\delta}^{(1)}$, $\sigma_{\delta\delta}^{(2)}$, $\sigma_{\varepsilon\varepsilon}$, θ_1, θ_2, σ_{aa} and ρ is nonsingular. This Jacobian is given by the matrix:

$$
\left(\begin{array}{ccccccccccc|cccc}
\bar{\omega}_1 & 0 & 0 & 0 & 0 & 0 & 0 & 0 & -\beta_0^{(1)} & 0 & 0 & & & & \\
0 & \bar{\omega}_1 & 0 & 0 & 0 & 0 & 0 & 0 & -\beta_1^{(1)} & 0 & 0 & & & & \\
0 & 0 & \bar{\omega}_1 & 0 & 0 & 0 & 0 & 0 & -\beta_2^{(1)} & 0 & 0 & & & & \\
0 & 0 & 0 & \bar{\omega}_2 & 0 & 0 & 0 & 0 & 0 & -\beta_0^{(2)} & 0 & & & & \\
0 & 0 & 0 & 0 & \bar{\omega}_2 & 0 & 0 & 0 & 0 & -\beta_1^{(2)} & 0 & & & 0 & \\
0 & 0 & 0 & 0 & 0 & \bar{\omega}_2 & 0 & 0 & 0 & -\beta_2^{(2)} & 0 & & & & \\
0 & 0 & 0 & 0 & 0 & 0 & \bar{\omega}_2 & 0 & 0 & -\beta_3^{(2)} & 0 & & & & \\
0 & 0 & 0 & 0 & 0 & 0 & 0 & \bar{\omega}_2 & 0 & -\beta_4^{(2)} & 0 & & & & \\
\hline
\omega_{yx}^{(1)} & \omega_{yx_{-1}}^{(1)} & \omega_{yx_{-2}}^{(1)} & \omega_{yx}^{(2)} & \omega_{yx_{-1}}^{(2)} & \omega_{yx_{-2}}^{(2)} & \omega_{yx_{-3}}^{(2)} & \omega_{yx_{-4}}^{(2)} & 0 & 0 & 1 & \frac{\partial\sigma_0}{\partial\theta_1} & \frac{\partial\sigma_0}{\partial\theta_2} & \frac{\partial\sigma_0}{\partial\sigma_{aa}} & \frac{\partial\sigma_0}{\partial\rho} \\
0 & \omega_{yx}^{(1)} & \omega_{yx_{-1}}^{(1)} & 0 & \omega_{yx}^{(2)} & \omega_{yx_{-1}}^{(2)} & \omega_{yx_{-2}}^{(2)} & \omega_{yx_{-3}}^{(2)} & 0 & 0 & -\gamma_1 & \frac{\partial\sigma_1}{\partial\theta_1} & \frac{\partial\sigma_1}{\partial\theta_2} & \frac{\partial\sigma_1}{\partial\sigma_{aa}} & \frac{\partial\sigma_1}{\partial\rho} \\
0 & 0 & \omega_{yx}^{(1)} & 0 & 0 & \omega_{yx}^{(2)} & \omega_{yx_{-1}}^{(2)} & \omega_{yx_{-2}}^{(2)} & 0 & 0 & -\gamma_2 & \frac{\partial\sigma_2}{\partial\theta_1} & \frac{\partial\sigma_2}{\partial\theta_2} & \frac{\partial\sigma_2}{\partial\sigma_{aa}} & \frac{\partial\sigma_2}{\partial\rho} \\
0 & 0 & 0 & 0 & 0 & 0 & \omega_{yx}^{(2)} & \omega_{yx_{-1}}^{(2)} & 0 & 0 & -\gamma_3 & \frac{\partial\sigma_3}{\partial\theta_1} & \frac{\partial\sigma_3}{\partial\theta_2} & \frac{\partial\sigma_3}{\partial\sigma_{aa}} & \frac{\partial\sigma_3}{\partial\rho} \\
0 & 0 & 0 & 0 & 0 & 0 & 0 & \omega_{yx}^{(2)} & 0 & 0 & 0 & \frac{\partial\sigma_4}{\partial\theta_1} & \frac{\partial\sigma_4}{\partial\theta_2} & \frac{\partial\sigma_4}{\partial\sigma_{aa}} & \frac{\partial\sigma_4}{\partial\rho} \\
\hline
 & & & & 0 & & & & & & & \frac{\partial\sigma_5}{\partial\theta_1} & \frac{\partial\sigma_5}{\partial\theta_2} & \frac{\partial\sigma_5}{\partial\sigma_{aa}} & \frac{\partial\sigma_5}{\partial\rho} \\
 & & & & & & & & & & & \frac{\partial\sigma_6}{\partial\theta_1} & \frac{\partial\sigma_6}{\partial\theta_2} & \frac{\partial\sigma_6}{\partial\sigma_{aa}} & \frac{\partial\sigma_6}{\partial\rho}
\end{array}\right)
$$

where $\bar{\omega}_i = (\omega_{xx}^{(i)} - \sigma_{\delta\delta}^{(i)})$, i = 1, 2. Notice that the partition of the Jacobian corresponds to the one for J_{22} in (4.9b), where J_D and J_A are zero matrices.

Consider the Laplace expansion of the Jacobian around the last four columns. In order to have a complementary minor different from zero, the minors obtained from the last four columns have to include the last two rows. Let us find out which ones of these minors are also different from zero themselves.

The minors are (4 x 4) determinants of the form

$$(4.23) \qquad \begin{vmatrix} \frac{\partial\sigma_{\tau_1}}{\partial\theta_1} & \frac{\partial\sigma_{\tau_1}}{\partial\theta_2} & \frac{\partial\sigma_{\tau_1}}{\partial\sigma_{aa}} & \frac{\partial\sigma_{\tau_1}}{\partial\rho} \\ \frac{\partial\sigma_{\tau_2}}{\partial\theta_1} & \frac{\partial\sigma_{\tau_2}}{\partial\theta_2} & \frac{\partial\sigma_{\tau_2}}{\partial\sigma_{aa}} & \frac{\partial\sigma_{\tau_2}}{\partial\rho} \\ \frac{\partial\sigma_5}{\partial\theta_1} & \frac{\partial\sigma_5}{\partial\theta_2} & \frac{\partial\sigma_5}{\partial\sigma_{aa}} & \frac{\partial\sigma_5}{\partial\rho} \\ \frac{\partial\sigma_6}{\partial\theta_1} & \frac{\partial\sigma_6}{\partial\theta_2} & \frac{\partial\sigma_6}{\partial\sigma_{aa}} & \frac{\partial\sigma_6}{\partial\rho} \end{vmatrix}$$

where τ_1 and τ_2 are combinations of the numbers 0, 1, 2, 3, and 4 (without loss of generality, assume $\tau_1 < \tau_2$). We shall prove that only the determinant for which $\tau_1 = 0$ and $\tau_2 = 1$ is different from zero.

Consider equation (4.21b). If follows that

$$(4.24) \qquad \sigma_\tau = \rho\sigma_{\tau-1} = \rho^{\tau-2}\,\sigma_2,$$

for $\tau > 2$. Expand the determinant by the elements of the last column. Let $\tau_1 \neq 0$. Then all the minors appearing in the expansion have at least two rows containing the partial derivatives of σ_τ's for $\tau > 2$. As (4.24) implies

$$\frac{\partial\sigma_\tau}{\partial\theta_i} = \rho^{\tau-2}\frac{\partial\sigma_2}{\partial\theta_i}, \qquad i = 1, 2$$

$$\frac{\partial\sigma_\tau}{\partial\sigma_{aa}} = \rho^{\tau-2}\frac{\partial\sigma_2}{\partial\sigma_{aa}},$$

it follows that all such minors will be zero. Thus in order for the determinant (4.23) to be different from zero, it has to be that $\tau_1 = 0$. Now, let $\tau_2 \neq 1$.

Again, all the minors in the expansion will have at least two rows with the partial derivatives of σ_τ's for $\tau > 2$; thus they will be zero also. Therefore, all the determinants of the form (4.23), different from the one for which $\tau_1 = 0$, $\tau_2 = 1$, are zero. Now, to see that the determinant

$$E_0 = \begin{vmatrix} \frac{\partial\sigma_0}{\partial\theta_1} & \frac{\partial\sigma_0}{\partial\theta_2} & \frac{\partial\sigma_0}{\partial\sigma_{aa}} & \frac{\partial\sigma_0}{\partial\rho} \\ \frac{\partial\sigma_1}{\partial\theta_1} & \frac{\partial\sigma_1}{\partial\theta_2} & \frac{\partial\sigma_1}{\partial\sigma_{aa}} & \frac{\partial\sigma_1}{\partial\rho} \\ \frac{\partial\sigma_5}{\partial\theta_1} & \frac{\partial\sigma_5}{\partial\theta_2} & \frac{\partial\sigma_5}{\partial\sigma_{aa}} & \frac{\partial\sigma_5}{\partial\rho} \\ \frac{\partial\sigma_6}{\partial\theta_1} & \frac{\partial\sigma_6}{\partial\theta_2} & \frac{\partial\sigma_6}{\partial\sigma_{aa}} & \frac{\partial\sigma_6}{\partial\rho} \end{vmatrix}$$

is different from zero, notice that (4.24) implies that E_0 can be written as:

$$E_0 = \begin{vmatrix} \frac{\partial\sigma_0}{\partial\theta_1} & \frac{\partial\sigma_0}{\partial\theta_2} & \frac{\partial\sigma_0}{\partial\sigma_{aa}} & \frac{\partial\sigma_0}{\partial\rho} \\ \frac{\partial\sigma_1}{\partial\theta_1} & \frac{\partial\sigma_1}{\partial\theta_2} & \frac{\partial\sigma_1}{\partial\sigma_{aa}} & \frac{\partial\sigma_1}{\partial\rho} \\ \frac{\partial\sigma_5}{\partial\theta_1} & \frac{\partial\sigma_5}{\partial\theta_2} & \frac{\partial\sigma_5}{\partial\sigma_{aa}} & \frac{\partial\sigma_5}{\partial\rho} \\ 0 & 0 & 0 & \sigma_5 \end{vmatrix}$$

Thus $E_0 \neq 0$ if

$$\begin{vmatrix} \frac{\partial\sigma_0}{\partial\theta_1} & \frac{\partial\sigma_0}{\partial\theta_2} & \frac{\partial\sigma_0}{\partial\sigma_{aa}} \\ \frac{\partial\sigma_1}{\partial\theta_1} & \frac{\partial\sigma_1}{\partial\theta_2} & \frac{\partial\sigma_1}{\partial\sigma_{aa}} \\ \frac{\partial\sigma_5}{\partial\theta_1} & \frac{\partial\sigma_5}{\partial\theta_2} & \frac{\partial\sigma_5}{\partial\sigma_{aa}} \end{vmatrix} \tag{4.25}$$

is different from zero. (Notice that this last determinant represents the minor E_{i0} used in the proof of Theorem 4.)

Using the relationship:

$$\sigma_5 = \rho^3 \; (\rho\sigma_1 + \theta_2\sigma_{aa}),$$

expression (4.25) can be simplified into

$$(4.26) \qquad \rho_3 \begin{vmatrix} \frac{\partial\sigma_0}{\partial\theta_1} & \frac{\partial\sigma_0}{\partial\theta_2} & \frac{\partial\sigma_0}{\partial\sigma_{aa}} \\ \frac{\partial\sigma_1}{\partial\theta_1} & \frac{\partial\sigma_1}{\partial\theta_2} & \frac{\partial\sigma_1}{\partial\sigma_{aa}} \\ 0 & \sigma_{aa} & \theta \end{vmatrix}$$

Finally, using the following relationships (implied by (4.21a) and (4.21b)):

$$\sigma_1 = \rho\sigma_0 + [\theta_1 + \theta_2 (\gamma_1 + \rho + \theta_1)] \sigma_{aa}$$

$$\sigma_0 = \rho\sigma_{yu_{-1}} + \{1+(\theta_1+\theta_2\gamma_1)(\gamma_1+\rho+\theta_1) + \theta_2[\gamma_2+\rho(\rho+\theta_1)+\theta_2]\} \sigma_{aa}$$

$$\sigma_{yu_{-1}} = \gamma_1\sigma_0 +\gamma_2\sigma_1+\gamma_3\sigma_2 + \frac{1}{1-\rho^2} \{\rho\theta_2^{\,2} + (\rho+\theta_1)(1+\rho\theta_1+\theta_2\rho^2 + \theta_2)\} \sigma_{aa}$$

$$\sigma_2 = \rho\sigma_1 + \theta_2\sigma_{aa},$$

it can be verified that the determinant given by expression (4.26) is different from zero.

In Chapter II we analyzed identification of an error-in-the-variables distributed lag model under the assumptions that the shock of the structural equation plus all the exogenous variables were independent white-noise variables. In Chapter III and IV we have removed the assumption of the white-noise shock. In Chapter III we found that the conditions for identification become more restrictive when the shock is a pure moving average process, and less restrictive when the process is a pure autoregression. In Chapter IV we have combined both processes into a mixed autoregressive-moving average process. We concluded that the combined effect varies according to the relative orders of the autoregressive and moving average polynomials.

In the next Chapter, we shall modify the assumption concerning the exogenous variables. As we shall see, while different autocorrelation functions for the shock may have opposite effects, for the case of an exogenous variable the effect has always the same direction (in the sense that the presence of autocorrelation always increase the state of identification of the model).

CHAPTER V

AUTOCORRELATED EXOGENOUS VARIABLES, WHITE NOISE SHOCK

The analysis of the previous chapters was developed under the assumption that the exogenous variables were independent white-noises. In the present chapter this assumption is dropped, and models with autocorrelated exogenous variables are considered. In order to isolate the identification effects due to the presence of autocorrelation in the exogenous variables from the ones implied by the presence of autocorrelation in the shock, in this chapter we shall assume that the latter is a white-noise variable.

To characterize the different autocorrelations functions of the exogenous variables, autoregressive-moving average (ARMA) processes will be used.

We begin the analysis by considering two illustrative examples.

1. SOME EXAMPLES

1.1 First Example

Consider the model given by the equations:

(5.1a) $$\eta_t = \gamma\eta_{t-1} + \beta\zeta_t + u_t$$

(5.1b) $$x_t = \zeta_t + \delta_t$$

(5.1c) $$y_t = \eta_t + \varepsilon_t \quad ,$$

where u_t, δ_t and ε_t are independent white-noise variables, independent also of ζ_t, and where stationarity implies $-1 < \gamma < 1$. In Section 1.2 of Chapter II (case d), the model was analyzed under a white-noise assumption for the exogenous variable ζ and it was found to be underidentified. Now assume, instead, that ζ follows a moving average process of order one, that is

(5.2) $$\zeta_t = b_t + \alpha b_{t-1} \ ,$$

where b_t is white-noise and, due to the invertibility assumption, $-1 < \alpha < 1$. The system of covariance equations corresponding to (5.1) will be

(5.3a) $\omega_{yx} = \gamma\omega_{xy_{-1}} + \beta(\omega_{xx} - \sigma_{\delta\delta})$

(5.3b) $\omega_{yx_{-1}} = \gamma\omega_{yx} + \beta\omega_{xx_{-1}}$

(5.3c) $\omega_{yx_{-2}} = \gamma\omega_{yx_{-1}}$

(5.3d) $\omega_{yy_{-1}} = \gamma(\omega_{yy} - \sigma_{\varepsilon\varepsilon}) + \beta\omega_{xy_{-1}}$

(5.3e) $\omega_{yy} = \gamma\omega_{yy_{-1}} + \beta\omega_{yx} + \sigma_{\varepsilon\varepsilon} + \sigma_{uu}$

plus a set of equations with γ appearing explicityly as the only parameter. Comparing this sytem with the one corresponding to the white-noise exogenous variable case, it is seen that the difference consists in the fact that now the equations of the system of covariance equations contain the terms $\omega_{xy_{-1}}$ and $\omega_{xx_{-1}}$, which were zero for the white-noise case.

Equation (5.2) yields an additional set of covariance equations. In particular

(5.4a) $\omega_{xx} = (1 + \alpha^2)\,\sigma_{bb} + \sigma_{\delta\delta}$

(5.4b) $\omega_{xx_{-1}} = \alpha\sigma_{bb}$,

The Jacobian of the system of equations (5.3) with respect to the parameters γ, β, $\sigma_{\delta\delta}$, $\sigma_{\varepsilon\varepsilon}$ and σ_{uu} is given by the matrix.

$$J_1 = \begin{pmatrix} \omega_{yx_{-1}} & 0 & 0 & 0 & 0 \\ \omega_{yx} & \omega_{xx_{-1}} & 0 & 0 & 0 \\ \omega_{xy_{-1}} & \omega_{xx}-\sigma_{\delta\delta} & -\beta & 0 & 0 \\ \omega_{yy}-\sigma_{\varepsilon\varepsilon} & \omega_{xy_{-1}} & 0 & -\gamma & 0 \\ \omega_{yy_{-1}} & \omega_{yx} & 0 & 0 & 1 \end{pmatrix}$$

with determinant equal to

$$\det J = \beta\gamma\,\omega_{xx_{-1}}\,\omega_{yx_{-1}} = \beta\sigma_{bb}\,[(1 + \gamma^2)\,\alpha + (1 + \alpha^2)\gamma]$$

Thus the parameters γ, β, $\sigma_{\delta\delta}$, $\sigma_{\varepsilon\varepsilon}$ and σ_{uu} are identified. Consider now the Jacobian of the system of equations (5.4) with respect to the parameters α and σ_{bb}, given by the matrix:

$$J_2 = \begin{pmatrix} 2\alpha\sigma_{bb} & 1 + \alpha^2 \\ \sigma_{bb} & \alpha \end{pmatrix}$$

As det $J_2 = (\alpha^2 - 1)\,\sigma_{bb}$, the invertibility condition implies det $J_2 \neq 0$. Hence the parameters α and σ_{bb} are also identified, and, consequently, the complete model implied by equations (5.1) and (5.2) is identified.

Thus the presence of autocorrelation in the exogenous variable, in the previous example, increases the state of identification of the model consisting of the system of equations (5.1). In particular, the system of τ-lag cross covariance equations for $\tau = 0$, 1 and 2, can be solved for the parameters γ, β, and $\sigma_{\delta\delta}$, due to the presence of the autocovariance $\omega_{xx_{-1}}$. Considering that this autocovariance will be also nonzero for autoregressive or higher-order moving average processes, it seems that the model would be identified also when the autocorrelation function of the exogenous variable is explained by these other types of stochastic processes.

1.2 Second Example

When the exogenous variables are assumed to be independent white-noise variables, we concluded in Chapter II, that the more exogenous variables are included in the model, the more restrictive are the conditions for identification. To illustrate how this result has to be modified when the exogenous variables are autocorrelated, consider a model similar to the one used in the first example, but with an additional exogenous variable, which is assumed to follow a first order autoregressive process. Thus, let the model be described by the equations:

(5.5a) $$\eta_t = \gamma\eta_{t-1} + \beta^{(1)}\,\zeta_t^{(1)} + \beta^{(2)}\,\zeta_t^{(2)} + u_t$$

(5.5b) $$\zeta_t^{(1)} = b_t^{(1)} + \alpha\, b_{t-1}^{(1)}$$

(5.5c) $$\zeta_t^{(2)} = \phi\,\zeta_{t-1}^{(2)} + b_t^{(2)} ,$$

together with the EIV equations (5.1b) and (5.1c). The variables u, ε, δ, $b^{(1)}$ and $b^{(2)}$ are independent white-noise variables, and stationarity and invertibility for the processes (5.5a, b and c) imply $-1 < \gamma < 1$, $-1 < \alpha < 1$ and $-1 < \phi < 1$.

Consider equation (5.5a). The τ-lag crosscovariance equations corresponding to $\zeta^{(1)}$, for $\tau = 0, 1, 2$, is given by equations (5.3a), (5.3b) and (5.3c), respectively (with the appropriate superindex 1 in the ω-covariances, in β and in $\sigma_{\delta\delta}$). The τ-lag crosscovariance equations corresponding to $\zeta^{(2)}$, for $\tau = 0, 1$, are given also by equations (5.3a) and (5.3b), respectively (with the superindex 2 in the ω-covariances and the β and $\sigma_{\delta\delta}$ parameters). The τ-lag autocovariance equations for $\tau = 0, 1$ are given by the expressions:

$$\omega_{yy} = \gamma\omega_{yy_{-1}} + \beta^{(1)}\,\omega^{(1)}_{yx} + \beta^{(2)}\,\omega^{(2)}_{yx} + \sigma_{\varepsilon\varepsilon} + \sigma_{uu}$$

$$\omega_{yy_{-1}} = \gamma(\omega_{yy} - \sigma_{\varepsilon\varepsilon}) + \beta^{(1)}\,\omega^{(1)}_{xy_{-1}} + \beta^{(2)}\omega^{(2)}_{xy_{-1}}$$

The Jacobian of the system of covariance equations mentioned in the previous paragraph with respect to the parameters γ, $\beta^{(1)}$, $\sigma^{(1)}_{\delta\delta}$, $\beta^{(2)}$, $\sigma^{(2)}_{\delta\delta}$, $\sigma_{\varepsilon\varepsilon}$ and σ_{uu} is given by the matrix:

$$J_1 = \begin{pmatrix} \omega^{(1)}_{yx_{-1}} & 0 & 0 & 0 & 0 & 0 & 0 \\ \omega^{(1)}_{yx} & \omega^{(1)}_{xx_{-1}} & 0 & 0 & 0 & 0 & 0 \\ \omega^{(1)}_{xy_{-1}} & \omega^{(1)}_{xx}-\sigma^{(1)}_{\delta\delta} & -\beta^{(1)} & 0 & 0 & 0 & 0 \\ \omega^{(2)}_{yx} & 0 & 0 & \omega^{(2)}_{xx_{-1}} & 0 & 0 & 0 \\ \omega^{(2)}_{xy_{-1}} & 0 & 0 & \omega^{(2)}_{xx}-\sigma^{(2)}_{\delta\delta} & -\beta^{(2)} & 0 & 0 \\ \omega_{yy}-\sigma_{\varepsilon\varepsilon} & \omega^{(1)}_{xy_{-1}} & 0 & \omega^{(2)}_{xy_{-1}} & 0 & -\gamma & 0 \\ \omega_{yy_{-1}} & \omega^{(1)}_{yx} & 0 & \omega^{(2)}_{yx} & 0 & 1 & 1 \end{pmatrix}$$

It follows that

$$\det J_1 = -\gamma\beta^{(1)}\,\beta^{(2)}\,\omega^{(1)}_{yx_{-1}}\,\omega^{(1)}_{xx_{-1}}\,\omega^{(2)}_{xx_{-1}} \quad ,$$

which after substituting for the covariances as functions of the parameters yields

$$\det J_1 = -\gamma\alpha\phi\beta^{(2)} [\beta^{(1)} \sigma_{bb}^{(1)}]^2 (\gamma+\alpha)(\gamma\alpha + 1) \frac{1}{1-\phi^2} \sigma_{bb}^{(2)} ,$$

which is different from zero.

Consider now equation (5.5b). The τ-lag autocovariance equations for $\tau = 0, 1$ yield equations (5.4a) and (5.4b), respectively (with the appropriate superindex 1), and the Jacobian of these two equations with respect to $\sigma_{bb}^{(1)}$ and α has a nonzero determinant equal to $(\alpha^2 - 1)\, \sigma_{bb}^{(1)}$.

Finally, consider equation (5.5c). The τ-lag autocovariance equations for $\tau = 0, 1$ are given by the expressions:

$$\omega_{xx}^{(2)} = \phi\omega_{xx_{-1}}^{(2)} + \sigma_{\delta\delta}^{(2)} + \sigma_{bb}^{(2)}$$

$$\omega_{xx_{-1}}^{(2)} = \phi(\omega_{xx}^{(2)} - \sigma_{\delta\delta}^{(2)})$$

The Jacobian of this system with respect to the parameters ϕ and $\sigma_{bb}^{(2)}$ is the matrix

$$J_2 = \begin{pmatrix} \omega_{xx_{-1}}^{(2)} & 1 \\ \omega_{xx}^{(2)} - \sigma_{\delta\delta}^{(2)} & 0 \end{pmatrix} ,$$

with determinant equal to $-(\omega_{xx}^{(2)} - \sigma_{\delta\delta}^{(2)})$.

It follows that the two-exogenous-variable model given by the system of equations (5.5) is identified. Thus, contrary to the white-noise exogenous variables case, the second example seems to indicate that models that contain more exogenous variables do not have to satisfy more restrictive conditions in order to be identified, as long as each exogenous variable presents some degree of autocorrelation. In the next two sections we derive formally the results for the general model. The analysis is facilitated if we consider first the case when the exogenous variables follow moving average processes.

2. MOVING AVERAGE PROCESSES

Consider Model V, where the structural equation is given by the expression

$$(5.6)\qquad G_p(L)\,\eta_t = \sum_{i=0}^{n} B_{q_i}^{(i)}(L)\,\zeta_t^{(i)} + u_t \ ,$$

and the exogenous variables follow moving average processes of the form

$$(5.7)\qquad \zeta_t^{(i)} = H_{h_i}^{(i)}(L)\, b_t^{(i)} \ , \qquad i = 1, \ldots, n,$$

where u_t, $b_t^{(i)}$ are independent white-noise variables, and the polynomials $G(L)$ and $H^{(i)}(L)$ satisfy the stationarity and invertibility conditions of assumptions 1 and 5b. Assume that all the exogenous variables have some degree of autocorrelation.

Assumption 6a. The orders of the polynomials are such that

$$h_i \neq 0, \text{ for } i = 1, \ldots, n.$$

Lemma 8. For the case of Model V, the parameters in $B_{q_i}^{(i)}(L)$, $H_{h_i}^{(i)}(L)$, $\sigma_{bb}^{(i)}$, $\sigma_{\delta\delta}^{(i)}$, and $G_p(L)$ are identified.

Proof: Equation (5.7) implies $\omega_{xx_{-\tau}}^{(i)} = 0$ for $\tau > h_i$. Denote by $\tau_0 = \max_i (q_i + h_i)$. It follows that the τ-lag autocovariance equation corresponding to equation (5.6), for $\tau > \tau_0$ is given by an equation of the form (2.10). Using the same reasoning as in Lemma 1, we conclude that the parameters $\gamma_1, \ldots, \gamma_p$ of the polynomial $G_p(L)$ are identified.

Now, for each one of the exogenous variables, consider the system of τ-lag crosscovariance equations corresponding to equation (5.6), for $\tau = 0,1, \ldots, q_i + 1$:

$$(5.8a)\qquad \omega_{yx_{-\tau}}^{(i)} = \sum_{j=1}^{p} \gamma_j \omega_{yx_{-\tau+j}} + \beta_\tau^{(i)}(\omega_{xx}^{(i)} - \sigma_{\delta\delta}^{(i)}) + \sum_{\substack{j=0\\ j\neq\tau}}^{q_i} \beta_j^{(i)}\,\omega_{xx_{-\tau+j}}^{(i)} \ , \qquad \tau = 0, 1, \ldots, q_i,$$

$$(5.8b)\qquad \omega_{yx_{-q_i-1}}^{(i)} = \sum_{j=1}^{p} \gamma_j\, \omega_{yx_{-q_i-1+j}}^{(i)} \sum_{j=0}^{q_i} \beta_j^{(i)}\,\omega_{xx_{-q_i-1+j}}^{(i)}$$

Assumption (6a) guarantees that the last equation contains, at least, one β-parameter (in particular, $\beta_{q_i}^{(i)}$). To prove that this system of $(q_i + 2)$ equations provides a locally isolated solution for $\beta_0^{(i)}, \ldots, \beta_{q_i}^{(i)}$ and $\sigma_{\delta\delta}^{(i)}$, we need to prove that the Jacobian of this system with respect to these parameters is non-singular. The Jacobian is given by matrix

$$J_x = \begin{pmatrix} \omega_{xx}-\sigma_{\delta\delta} & \omega_{xx_{-1}} & \omega_{xx_{-2}} & \cdots & \omega_{xx_{-q}} & -\beta_0 \\ \omega_{xx_{-1}} & \omega_{xx}-\sigma_{\delta\delta} & \omega_{xx_{-1}} & \cdots & \omega_{xx_{-q+1}} & -\beta_1 \\ \omega_{xx_{-2}} & \omega_{xx_{-1}} & \omega_{xx}-\sigma_{\delta\delta} & \cdots & \omega_{xx_{-q+2}} & -\beta_2 \\ \vdots & \vdots & \vdots & \ddots & \vdots & \vdots \\ & & & & \omega_{xx}-\sigma_{\delta\delta} & -\beta_q \\ \omega_{xx_{-q-1}} & \omega_{xx_{-q}} & \omega_{xx_{-q+1}} & \cdots & \omega_{xx_{-1}} & 0 \end{pmatrix}$$

where, for the sake of simplicity, the subscript i has been deleted from the expressions.

The parameter $\sigma_{\delta\delta}$ appears only in the elements of the main diagonal except in the last one which is zero. Expanding the determinant of J_x by the elements of the last column, it is easily seen that the coefficient of $(\sigma_{\delta\delta}^{q+1})$ in this expansion is given by the expression:

$$(-1)^{q+1}\,[\beta_0\,\omega_{xx_{-q-1}} + \beta_1\,\omega_{xx_{-q}} + \ldots + \beta_{q-1}\,\omega_{xx_{-2}} + \beta_q\,\omega_{xx_{-1}}]$$

It follows that, for the determinant of J_x to be (identically) zero, the equation

$$(5.9) \qquad \beta_0\omega_{xx_{-q-1}} + \beta_1\omega_{xx_{-q}} + \ldots + \beta_q\omega_{xx_{-1}} = 0$$

has to hold.

Equation (5.9) is a covariance equation generated by multiplying the equation

$$\beta_0\zeta_t + \beta_1\zeta_{t-1} + \ldots + \beta_q\zeta_{t-q} = w_t$$

by $\zeta_{t-(q+1)}$ and taking expectations. Notice that w_t represents a function that has to uncorrelated with $\zeta_{t-(q+1)}$, according to equation (5.9). But equation (5.6) implies that w_t has to include (at least) the variable η_t, which, under our assumptions, is correlated with $\zeta_{t-(q+1)}$. Thus (5.9) contradicts (5.6), which proves that J_x is nonsingular.[1/] Consequently, the parameters in the polynomial $\beta^{(i)}_{q_i}(L)$ and $\sigma^{(i)}_{\delta\delta}$ are identified for i = 1, ..., n.

Finally, consider the system of τ-lag autocovariance equations corresponding to equation (5.7), for $\tau = 0, 1, \ldots, h_i$. Deleting again the index i for notational simplicity, this sytem of equations has the form:

$$\text{(5.10a)} \qquad \omega_{xx} = (1 + \alpha_1^2 + \ldots + \alpha_h^2)\, \sigma_{bb} + \sigma_{\delta\delta}$$

$$\text{(5.10b)} \qquad \omega_{xx_{-\tau}} = (\alpha_\tau + \alpha_1\alpha_{\tau+1} + \ldots + \alpha_{h-\tau}\alpha_h)\, \sigma_{bb},\ \tau = 1, 2, \ldots, h.$$

The proof that this system of (h+1) equations can be solved for the (h+1) parameters $\alpha_1, \ldots, \alpha_h$ and σ_{bb}, is identical to the proof of Lemma 2. Thus the parameters in the polynomials $H^{(i)}_{h_i}(L)$ and $\sigma^{(i)}_{bb}$ are identified. This concludes the proof of Lemma 8.

The only parameters of Model V that are not covered by Lemma 8 are the two variances $\sigma_{\varepsilon\varepsilon}$ and σ_{uu}. The following Theorem completes the analysis of the identification of Model V.

<u>Theorem 5</u>: Under assumption (6a), Model V is identified, if and only if $p \neq 0$.

If p = 0 it is easily seen that the parameters $\sigma_{\varepsilon\varepsilon}$ and σ_{uu} only appear in the 0-lag autocovariance equation corresponding to equation (5.6). Thus the model cannot be identified, which proves necessity.

To prove sufficiency, consider the τ-lag autocovariance equations corresponding to equation (5.6), for τ = 0, 1. When $p \neq 0$, these two equations are given by

---

1/ Notice that if $\sigma_{\delta\delta} = 1$ the argument breaks down, as then $\sigma_{\delta\delta}^{q+1} = \sigma_{\delta\delta}^{q} = \ldots = \sigma_{\delta\delta}$. But since the only constraint on $\sigma_{\delta\delta}$ implied by our assumptions is $\sigma_{\delta\delta} > 0$, the equation $\sigma_{\delta\delta} = 1$ represents a zero measure set.

$$\omega_{yy} = \sum_{j=1}^{p} \gamma_j \, \omega_{yy_{-j}} + \sum_{i=1}^{n} \sum_{j=0}^{q_i} \beta_j^{(i)} \, \omega_{yx_{-j}}^{(i)} + \sigma_{uu} + \sigma_{\varepsilon\varepsilon}$$

$$\omega_{yy_{-1}} = \gamma_1 \, (\omega_{yy} - \sigma_{\varepsilon\varepsilon}) + \sum_{j=2}^{p} \gamma_j \, \omega_{yy_{-j}} + \sum_{i=1}^{n} \sum_{j=0}^{q_i} \beta_j^{(i)} \, \omega_{yx_{-j+1}}^{(i)}$$

and the Jacobian of this two equations with respect to the parameters $\sigma_{\varepsilon\varepsilon}$ and σ_{uu} is given by the matrix:

$$\begin{pmatrix} 1 & 1 \\ -\gamma_1 & 0 \end{pmatrix}$$

Therefore, when $p \neq 0$ all the parameters of Model V are identified, and Theorem 5 is proved.

3. AUTOREGRESSIVE-MOVING AVERAGE PROCESSES

In the previous section we considered a model in which the exogenous variables were autocorrelated. In particular, we assumed that these autocorrelations were explained by moving average processes, which implied that, for each exogenous variable, only a finite number of autocorrelations were assumed to be nonzero. More generally, in this section we consider models where the autocorrelation function of the exogenous variables may extend over an infinite horizon.[2/] We shall assume that each exogenous variable follows an autoregressive-moving average process. The patterns of autocorrelation of different exogenous variables will be allowed to be different, in general, and so will the orders of the underlying ARMA processes.

Thus, we consider now Model VI, where the exogenous variables follow stationary ARMA processes given by

(5.11) $$M_{m_i}^{(i)}(L)\zeta_t^{(i)} = H_{h_i}^{(i)}(L)b_t^{(i)} ,$$

2/ Even though the covariances do not vanish for any finite lag, the stationarity assumption (assumption 5b, Chapter I) implies that the autocorrelation function has to damp out as the magnitude of the lag increases.

where u_t, $b_t^{(i)}$ and $b_t^{(i)}$ are independent white-noise variables. The structural equation is given by equation (5.6).

As in the previous section, we rule out the possibility of white-noise exogenous variables. But assumption (6a) is replaced by

Assumption 6b: The orders of the autoregressive polynomials are such that $m_i \neq 0$, for $i = 1, \ldots, n$.

Notice that the "pure autoregressive" model is a particular case of Model VI. We shall see that the identifiability of Model V and Model VI are very similar.

Lemma 9: For the case of Model VI, the parameters in the polynomials $B_{q_i}^{(i)}(L)$, $M_{m_i}^{(i)}(L)$, $H_{h_i}^{(i)}$, $G_p(L)$ and the variances $\sigma_{bb}^{(i)}$, $\sigma_{\delta\delta}^{(i)}$, are identified.

Proof: For the ith exogenous variable, the τ-lag crosscovariance equation corresponding to equation (5.6) for $\tau > q_i$ has form:

$$\omega_{yx_{-\tau}}^{(i)} = \sum_{j=1}^{p} \gamma_j \, \omega_{yx_{-\tau+j}}^{(i)} + \sum_{j=0}^{q_i} \beta_j^{(i)} \, \omega_{xx_{-\tau+j}}^{(i)} , \tag{5.12}$$

and assumption (6b) guarantees that all the lagged autocovariances $\omega_{xx_{-\tau+j}}$ are different from zero. Consider the system of all such covariance equations. If this system does not contain a subsystem of $(p + q_i + 1)$ equations that can be solved uniquely for the parameters $\gamma_1, \ldots, \gamma_p, \beta_0^{(i)}, \ldots, \beta_{q_i}^{(i)}$, then there exists a set of constants $\pi_0, \pi_1, \ldots, \pi_{p-1}, \mu_0, \mu_1, \ldots, \mu_{q_i}$ such that:

$$\pi_0 \omega_{yx_{-\tau+1}} + \pi_1 \omega_{yx_{-\tau+2}}^{(i)} + \ldots + \pi_{p-1} \omega_{yx_{-\tau+p}}^{(i)} + \mu_0 \omega_{xx_{-\tau}}^{(i)} + \mu_1 \omega_{xx_{-\tau+1}}^{(i)} + \ldots + \mu_{q_i} \omega_{xx_{-\tau+q_i}}^{(i)} \tag{5.13}$$

for $\tau > q_i$. Deleting the index i, in terms of the variable ω_{yx}, expression (5.13) represents a (nonhomogenous) linear difference equation. The solution can be expressed as

$$\omega_{yx_{-\tau}} = C_t \, (\tau - t) + I_t \, (\tau - t), \qquad (\tau \geq q_i) ,$$

where $C_t \, (\tau - t)$ is the complementary function and $I_t \, (\tau - t)$ is a particular integral. Thus C_t $(\tau - t)$ is the solution of the homogenous linear difference equation:

$$(5.14) \qquad \pi_0 \omega_{yx_{-\tau}} + \pi_1 \omega_{yx_{-\tau+1}} + \ldots + \pi_{p-1} \omega_{yx_{-\tau+p-1}} = 0 , \quad (\tau \geq q_i),$$

of order $(p - 1)$, at most.[3/]

But, the variable ω_{yx} follows a non-homogenous difference equation given by equation (5.12). The complementary function of the solution to this difference equation is given by the solution to the homogenous linear difference equation:

$$(5.15) \qquad \omega_{yx_{-\tau}} = \gamma_1 \omega_{yx_{-\tau+1}} + \ldots + \gamma_p \omega_{yx_{-\tau+p}} ,$$

of order p, for any value of τ. In Lemma 1 we proved that the solutions to the two equations (5.14) and (5.15) cannot be the same, thus the complementary functions of the solutions to (5.12) and (5.13), for $\tau \geq q_i$, contradict each other. It follows that the system of equations (5.12) for $\tau = q_i + 1, q_i + 2, \ldots$ has to contain a subsystem of $(p + q_i + 1)$ equations that can be solved uniquely for the parameters in the polynomials $G_p(L)$ and $B^{(i)}_{q_i}(L)$.

Now, the τ-lag autocovariance equation corresponding to equation (5.6), for $\tau \leq q_i$,

$$\omega^{(i)}_{yx_{-\tau}} = \sum_{j=1}^{p} \gamma_j \omega_{yx_{-\tau+j}} + \sum_{\substack{j=0 \\ j \neq \tau}}^{q_i} \beta^{(i)}_j \omega^{(i)}_{xx_{-\tau+j}} + \beta^{(i)}_\tau (\omega^{(i)}_{xx} - \sigma^{(i)}_{\delta\delta})$$

can be solved for the parameter $\sigma^{(i)}_{\delta\delta}$. Once this parameter is identified, the system of the

a) τ-lag autocovariance equations corresponding to equation (5.11), for $\tau = h_i + 1, \ldots, h_i + m_i$, and

b) τ-lag autocovariance equations corresponding to (5.11), for $\tau = 0, 1, \ldots, h_i$,

can be solved for the m_i parameters in the polynomial $M^{(i)}_{m_i}(L)$, and the $(h_i + 1)$ parameters in the polynomial $H^{(i)}_{h_i}(L)$ and $\sigma^{(i)}_{bb}$, respectively. This completes the proof of the Lemma.

3/ The "at most" qualification stems from the fact that some of the π-coefficients in equation (5.14) may be zero.

Theorem 6: Under assumption (6b), the necessary and sufficient condition for Model VI to be identified is given by

$$p \neq 0.$$

The proof of Theorem 6 is identical to the proof of Theorem 5.[4/]

4. SOME FINAL REMARKS

In Chapter II we derived the conditions for identification of an error-in-variables distributed lag model when the shock and the exogenous variables are independent white-noises. Chapters III and IV extended the analysis to models with autocorrelated shock. It was found that different patterns of autocorrelation, corresponding to moving average or autoregressive processes, have opposite effects as far as identification is concerned. In this chapter the white-noise assumption for the shock is maintained, and, instead, the exogenous variables are assumed to be autocorrelated. In such cases, different patterns of autocorrelation, as represented by moving average autoregressive or mixed autoregressive-moving average processes, have the same effect on the identification of the model. In fact, autocorrelation in an exogenous variable measured with error identifies the variance of

---

4/ Thus, under assumption (6a) or (6b), the only situation in which Model V or VI are underidentified is when $p = 0$. In this case the only parameters that are not identified are the variances σ_{uu} and $\sigma_{\varepsilon\varepsilon}$. Yet, as the other parameters are identified, the sum $(\sigma_{uu} + \sigma_{\varepsilon\varepsilon})$ is identified also through the 0-lag autocovariance equation:

$$\omega_{yy} = \sum_{j=1}^{p} \gamma_j \omega_{yy_{-j}} + \sum_{i=1}^{n} \sum_{j=0}^{q_i} \beta_j^{(i)} \omega_{xy_{-j}}^{(i)} + (\sigma_{uu} + \sigma_{\varepsilon\varepsilon}).$$

Thus the only underidentification present is due to the fact that the measurement error of the endogenous variable is not distinguishable from the shock of the equation. The same result is true for a "contemporaneous" model where only the endogenous variable is measured with error (see Geraci [1974], p. 95).

that error. As a consequence, errors of measurement in exogenous variables do not bring underidentification as long as the variable is autocorrelated. It follows that when all exogenous variables are autocorrelated, the only possible source of underidentification becomes then the error of measurement of the endogenous variables. Yet whenever a lagged value of the endogenous variable is included in the structural equation, all the parameters of the model are identified.5/

The requirement that all exogenous variables are autocorrelated can be relaxed easily. When some of the exogenous variables are allowed to be white-noise, theorems 1 and 6 can be combined.

Let the number of white-noise exogenous variables be n_1, so that $0 \leq n_1 \leq n$. Without loss of generality, assume that these variables are indexed $i = 1, 2, \ldots n_1$.

Theorem 6 : Consider only the orders $(q_1, q_2, \ldots, q_{n_1})$ of the lag polynomials of the exogenous variables that are white-noise. Arrange the $(n_1 + 1)$ numbers $(p, q_1, \ldots, q_{n_1})$ in a nondecreasing sequence, and let q_i^{**} denote the one occupying the ith place in this sequence. The model is identified if and only if:

$$q_i^{**} \geq i, \quad i = 1, 2, \ldots, n_1 + 1.$$

We skip the proof of the theorem since it is a trivial extension of the proofs of theorem 1 and 2. Note that theorem 1 corresponds to the case $n_1 = n$, while theorem 2 corresponds to $n_1 = 0$.

In the next chapter the previous results are all combined. We shall consider models where some of the exogenous variables may be autocorrelated and some may be white-noise, and where the shock may or may not be autocorrelated.

5/ The fact that autocorrelation in the exogenous variables brings identification to dynamic shock-error models is also implicit in Hurwicz [1949] and Hsiao [1977]. Yet both authors only consider identification of the structural model, and not identification of the processes generating the autocorrelation of the exogenous variables. Even though these processes may lack an economic interpretation, the efficient estimation of the overall model is improved if the stochastic processes for the exogenous variables are specified (see Espasa [1977]). Also, this specification is also needed if the model is used to obtain forecasts.

CHAPTER VI

AUTOCORRELATED SHOCK: AUTOCORRELATED EXOGENOUS VARIABLES. THE GENERAL MODEL

In the first section of this Chapter we consider identification of a model where the shock and each one of the exogenous variables present some degree of autocorrelation. The necessary and sufficient conditions for identification are derived, and the analysis is illustrated with two examples. Then we proceed to consider a general model where autocorrelation may or may not be present in the shock and in any number of exogenous variables. The analysis of this model brings together the results of all previous chapters.

1. AUTOCORRELATED SHOCK AND AUTOCORRELATED EXOGENOUS VARIABLES

1.1 The General Case

Consider model VII, given by the equations:

(6.1a) $$G_p(L)\eta_t = \sum_{i=1}^{n} B_{q_i}^{(i)}(L)\,\zeta_t^{(i)} + u_t$$

(6.1b) $$R_r(L)\,u_t = S_s(L)\,a_t$$

(6.1c) $$M_{m_i}^{(i)}(L)\,\zeta_t^{(i)} = H_{h_i}^{(i)}(L)\,b_t^{(i)} \qquad i = 1, 2, \ldots, n$$

(6.1d) $$x_t^{(i)} = \zeta_t^{(i)} + \delta_t^{(i)}$$

(6.1e) $$y_t = \eta_t + \varepsilon_t,$$

which were defined already in Chapter I, together with the set of assumptions 1, 2, 3, 4b, 5b. We shall combine assumptions (6a) and (6.b) into a slightly more general one:

Assumption 6c: For every i (i = 1, 2, ..., n) either m_i or h_i are nonzero.

The conditions for identification of model VII are summarized in Lemma 10 and Theorem 7.

Lemma 10: The coefficients of the polynomials $G_p(L)$, $B_{q_i}^{(i)}(L)$, $R_r(L)$, $M_{m_i}^{(i)}(L)$, $H_{h_i}^{(i)}(L)$, $S_s(L)$, and the variances $\sigma_{\delta\delta}^{(i)}$, $\sigma_{bb}^{(i)}$ are always identified.

Proof: Due to the independence of the variables ζ and a, the crosscovariance equations corresponding to equation (6.1a) are identical to the crosscovariance equations corresponding to equation (5.6) of Model VI. The system of autocovariance equations corresponding to (6.1c) is also identical to the one corresponding to (5.11) of Model VI. Thus by using Lemma 9, we know that the coefficients of the polynominals $G_p(L)$, $B_{q_i}^{(i)}(L)$, $M_{m_i}^{(i)}(L)$ and $S_s(L)$, plus the variances $\sigma_{\delta\delta}^{(i)}$ and $\sigma_{bb}^{(i)}$ are identified. Therefore we only have to prove that the coefficients of $R_r(L)$ are identified also.

For $\tau > p$, the τ-lag autocovariance equation corresponding to equation (6.1a) yields:

$$(6.2) \qquad \omega_{yy_{-\tau}} = \sum_{j=1}^{p} \gamma_j\, \omega_{yy_{-\tau+p}} + \sum_{i=1}^{n} \sum_{j=0}^{q_i} \beta_j^{(i)}\, \omega_{xy_{-\tau+j}}^{(i)} + \sigma_\tau \quad ,$$

where $\sigma_\tau = E(u_t\, y_{t-\tau})$. As the γ and β parameters are identified, so are the covariances $\sigma_\tau, \tau > p$. Consider now equation (6.1b). Multiplying both sides of the equation by $y_{t-\tau}$, for $\tau > \max(p,s)$, and taking expectations, yields the expression

$$(6.3) \qquad \sigma_\tau = \rho_1\, \sigma_{\tau-1} + \ldots + \rho_r\, \sigma_{\tau-r}$$

Letting $\tau = \max(p,s) + r+1, \ldots, \max(p,s) + 2r$, a linear system is obtained, which can be solved for the parameters $\rho_1, \ldots, \rho_r$ as functions of crosscovariances σ_τ (with $\tau > \max(p,s)$). Since these covariances are identified so are the parameters $\rho_1, \ldots, \rho_r$, which completes the proof of the Lemma.

The only parameters that are not covered by Lemma 10 are the coefficients of the polynominal $S_s(L)$, that is the θ-parameters, plus the variances $\sigma_{\varepsilon\varepsilon}$ and σ_{aa}. Identification of these parameters is considered in the following Theorem.

Theorem 7. Model VII (with autocorrelated shock and autocorrelated exogenous variables) is identified if and only if

$$p + r > s.$$

Proof of Theorem 7:

The proof is simplified if we consider the transformed equation:

(6.4) $$\Lambda^{(0)}_{p+r}(L)\ \eta_t = \sum_{i=1}^{n} \Lambda^{(i)}_{q_i+r}(L)\ \zeta^{(i)}_t + S_s(L)\ a_t,$$

where

(6.5a) $$\Lambda^{(0)}_{p+r}(L) = G_p(L)\ R_r(L)\ ,$$

(6.5b) $$\Lambda^{(i)}_{q_i+r}(L) = B^{(i)}_{q_i}(L)\ R_r(L)$$

and $\lambda^{(i)}_j$ is the coefficient of L^j in the polynominal $\Lambda^{(i)}_{q_i+r}(L)$.

a) Necessity: We shall prove that if the condition $p+r > s$ is not satisfied Model VII cannot be identified. The parameters $\theta_1, \ldots, \theta_s, \sigma_{aa}$ and $\sigma_{\varepsilon\varepsilon}$ are not contained in the crosscovariance equations for equation (6.4), nor in the covariance equations for the system (6.1c). Therefore, for Model VII to be identified, the system of autocovariance equations corresponding to (6.4) has to provide a subsystem that can be solved for these (s + 2) parameters. The (s + 1) parameters $\theta_1, \ldots, \theta_s$ and σ_{aa} are contained only in the τ-lag autocovariance equations for $\tau = 0, 1, \ldots, s$. The parameter $\sigma_{\varepsilon\varepsilon}$ is contained only in the τ-lag autocovariance equation for $\tau = 0, 1, \ldots, p + r$. Thus, if $p + r \leqq s$, (s + 2) of the parameters are contained in only (s + 1) equations, and the model is not identified.

b) Sufficiency: Lemma 10 implies that all the parameters except $\theta_1,\ldots, \theta_s, \sigma_{aa}$ and $\sigma_{\varepsilon\varepsilon}$ are identified. We shall prove that, when $p + r > s$, the system of τ-lag autocovariance equations for $\tau = 0, 1, \ldots, s + 1$, can be solved for these (s + 2) parameters.

It is easily seen that the Jacobian of this system of autocovariance equations with respect to $\theta_1, \ldots, \theta_s, \sigma_{aa}$ and $\sigma_{\varepsilon\varepsilon}$ can be written as:

$$J = \left(\begin{array}{c|c} J^* & \underline{\lambda}^{(0)} \\ \hline \underline{0}' & -\lambda^{(0)}_{s+1} \end{array}\right)$$

where $\underline{\lambda}^{(0)} = (1, -\lambda^{(0)}_1, \ldots, -\lambda^{(0)}_s)'$, $\lambda^{(0)}_i$ is the coefficient of L^i in the polynominal $\Lambda^{(0)}_{p+r}(L)$, and J* is the Jacobian of the system of τ-lag autocovariance equations for $\tau = 0, 1, \ldots, s$, with respect to $\theta_1, \ldots, \theta_s$ and σ_{aa}. As J* was proved nonsingular in Lemma 2 and $p+r > s$ implies $\Lambda^{(0)}_{s+1} \neq 0$, it follows that J is also nonsingular. This finishes the proof of Theorem 7.

When no exogenous variables are present, Theorem 7 and 4 become identical. To see that, notice that

a) when $r > s$, the conditions of Theorem 4 becomes $p \geqq 0$, which is always satisfied. Trivially, when $r > s$, the condition $p+r > s$ of Theorem 7 is always satisfied also

b) when $r \leqq s$, both Theorems yield the condition $p+r > s$.

A Remark on the Proof of Theorem 7.

Contrary to the models considered in Chapters III and IV, the analysis of both the necessary and sufficient conditions for identification of Model VII can be performed through the transformed equation (6.4). This difference between the analysis of identification of Model VII and Models III and IV is due to the fact that, for the case of Model VII, the correlation of the exogenous variables identifies the parameters of the B-polynomials (together with the variances $\sigma_{\delta\delta}$). Thus all the parameters of the G and B-polynomials (i.e., of the Λ-polynomials are identified for the case of Model VII, and as far as identification is concerned, we do not have to worry about the constraints that expression (6.5a) and (6.5b) imply for the λ-coefficients. Still, a better understanding of the identification properties of Model VII can be achieved by considering the system of covariance equations for the original equations (in particular, (6.1a)), as we did in Chapter IV.

Since the $\sigma_{\varepsilon\varepsilon}$, θ, σ_{aa} and ρ-parameters do not appear in the crosscovariance equations corresponding to (6.1c), it follows that identification of Model VII requires that the system of autocovariance equations for (6.1a) contains a subsystem that can be solved for those $(s + r + 2)$ parameters.

Consider, in particular, the first $(r + s + 2)$ autocovariance equations. The determinant of the Jacobian of this system with respect to the parameters $\sigma_{\varepsilon\varepsilon}, \theta_1, \ldots, \theta_s, \sigma_{aa}, \rho_1, \ldots, \rho_r$ can be expanded around the last r columns, by using the Laplace Expansion Theorem. These last r columns contain the derivatives with respect to the ρ-parameters. For the Jacobian to be nonsingular at least one of these (s + 2) x (s + 2) minors formed with the first (s + 2) columns has to be nonzero. Consider the minor obtained by deletting the last r columns and the last r rows. The (τ, j)-th element of this minor is given by the partial derivative of the τ-lag autocovariance equation with respect to the parameters:

$$\begin{cases} \sigma_{\varepsilon\varepsilon} & \text{if } j=1 \\ \theta_j & \text{if } j=2, \ldots, s+1 \\ \sigma_{aa} & \text{if } j = s+2, \end{cases}$$

for $\tau = 0, 1, \ldots, s + 2$. Let $p + r \leqq s$. It is easily seen that the last (r + 1) rows of the minor correspond to $\tau = s - r + 1, s - r + 2, \ldots, s + 1$. The condition $p + r \leqq s$ implies $p < s - r + 1$, thus the τ-lag autocovariance equation for $\tau \geqq s - r + 1$ satisfies equation (6.2). Therefore, the (τ, j) element of the minor, for $\tau \geqq s - r + 1$ and $j \geqq 2$, is given by

$$\begin{cases} \dfrac{\partial\sigma_\tau}{\partial\theta_j} & \text{if } j = 2, \ldots, s+1 \\ \dfrac{\partial\sigma_\tau}{\partial\sigma_{aa}} & \text{if } j = s+2 \end{cases}$$

Since for $\tau \geqq s - r + 1 > p$ equation (6.3) is satisfied, if follows that

$$\frac{\partial\sigma_\tau}{\partial\theta_j} = \sum_{k=1}^{r} \rho_k \frac{\partial\sigma_{\tau-k}}{\partial\theta_j} \tag{6.6a}$$

$$\frac{\partial\sigma_\tau}{\partial\sigma_{aa}} = \sum_{k=1}^{r} \rho_k \frac{\partial\sigma_{\tau-k}}{\partial\sigma_{aa}} \tag{6.6b}$$

Also, for $\tau > p$, the τ th element of the first column of the minor is zero. Thus the last (r + 1) rows of the minor are as follows:

$$\begin{pmatrix} 0 & \frac{\partial\sigma_{\tau-r}}{\partial\theta_1} & \cdots & \frac{\partial\sigma_{\tau-r}}{\partial\sigma_{aa}} \\ \vdots & \vdots & & \vdots \\ 0 & \frac{\partial\sigma_{\tau-1}}{\partial\theta_1} & \cdots & \frac{\partial\sigma_{\tau-1}}{\partial\sigma_{aa}} \\ & & & \\ 0 & \frac{\partial\sigma_{\tau}}{\partial\theta_1} & \cdots & \frac{\partial\sigma_{\tau}}{\partial\sigma_{aa}} \end{pmatrix}$$

Equations (6.6a) and (6.6b) state that the last row is a linear combination of the previous r rows. This implies that the minor consisting of the first (s + 2) rows and the first (s + 2) columns of the Jacobian of the system of τ-lag autocovariance equations (for $\tau = 0, 1, \ldots, r+s+1$) with respect to $\sigma_{\varepsilon\varepsilon}$, $\theta_1, \ldots, \theta_s, \sigma_{aa}, \rho_1, \ldots, \rho_r$, is zero. Any other minor in the expansion of this determinant around the last r columns has to contain the derivatives of τ-lag autocovariance equation for values of $\tau > s+1$ ($> p$). Thus they can be proved to be zero in a similar way. This implies that the Jacobian of the system of τ-lag autocovariance equations for $\tau = 0, 1, \ldots, r+s+1$ with respect to the parameters $\sigma_{\varepsilon\varepsilon}$, $\theta_1, \ldots, \theta_s, \sigma_{aa}, \rho_1, \ldots, \rho_r$ has to be singular.

Consider now any other system of (r+s+r) autocovariance equation. As it has to contain τ-lag autocovariance equations for values of $\tau > r+s+1$, corresponding to these equations the Jacobian of this system with respect to the above parameters has new rows of the type:

$$\begin{pmatrix} 0 & \frac{\partial\sigma_{\tau}}{\partial\theta_1} & \cdots & \frac{\partial\sigma_{\tau}}{\partial\theta_s} & \frac{\partial\sigma_{\tau}}{\partial\sigma_{aa}} \end{pmatrix}.$$

The nonzero elements of this row satisfy equations (6.6a) and (6.6b). Thus, when $p+r > s$, any other system of autocovariance equations also has a singular Jacobian with respect to the $\sigma_{\varepsilon\varepsilon}$, θ, σ_{aa} and ρ-parameters.

Next we proceed to analyse two examples. The first one will illustrate the analysis through the original equations, (6.1a) to (6.1e). The second one illustrates the analysis in terms of the transformed model, where equation (6.1a) and (6.1b) are combined into (6.4).

1.2 Some Examples

First Example

To illustrate Lemma 10 and the "necessity" part of Theorem 7, consider the model:

(6.7a) $\eta_t = \gamma\eta_{t-1} + \beta\zeta_t + u_t$

(6.7b) $u_t = \rho u_{t-1} + a_t + \theta_1 a_{t-1} + \theta_2\, a_{t-2}$

(6.7c) $\zeta_t = b_t + \alpha b_{t-1}$

where a_t and b_t are independent white-noise variables, and the admissible parameter space is restricted by the constraints

$$-1 < \rho < 1 \quad ; \quad -1 < \gamma < 1 \quad ; -1 < \alpha < 1$$

$$-(\theta_2 + \theta_1) < 1 \ ; \quad \theta_1 - \theta_2 < 1 \quad ; -1 < -\theta_2 < 1,$$

representing the stationarity and invertibility conditions for the stochastic processes. The errors-in-variables equations (6.1d) and (6.1e) are assumed to hold. As p = 1, r = 1, s = 2, it follows that the condition of Theorem 7 is not met, so that the model is not identified.

Consider the system of τ-lag crosscovariance equations corresponding to equation (6.7a), for τ = 0, 1, 2.

$$\omega_{yx} = \gamma\omega_{xy} + \beta(\omega_{xx} - \sigma_{\delta\delta})$$

$$\omega_{yx_{-1}} = \gamma\omega_{yx} + \beta\ \omega_{xx_{-1}}$$

$$\omega_{yx_{-2}} = \gamma\omega_{yx_{-1}}$$

The Jacobian of this system with respect to the parameters γ, β and $\sigma_{\delta\delta}$ is given by the matrix:

$$\begin{pmatrix} \omega_{xy_{-1}} & \omega_{xx}-\sigma_{\delta\delta} & -\beta \\ \omega_{yx} & \omega_{xx_{-1}} & 0 \\ \omega_{yx_{-1}} & 0 & 0 \end{pmatrix}$$

with determinant equal to

$$\beta\, \omega_{yx_{-1}}\, \omega_{xx_{-1}} = \alpha\beta^2\, \sigma_{bb}^{\ 2}\, [\gamma\ (1 + \alpha^2) + \alpha]$$

Thus the parameters β, γ and $\sigma_{\delta\delta}$ are identified. Now, the system of τ-lag autocovariance equation corresponding to equation (6.7c), for $\tau = 0, 1$, is given by equations (5.4a) and (5.4b), and the Jacobian of this system with respect to α and σ_{bb} had determinant equal to $(\alpha^2 - 1)\,\sigma_{bb}$; hence the parameters α and σ_{bb} are also identified.

The rest of the parameters: ρ, θ_1, θ_2, σ_{aa} and $\sigma_{\varepsilon\varepsilon}$ only appear in the autocovariance equations corresponding to equation (6.7a). Thus the model consisting of the system of equations (6.7) is identified only if the system of these autocovariance equations can be solved for the five parameters ρ, θ_1, θ_2, σ_{aa} and $\sigma_{\varepsilon\varepsilon}$. Consider the first five autocovariance equations:

$$\begin{aligned}
\omega_{yy} &= \gamma\omega_{yy_{-1}} + \beta\omega_{xy} + \sigma_0 + \sigma_{\varepsilon\varepsilon} \\
\omega_{yy_{-1}} &= \gamma(\omega_{yy} - \sigma_{\varepsilon\varepsilon}) + \beta\omega_{yx_{-1}} + \sigma_1 \\
\omega_{yy_{-2}} &= \gamma\omega_{yy_{-1}} + \sigma_2 \\
\omega_{yy_{-3}} &= \gamma\omega_{yy_{-2}} + \sigma_3 \\
\omega_{yy_{-4}} &= \gamma\omega_{yy_{-3}} + \sigma_4
\end{aligned}$$

where $\sigma_\tau = E(u_t\, y_{t-\tau})$. The Jacobian of this system with respect to the parameters $\sigma_{\varepsilon\varepsilon}$, θ_1, θ_2, σ_{aa} and ρ is given by the matrix

$$J_1 = \begin{pmatrix}
1 & \frac{\partial\sigma_0}{\partial\theta_1} & \frac{\partial\sigma_0}{\partial\theta_2} & \frac{\partial\sigma_0}{\partial\sigma_{aa}} & \frac{\partial\sigma_0}{\partial\rho} \\
-\gamma & \frac{\partial\sigma_1}{\partial\theta_1} & \frac{\partial\sigma_1}{\partial\theta_2} & \frac{\partial\sigma_1}{\partial\sigma_{aa}} & \frac{\partial\sigma_1}{\partial\rho} \\
0 & \frac{\partial\sigma_2}{\partial\theta_1} & \frac{\partial\sigma_2}{\partial\theta_2} & \frac{\partial\sigma_2}{\partial\sigma_{aa}} & \frac{\partial\sigma_2}{\partial\rho} \\
0 & \frac{\partial\sigma_3}{\partial\theta_1} & \frac{\partial\sigma_3}{\partial\theta_2} & \frac{\partial\sigma_3}{\partial\sigma_{aa}} & \frac{\partial\sigma_3}{\partial\rho} \\
0 & \frac{\partial\sigma_4}{\partial\theta_1} & \frac{\partial\sigma_4}{\partial\theta_2} & \frac{\partial\sigma_4}{\partial\sigma_{aa}} & \frac{\partial\sigma_4}{\partial\rho}
\end{pmatrix}$$

From equation (5.7b) it follows that

$$(6.9) \qquad \sigma_{\tau+1} = \rho\sigma_\tau , \qquad \tau \geqq 2,$$

which implies that J_1 can be rewritten as:

$$\begin{pmatrix} 1 & \frac{\partial\sigma_0}{\partial\theta_1} & \frac{\partial\sigma_0}{\partial\theta_2} & \frac{\partial\sigma_0}{\partial\sigma_{aa}} & \frac{\partial\sigma_0}{\partial\rho} \\ -\gamma & \frac{\partial\sigma_1}{\partial\theta_1} & \frac{\partial\sigma_1}{\partial\theta_2} & \frac{\partial\sigma_1}{\partial\sigma_{aa}} & \frac{\partial\sigma_1}{\partial\rho} \\ 0 & \frac{\partial\sigma_2}{\partial\theta_1} & \frac{\partial\sigma_2}{\partial\theta_2} & \frac{\partial\sigma_2}{\partial\sigma_{aa}} & \frac{\partial\sigma_2}{\partial\rho} \\ 0 & \rho\frac{\partial\sigma_2}{\partial\theta_1} & \rho\frac{\partial\sigma_2}{\partial\theta_2} & \rho\frac{\partial\sigma_2}{\partial\sigma_{aa}} & \sigma_2 + \frac{\partial\sigma_2}{\partial\rho} \\ 0 & \rho^2\frac{\partial\sigma_2}{\partial\theta_1} & \rho^2\frac{\partial\sigma_2}{\partial\theta_2} & \rho^2\frac{\partial\sigma_2}{\partial\sigma_{aa}} & 2\rho\sigma_2 + 2\frac{\partial\sigma_2}{\partial\rho} \end{pmatrix}$$

and it is seen that, except for the elements of the last column, the last rows are linear combinations of the third row. Thus expanding det J_1, around the elements of the last column (i.e., the column corresponding to the partial derivative of the autocovariance equations with respect to ρ), all the (4 x 4) minors appearing in this expansion have to contain at least two rows that are linear combinations of each other. Thus det $J_1 = 0$.

Now, for $\tau > 4$, the τ-lag autocovariance equation corresponding to (6.7a) is given by

$$(6.10) \qquad \omega_{yy_{-\tau}} = \gamma\omega_{yy_{-\tau+1}} + \sigma_\tau , \qquad (\tau > 4)$$

and equation (6.9) holds. It follows that if one of the autocovariance equations of the system (6.8) is substituted with the use of (6.10), the new Jacobian will be equal to J_1, with one of its rows substituted by

$$\left(\rho^{\tau-2}\frac{\partial\sigma_2}{\partial\theta_1},\ \rho^{\tau-2}\frac{\partial\sigma_2}{\partial\theta_2},\ \rho^{\tau-2}\frac{\partial\sigma_2}{\partial\sigma_{aa}},\ \frac{\partial\sigma_\tau}{\partial\rho} \right)$$

Therefore, it will still be true that the minors appearing in the expansion of the determinant of the Jacobian around the elements of the last row will have two rows proportional to each other. Thus, no combination of five τ-lag autocovariance equations has a nonsingular Jacobian with respect to the parameters $\sigma_{\varepsilon\varepsilon}$, θ_1, θ_2,

σ_{aa} and ρ, and the model is not identified.

Second Example

A second example will illustrate the "sufficiency" part of Theorem 7. Consider the model consisting of equations (6.7a), (6.7c), (6.1d), (6.1e) plus the equation

(6.11) $$u_t = \rho u_{t-1} + a_t + \theta a_{t-1}$$

instead of (6.7b). As p = 1, r = 1, s = 1, the condition p+r > s is met and, according to Theorem 7, the model should be identified.

The crosscovariance equations corresponding to (6.7a) and the autocovariance equations corresponding to (6.7c) are the same as the ones derived in the previous example. Hence, the parameters γ, β, α, σ_{bb} and $\sigma_{\delta\delta}$ are identified. Combining equations (6.7a) and (6.11), the following equation is obtained:

(6.12) $$\eta_t = \lambda_1^{(0)} \eta_{t-1} + \lambda_2^{(0)} \eta_{t-2} + \lambda_0^{(1)} \zeta_t + \lambda_1^{(1)} \zeta_{t-1} + a_t + \theta a_{t-1},$$

where

$$\lambda_1^{(0)} = \gamma + \rho \quad ; \quad \lambda_0^{(1)} = \beta$$

$$\lambda_2^{(0)} = -\gamma\rho \quad ; \quad \lambda_1^{(1)} = -\rho\beta$$

Corresponding to (6.12), the system of τ-lag autocovariance equations for τ = 0, 1, 2, 3 is given by:

$$\omega_{yy} = \lambda_1^{(0)} \omega_{yy_{-1}} + \lambda_2^{(0)} \omega_{yy_{-2}} + \lambda_0^{(1)} \omega_{yx} + \lambda_1^{(1)} \omega_{yx_{-1}} + [1 + \theta(\lambda_1^{(0)} + \theta)] \sigma_{aa} + \sigma_{\varepsilon\varepsilon}$$

$$\omega_{yy_{-1}} = \lambda_1^{(0)} (\omega_{yy} - \sigma_{\varepsilon\varepsilon}) + \lambda_2^{(0)} \omega_{yy_{-1}} + \lambda_0^{(1)} \omega_{xy_{-1}} + \lambda_1^{(1)} \omega_{yx} + \theta\sigma_{aa}$$

$$\omega_{yy_{-2}} = \lambda_1^{(0)} \omega_{yy_{-1}} + \lambda_2^{(0)} (\omega_{yy} - \sigma_{\varepsilon\varepsilon}) + \lambda_1^{(1)} \omega_{xy_{-1}}$$

$$\omega_{yy_{-3}} = \lambda_1^{(0)} \omega_{yy_{-2}} + \lambda_2^{(0)} \omega_{yy_{-1}} ,$$

where use has been made of the fact that $\sigma_{ya} = \sigma_{aa}$, $\sigma_{ya_{-1}} = (\lambda_1^{(0)} + \theta)\sigma_{aa}$, and

$\sigma_{ay_{-1}} = 0$. The Jacobian of this sytem with respect to the parameters θ, σ_{aa}, $\sigma_{\varepsilon\varepsilon}$ and ρ is equal to the (4 x 4) matrix:

$$\begin{pmatrix} (\gamma+\rho+2\theta)\,\sigma_{aa} & 1+\theta\,(\gamma+\rho+\theta) & 1 & \omega_{yy_{-1}} - \gamma\omega_{yy_{-2}} - \beta\omega_{yx_{-1}} + \theta\sigma_{aa} \\ \sigma_{aa} & \theta & -(\gamma+\rho) & \omega_{yy} - \gamma\omega_{yy_{-1}} - \beta\omega_{yx} \\ 0 & 0 & \gamma\rho & \omega_{yy_{-1}} - \gamma\omega_{yy_{-1}} - \beta\omega_{xy_{-1}} \\ 0 & 0 & 0 & \omega_{yy_{-2}} - \gamma\omega_{yy_{-1}} \end{pmatrix}$$

Partition this matrix as:

$$J = \begin{pmatrix} J_{11} & J_{12} \\ J_{21} & J_{22} \end{pmatrix}$$

where each J_{ij} (i, j, = 1, 2) is a (2 x 2) matrix. The Jacobian J_1 will be nonsingular if and only if the determinants of J_{11} and J_{22} are nonzero (notice that all the elements of J_{21} are zero). The determinant of J_{11} is equal to $(\theta^2 - 1)\,\sigma_{aa}$, thus nonzero. Noticing that equation (6.7a) implies

$$\omega_{yy_{-1}} - \gamma\omega_{yy} - \beta\omega_{xy_{-1}} = -\gamma\sigma_{\varepsilon\varepsilon} + \sigma_1$$

$$\omega_{yy_{-2}} - \gamma\omega_{yy_{-1}} = \sigma_2 \ ,$$

the determinant of J_{22} is equal to $(\gamma\rho\sigma_2)$. To express σ_2 as a function of the parameters, from equations (6.7a) and (6.7b) it is found that

$$\sigma_{uu} = \frac{1+2\theta\rho+\theta}{1-\rho^2}\,\sigma_{aa}$$

$$\sigma_0 = \frac{\gamma\theta\sigma_{aa} + \sigma_{uu}}{1-\gamma\rho}$$

$$\sigma_1 = \rho\sigma_0 + \theta\sigma_{aa}$$

$$\sigma_2 = \rho\sigma_1 \ .$$

Therefore:

$$\sigma_2 = \frac{\rho\ (\theta+\rho)(1+\rho\theta)}{(1-\gamma\rho)(1-\rho^2)}\ \sigma_{aa}$$

It follows that det $J_{22} \neq 0$, which implies that det $J_1 \neq 0$, and the model is identified.

2. THE GENERAL MODEL

In Chapters II, III and IV we analysed models where the exogenous variables were independent white-noise variables. In Chapter V and in the previous section we considered models where all the exogenous variables were autocorrelated. Finally, in this section we consider a general model, where some of the exogenous variables may be white-noise and some may be autocorrelated.

2.1 The General Result

Assume that the number of exogenous variables that are independently distributed white-noise exogenous variables is n_1, and $0 \leq n_1 \leq n$. Let the subindex $i=1,2,\ldots,n_1$ designate the white-noise exogenous variables, and $i=n_1+1, n_1+2,\ldots,n$ designate the autocorrelated ones. The model considered (Model VIII) is described by the equations.

(6.13a) $$G_p(L)\ \eta_t = \sum_{i=1}^{n} B_{q_i}^{(i)}(L)\ \zeta_t^{(i)} + u_t$$

(6.13b) $$R_r(L)\ u_t = S_s(L)\ a_t$$

(6.13c) $$M_{m_i}^{(i)}(L)\ \zeta_t^{(i)} = H_{h_i}^{(i)}(L)\ b_t^{(i)}\ , \quad i = n_1+1,\ n_1+2,\ \ldots,\ n$$

(6.13d) $$x_t^{(i)} = \zeta_t^{(i)} + \delta_t^{(i)},\quad i = 1,\ 2,\ \ldots,\ n$$

(6.13e) $$y_t = \eta_t + \varepsilon_t\ ,$$

and by the set of assumptions 1, 2, 3, 4b, 5b of Chapter I.

<u>Lemma 11</u>: The coefficients of the polynominals $R_r(L)$, $G_p(L)$, $M_{m_i}^{(i)}(L)$, $H_{h_i}^{(i)}(L)$, $B_{q_i}^{(i)}(L)$ and the variances $\sigma_{\delta\delta}^{(i)}$, $\sigma_{bb}^{(i)}$, for $i = n_1 + 1,\ n_1 + 2,\ \ldots,\ n$, are always identified.

Proof of Lemma 11: The proof is identical to the one used for Lemma 10, except for the fact that, in Lemma 11, only the covariance equations corresponding to the exogenous variables with subindexes $i = n_1 + 1, n_1 + 2, \ldots, n$, are considered.

Theorem 8: Consider the orders $(q_1, q_2, \ldots, q_{n_1})$ of the polynominals of the exogenous variables that are white-noise. Arrange the set of numbers $(p, q_1, q_2, \ldots, q_{n_1})$ in nondecreasing order, and let q_j^{**} denote the one occupying the j th place in this new sequence (i.e., $q_1^{*} \leqq q_2^{**} \leqq \ldots \leqq q_{n_1+1}^{**}$). Model VIII is identified if and only if:

a) when $r > s$, $q_j^{**} \geqq j - 1$

b) when $r \leqq s$, $q_j^{**} \geqq j + s - r$

for $i = 1, 2, \ldots, n_1 + 1$.

Proof of Theorem 8: The only parameters that are not covered by Lemma 11 are $\beta_0^{(i)}, \beta_1^{(i)}, \ldots, \beta_{q_1}^{(i)}, \sigma_{\delta\delta}^{(i)}$ $(i = 1, 2, \ldots, n_1)$ $\sigma_{\varepsilon\varepsilon}, \sigma_{aa}, \theta_1, \theta_2, \ldots, \theta_s$. These $(\sum_{i=1}^{n_1} q_i + 2n_1 + 2 + s)$ parameters will be identified if and only if they are the solution of some set of crosscovariance equations (corresponding to the exogenous variables that are white-noise) and autocovariance equations (for equation (6.13a)). Denote by J_1 the Jacobian of this system of equations with respect to the above parameters.

Consider now the model given by the equation:

$$(6.13a') \quad G_p(L)\,\eta_t = \sum_{i=1}^{n_1} B_{q_i}^{(i)}(L)\,\zeta_t^{(i)} + u_t$$

together with equations (6.13b, d and e). Denote by J_2 the Jacobian of the system of auto and crosscovariance equations for this model with respect to the parameters $\beta_0^{(i)}, \beta_1^{(i)}, \ldots, \beta_{q_i}^{(i)}, \sigma_{\delta\delta}^{(i)}$ $(i = 1, 2, \ldots, n_1)$, $\sigma_{\varepsilon\varepsilon}, \sigma_{aa}, \theta_1, \theta_2, \ldots, \theta_s$. It is easily verified that $J_2 = J_1$, thus the necessary and sufficient conditions for J_1 to have rank equal to $(\sum_{i=1}^{n_1} q_i + 2n_1 + 2 + s)$ are the same as the necessary and sufficient conditions for J_2 to have this rank also. Since the model consisting of (6.13a , b, d and e) is a particular case of Model IV, these conditions are

a) when $r > s$, $q_j^* \geqq j - 1$

b) when $r \leqq s$, $q_j^* \geqq j + s - r$,

for $j = 1, 2, \ldots, n_1 + 1$. Since the q_j^*'s of the latter model are the same ones as the q_j^{**} of Theorem 8, the proof is complete.

A Remark on Theorem 8

Theorems 1 to 7 can be derived as particular cases of Theorem 8. To verify this statement, the following Table derives the necessary and sufficient conditions for the identification of Models I to VII as particular cases of Theorem 8, and compares these conditions with the ones obtained in Theorem 1 to 7.

Model		Application of Theorem 8	
I	$n_1 = n$ $r = s = 0$	$q^* \geqq j$ $j = 1,2, \ldots, n+1$	Theorem 1
II	$n_1 = n$ $r = 0,\ s>0$	$q_j^* \geqq j + s$ $j = 1,2, \ldots, n+1$	Theorem 2
III	$n_1 = n$ $r>0,\ s = 0$	$q_j^* \geqq j - 1$ $j=1,2, \ldots, n+1$	Theorem 3
IV	$n_1 = n$ $r \geqq 0,\ s \geqq 0$	a) $r>s$, $q_j^* \geqq j-1$ b) $r \leqq s$, $q_j^* \geqq j+s-r$ $j=1,2, \ldots, n+1$	Theorem 4
V and VI	$n_1 = 0$ $r = s = 0$	$p \geqq 1$	Theorems 5 and 6
VII	$n_1 = 0$ $r \geqq 0,\ s \geqq 0$	$p \geqq 1+s-r$	Theorem 7

2.2 An Example

We shall analyse a model with two exogenous variables, when one of them presents autocorrelation and the other is distributed as white-noise. The shock will be assumed to follow an ARMA (1,1) process.

Let the equations describing the model be given by:

(6.14a) $\eta_t = \gamma\eta_{t-1} + \beta_0^{(1)}\zeta_t^{(1)} + \beta_1^{(1)}\zeta_{t-1}^{(1)} + \beta_2^{(1)}\zeta_{t-2}^{(1)} + \beta_0^{(2)}\zeta_t^{(2)} + u_t$

(6.14b) $u_t = \rho u_{t-1} + a_t + \theta a_{t-1}$

(6.14c) $\zeta_t^{(2)} = b_t + \alpha b_{t-1}$

$$x_t^{(i)} = \zeta_t^{(i)} + \delta_t^{(i)} \qquad i = 1, 2$$

$$y_t = \eta_t + \varepsilon_t ,$$

and the stationarity and invertibility assumptions imply that the parameters γ, ρ, θ and α are smaller than one in absolute value.

Since for this example, $n = 2$, $n_1 = 1$, $r = s = 1$, according to Theorem 8 the necessary and sufficient conditions for the model to be identified are: $q_i^{**} = 1$, $q_2^{**} = 2$. As $p = 1$ and $q_1 = 2$ (notice that $\zeta^{(1)}$ is the white-noise exogenous variable) the conditions are satisfied and the model should be identified.

Consider first the following system of covariance equations:

a) 3-lag crosscovariance equation for the variable $\zeta^{(1)}$:

$$\omega_{yx_{-3}}^{(1)} = \gamma\omega_{yx_{-2}}^{(1)}$$

b) 0 and 1-lag crosscovariance equations for the variable $\zeta^{(2)}$:

$$\omega_{yx}^{(2)} = \gamma\omega_{yx_{-1}}^{(2)} + \beta_0^{(2)} (\omega_{xx}^{(2)} - \sigma_{\delta\delta}^{(2)})$$

$$\omega_{yx_{-1}}^{(2)} = \gamma\omega_{yx}^{(2)} + \beta_0^{(2)} \omega_{xx_{-1}}^{(2)}$$

c) 0 and 1-lag autocovariance equations for the variable $\zeta^{(2)}$ (in equation (6.14e)).

$$\omega_{xx}^{(2)} = (1 + \alpha^2)\,\sigma_{bb} + \sigma_{\delta\delta}^{(2)}$$

$$\omega_{xx_{-1}}^{(2)} = \alpha\,\sigma_{bb}$$

The Jacobian of these five equations with respect to the parameters γ, $\beta_0^{(2)}$, $\sigma_{\delta\delta}^{(2)}$, σ_{bb} and α is given by the matrix:

$$J_1 = \begin{pmatrix} \omega^{(1)}_{yx_{-2}} & 0 & 0 & 0 & 0 \\ \omega^{(2)}_{xy_{-1}} & \omega^{(2)}_{xx} - \sigma^{(2)}_{\delta\delta} & -\beta^{(2)}_0 & 0 & 0 \\ \omega^{(2)}_{yx} & \omega^{(2)}_{xx_{-1}} & 0 & 0 & 0 \\ 0 & 0 & 1 & 1+\alpha^2 & 2\alpha\,\sigma_{bb} \\ 0 & 0 & 0 & \alpha & \sigma_{bb} \end{pmatrix}$$

with determinant equal to:

$$\det J_1 = (1-\alpha^2)\,\omega^{(1)}_{yx_{-2}}\ \omega^{(2)}_{xx_{-1}}\ \beta^{(2)}_0\ \sigma_{bb}.$$

And, considering that

$$\omega^{(1)}_{yx_{-2}} = (\gamma^2\beta^{(1)}_0 + \gamma\beta^{(1)}_1 + \beta^{(1)}_2)\quad(\omega^{(1)}_{xx} - \sigma^{(1)}_{\delta\delta})$$

$$\omega^{(2)}_{xx_{-1}} = \alpha\,\sigma_{bb}\,,$$

it follows that $\det J_1 \neq 0$, and the parameters γ, $\beta^{(2)}_0$, $\sigma^{(2)}_{\delta\delta}$, σ_{bb} and α are identified.

If the rest of the covariance equations contains a subsystem that can be solved for the parameters $\beta^{(1)}_0$, $\beta^{(1)}_1$, $\beta^{(1)}_2$, $\sigma^{(1)}_{\delta\delta}$, $\sigma_{\varepsilon\varepsilon}$, ρ, θ and σ_{aa}, the model is identified. Consider the following system of covariance equations:

a) 0, 1 and 2-lag crosscovariance equations for the exogenous variable $\zeta^{(1)}$:

$$\omega^{(1)}_{yx} = \beta^{(1)}_0\,(\omega^{(1)}_{xx} - \sigma^{(1)}_{\delta\delta})$$

$$\omega^{(1)}_{yx_{-1}} = \gamma\omega^{(1)}_{yx} + \beta^{(1)}_1\,(\omega^{(1)}_{xx} - \sigma^{(1)}_{\delta\delta})$$

$$\omega^{(1)}_{yx_{-2}} = \gamma\omega^{(1)}_{yx_{-1}} + \beta^{(1)}_2\,(\omega^{(1)}_{xx} - \sigma^{(1)}_{\delta\delta})$$

b) 0, 1, 2, 3 and 4-lag autocovariance equations (for equation (6.14a))

$$\omega_{yy} = \gamma\omega_{yy_{-1}} + \beta^{(1)}_0\,\omega^{(1)}_{yx} + \beta^{(1)}_1\,\omega^{(1)}_{yx_{-1}} + \beta^{(1)}_2\,\omega^{(1)}_{yx_{-2}} + \beta^{(2)}_0\,\omega^{(2)}_{yx} + \sigma_0 + \sigma_{\varepsilon\varepsilon},$$

$$\omega_{yy_{-1}} = \gamma(\omega_{yy} - \sigma_{\varepsilon\varepsilon}) + \beta_1^{(1)} \omega_{yx}^{(1)} + \beta_2^{(1)} \omega_{yx_{-1}} + \sigma_1$$

$$\omega_{yy_{-2}} = \omega_{yy_{-1}} + \beta_2^{(1)} \omega_{yx}^{(1)} + \sigma_2$$

$$\omega_{yy_{-3}} = \omega_{yy_{-2}} + \sigma_3$$

$$\omega_{yy_{-4}} = \omega_{yy_{-3}} + \sigma_4 \quad ,$$

where, as before, $\sigma_\tau = E(u_t y_{t-\tau})$

The Jacobian of this system with respect to the parameters $\beta_0^{(1)}$, $\beta_1^{(1)}$, $\beta_2^{(1)}$, $\sigma_{\delta\delta}^{(1)}$, $\sigma_{\varepsilon\varepsilon}$, θ, σ_{aa} and ρ is given by the matrix:

$$J_2 = \begin{pmatrix}
\omega_{xx}^{(1)} - \sigma_{\delta\delta}^{(1)} & 0 & 0 & -\beta_0^{(1)} & 0 & 0 & 0 & 0 \\
0 & \omega_{xx}^{(1)} - \sigma_{\delta\delta}^{(1)} & 0 & -\beta_1^{(1)} & 0 & 0 & 0 & 0 \\
0 & 0 & \omega_{xx}^{(1)} - \sigma_{\delta\delta}^{(1)} & -\beta_2^{(1)} & 0 & 0 & 0 & 0 \\
\omega_{yx}^{(1)} & \omega_{yx_{-1}}^{(1)} & \omega_{yx_{-2}}^{(1)} & 0 & 1 & \frac{\partial\sigma_0}{\partial\theta} & \frac{\partial\sigma_0}{\partial\sigma_{aa}} & \frac{\partial\sigma_0}{\partial\rho} \\
0 & \omega_{yx}^{(1)} & \omega_{yx_{-1}}^{(1)} & 0 & -\gamma & \frac{\partial\sigma_1}{\partial\theta} & \frac{\partial\sigma_1}{\partial\sigma_{aa}} & \frac{\partial\sigma_1}{\partial\rho} \\
0 & 0 & \omega_{yx}^{(1)} & 0 & 0 & \frac{\partial\sigma_2}{\partial\theta} & \frac{\partial\sigma_2}{\partial\sigma_{aa}} & \frac{\partial\sigma_2}{\partial\rho} \\
0 & 0 & 0 & 0 & 0 & \frac{\partial\sigma_3}{\partial\theta} & \frac{\partial\sigma_3}{\partial\sigma_{aa}} & \frac{\partial\sigma_3}{\partial\rho} \\
0 & 0 & 0 & 0 & 0 & \frac{\partial\sigma_4}{\partial\theta} & \frac{\partial\sigma_4}{\partial\sigma_{aa}} & \frac{\partial\sigma_4}{\partial\rho}
\end{pmatrix}$$

If the matrix J_2 is nonsingular, the model is identified. Expanding the determinant of J_2 around the last three rows, it is seen that the only minors (formed with these last three rows) that do not have a row of zeros, or a complementary minor with a row of zeros, are the following ones:

$$E_1 = \begin{vmatrix}
\frac{\partial\sigma_0}{\partial\theta} & \frac{\partial\sigma_0}{\partial\sigma_{aa}} & \frac{\partial\sigma_0}{\partial\rho} \\
\frac{\partial\sigma_3}{\partial\theta} & \frac{\partial\sigma_3}{\partial\sigma_{aa}} & \frac{\partial\sigma_3}{\partial\rho} \\
\frac{\partial\sigma_4}{\partial\theta} & \frac{\partial\sigma_4}{\partial\sigma_{aa}} & \frac{\partial\sigma_4}{\partial\rho}
\end{vmatrix}$$

$$E_2 = \begin{vmatrix} \frac{\partial\sigma_1}{\partial\theta} & \frac{\partial\sigma_1}{\partial\sigma_{aa}} & \frac{\partial\sigma_1}{\partial\rho} \\ \frac{\partial\sigma_3}{\partial\theta} & \frac{\partial\sigma_3}{\partial\sigma_{aa}} & \frac{\partial\sigma_3}{\partial\rho} \\ \frac{\partial\sigma_4}{\partial\theta} & \frac{\partial\sigma_4}{\partial\sigma_{aa}} & \frac{\partial\sigma_4}{\partial\rho} \end{vmatrix}$$

$$E_3 = \begin{vmatrix} \frac{\partial\sigma_2}{\partial\theta} & \frac{\partial\sigma_2}{\partial\sigma_{aa}} & \frac{\partial\sigma_2}{\partial\rho} \\ \frac{\partial\sigma_3}{\partial\theta} & \frac{\partial\sigma_3}{\partial\sigma_{aa}} & \frac{\partial\sigma_3}{\partial\rho} \\ \frac{\partial\sigma_4}{\partial\theta} & \frac{\partial\sigma_4}{\partial\sigma_{aa}} & \frac{\partial\sigma_4}{\partial\rho} \end{vmatrix}$$

Equation (6.14b) implies:

$$\sigma_\tau = \rho\, \sigma_{\tau-1} \quad ,$$

for $\tau > 1$. Thus

$$\text{(6.15a)} \quad \frac{\partial\sigma_4}{\partial\theta} = \rho \frac{\partial\sigma_3}{\partial\theta} = \rho^2 \frac{\partial\sigma_2}{\partial\theta} = \rho^3 \frac{\partial\sigma_1}{\partial\theta}$$

$$\text{(6.15b)} \quad \frac{\partial\sigma_4}{\partial\sigma_{aa}} = \rho \frac{\partial\sigma_3}{\partial\sigma_{aa}} = \rho^2 \frac{\partial\sigma_2}{\partial\sigma_{aa}} = \rho^3 \frac{\partial\sigma_1}{\partial\sigma_{aa}}$$

and expanding E_2 and E_3 around the elements of the last column, all the minors contain two rows that are proportional. Therefore:

$$E_2 = E_3 = 0$$

Now, using (6.15a and b) the determinant of E_1 can be rewritten:

$$E_1 = \begin{vmatrix} \frac{\partial\sigma_0}{\partial\theta} & \frac{\partial\sigma_0}{\partial\sigma_{aa}} & \frac{\partial\sigma_0}{\partial\rho} \\ \frac{\partial\sigma_3}{\partial\theta} & \frac{\partial\sigma_3}{\partial\sigma_{aa}} & \frac{\partial\sigma_3}{\partial\rho} \\ \rho \frac{\partial\sigma_3}{\partial\theta} & \rho \frac{\partial\sigma_3}{\partial\sigma} & \rho \frac{\partial\sigma_3}{\partial\rho} + \sigma_3 \end{vmatrix} = \sigma_3 \begin{vmatrix} \frac{\partial\sigma_0}{\partial\theta} & \frac{\partial\sigma_0}{\partial\sigma_{aa}} \\ \frac{\partial\sigma_3}{\partial\theta} & \frac{\partial\sigma_3}{\partial\sigma_{aa}} \end{vmatrix}$$

and, as

$$\sigma_3 = \rho^2\, \sigma_1 = \rho^2\, (\rho\sigma_0 + \theta\sigma aa),$$

the expression can be further simplified to:

$$E_1 = \rho^2 \sigma_3 \begin{vmatrix} \frac{\partial\sigma_0}{\partial\theta}, & \frac{\partial\sigma_0}{\partial\sigma_{aa}} \\ \sigma_{aa} & \theta \end{vmatrix}$$

It can be verified that equations (6.14a and b) imply:

$$\sigma_0 = [1 + \frac{(\theta+\rho)^2}{1-\rho^2} + \frac{\gamma}{1-\gamma\rho} \frac{(\theta+\rho)(1+\rho\theta)}{1-\rho^2}] \sigma_{aa} ,$$

from which

$$E_1 = \rho^2\sigma_3 \left[\frac{(1-\theta + 2\rho\theta - \rho + \rho^2 - \rho^2\theta - \rho\theta^2)\gamma}{(1-\gamma\rho)(1-\rho^2)} - \frac{\theta^2 + \rho^2}{1-\rho^2} - 1\right] \sigma_{aa},$$

so that $E_1 \neq 0$. In det J_2, the complementary minor of E_1 is given by the determinant

$$A_1 = \begin{vmatrix} \omega_{xx}^{(1)} - \sigma_{\delta\delta}^{(1)} & 0 & 0 & -\beta_0^{(1)} & 0 \\ 0 & \omega_{xx}^{(1)} - \sigma_{\delta\delta}^{(1)} & 0 & -\beta_1^{(1)} & 0 \\ 0 & 0 & \omega_{xx}^{(1)} - \sigma_{\delta\delta}^{(1)} & -\beta_2^{(1)} & 0 \\ 0 & \omega_{yx}^{(1)} & \omega_{yx_{-1}}^{(1)} & 0 & -\gamma \\ 0 & 0 & \omega_{yx}^{(1)} & 0 & 0 \end{vmatrix}$$

which is equal to (in absolute value)

$$\gamma\, \beta_2^{(1)}\, \omega_{yx}^{(1)}\, (\omega_{xx}^{(1)} - \sigma_{\delta\delta}^{(1)})^2 = \gamma\, \beta_0^{(1)}\, \beta_2^{(1)}\, (\omega_{xx}^{(1)} - \sigma_{\delta\delta}^{(1)})^3 .$$

Thus the Laplace expansion of det J_2 around the last three columns is equal to the product of E_1 and A_1, hence, different from zero (a.e.). It follows that the model is identified.

(Notice that if we consider the model:

$$\eta_t = \gamma\eta_{t-1} + \beta_0^{(1)} \zeta_t^{(1)} + \beta_1^{(1)} \zeta_{t-1}^{(1)} + \beta_2^{(1)} \zeta_{t-2}^{(1)} + u_t$$

together with (6.14b) and the errors-in-the-variables equations, the system of τ-lag autocovariance equations for $\tau = 0, 1, 2, 3$ and 4, has a Jacobian with respect to the parameters $\beta_0^{(1)}$, $\beta_1^{(1)}$, $\beta_2^{(1)}$, $\sigma_{\delta\delta}^{(1)}$, $\sigma_{\varepsilon\varepsilon}$, θ, σ_{aa} and ρ also equal to the matrix J_2).

CHAPTER VII

SOME EXTENSIONS OF THE GENERAL MODEL

The analysis of identification performed in the previous chapters was directed towards the interaction of an errors-in-the-variables assumption with the dynamic properties of a model. Thus we analysed the effects of lagged variables in the structural equation and the effects of different patterns of autocorrelation for the shock and for the exogenous variables. By using relatively simple models, the identification properties of the dynamic features of the model could be isolated somewhat easily. Yet it seems worthwhile to see how the analysis could be extended to cover more general assumptions.

In particular, four possible extensions are considered. First, the independence of the exogenous variables is removed and Theorem 8 is modified in order to cover a model where the exogenous variables follow jointly a multivariate time series process. Second, Theorem 1 is extended to a nonstationary model, characterized by homogenous nonstationarity. The third extension deals with a model that includes a priori zero restrictions on the coefficients of the structural equation, as would happen, for example, if seasonality was present. Finally, we consider a model where the errors of measurement are autocorrelated.

1. CORRELATION BETWEEN EXOGENOUS VARIABLES

The general model we have considered in the previous chapter allows for the exogenous variables to be autocorrelated. But the independence of the shocks $b_t^{(i)}$, implies independence among the exogenous variables. This assumption may seem somewhat restrictive, but, as we shall see in this section, under relatively mild assumptions, Theorem 8 extends to cover the case of a more general model, where the exogenous variables follow a multivaritate time series process.

Let the model be described by equations (6.13a, b, d and e) and let the system of independent equations in (6.13c) be substituted by

(7.1) $$M(L)\underset{\sim}{\zeta}_t = H(L)\underline{b}_t,$$

where M(L) and H(L) are (n x n) matrices, whose elements are finite polynomials in the lag operator. 1/ The typical elements of M(L) and H(L) are, respectively, $M^{(i,j)}_{m_{ij}}(L)$ and $H^{(i,j)}_{h_{ij}}(L)$, where m_{ij} and h_{ij} denote the order of the polynomials. The process given by (7.1) is assumed jointly stationary and invertible; the vector $\underline{b}_t$ is a vector of n independent white-noise variables, with variances $\sigma^{(1)}_{bb}, \ldots, \sigma^{(n)}_{bb}$.

Now, the crosscovariance equations for equations (6.13a) are modified to look like:

$$\omega^{(i)}_{yx_{-\tau}} = \sum_{j=1}^{p} \gamma_j \omega^{(i)}_{yx_{-\tau+j}} + \sum_{\ell=1}^{n} \sum_{j=0}^{q_\ell} \beta_j^{(\ell)} (\omega^{(\ell,i)}_{xx_{-\tau+j}} - d^{(\ell,i)}_{\tau,j} \sigma^{(i)}_{\delta\delta})$$

where $\omega^{(\ell,i)}_{xx_{-\tau+j}}$ is the $(\tau - j)$-lag crosscovariance between the variables $x^{(\ell)}$ and $x^{(i)}$, and $d^{(\ell,i)}_{\tau,j} = 1$ for $\ell = i$, $\tau = j$, and $d^{(\ell,i)}_{\tau,j} = 0$ otherwise.

The autocovariance equations for equation (6.13a), remain basically unaffected.

It follows that, as for the case of model VII, if no exogenous variable is white-noise, the crosscovariance equations for (6.13a) will identify the γ and β-parameters, plus the variances of the errors of measurement affecting the exogenous variables $(\sigma^{(1)}_{\delta\delta}, \ldots, \sigma^{(n)}_{\delta\delta})$. Therefore, once these variances are identified, the system given by (7.1) becomes also identified.

Since the autocovariance equations reamin unaffected, it follows that, if the multivariate process generating the exogenous variables implies that no such variable is white-noise, Theorem 7 can be applied and the model will be identified if $p + r \geq s$.

To see under what conditions the system (7.1) contains a variable $\zeta^{(i)}_t$ that is white-noise, let us assume that the matrix M(L) is nonsingular and write (7.1) as

$$\text{(7.1a)} \quad \underline{\zeta}_t = M(L)^{-1} H(L)\underline{b}_t = \pi(L)\underline{b}_t ,$$

where $\pi(L)$ is a (n x n) matrix of polynomials in L. The system of equations (7.1a) can be rewritten

1/ This is the model considered by Quenouille [1957] and Zellner and Palm [1974].

$$\zeta_t^{(i)} = \sum_{j=1}^{n} \pi_{ij}(L)\, b_t^{(j)}$$

where $\pi_{ij}(L)$ is the (i,j)th element of the matrix $\pi(L)$. Hence for a ζ-variable to be white-noise it has to be that, for some i, each of the n polynomials $\pi_{i1}(L), \ldots, \pi_{in}(L)$ has only one non-zero term. Since the matrix $\pi(L)$ is the product of $M(L)^{-1}$ and H(L), this is not likely to happen. Trivially, when each equation in the system (7.1) contains either an autoregressive or a moving-average structure, the following result holds.

Theorem 9:

When no exogenous variable is white-noise, the model consisting of equations (6.13a, b, d and e) and (7.1), is identified if $p + r > s$.

All previous Theorems listed conditions that were both necessary and sufficient. On the contrary, Theorem 9 states only sufficient conditions for identification. To see that there can be situations when this condition is not satisfied, but the model still is identified, consider the following case:

$$\eta_t = \gamma\eta_{t-1} + \beta_0^{(1)}\, \zeta_t^{(1)} + \beta_1^{(1)}\, \zeta_{t-1}^{(1)} + \beta_0^{(2)}\, \zeta_t^{(2)} + u_t$$

$$\zeta_t^{(1)} = \phi_1\zeta_{t-1}^{(1)} + \phi_2\zeta_t^{(2)} + b_t^{(1)}$$

$$\zeta_t^{(2)} = b_t^{(2)} ,$$

where u, $b^{(1)}$ and $b^{(2)}$ are independent white-noise variables. [2/] For this model the conditions of theorem 9 are not satisfied, since the variable $\zeta_t^{(2)}$ is white-noise, but is is straightforward to verify that the system of covariance equations:

$$\omega_{yx}^{(1)} = \gamma\omega_{y_{-1}x}^{(1)} + \beta_0^{(1)}\,(\omega_{xx}^{(1,1)} - \sigma_{\delta\delta}^{(1)}) + \beta_1^{(1)}\,\omega_{xx_{-1}}^{(1,1)} + \beta_0^{(2)}\,\omega_{xx}^{(1,2)}$$

2/ Notice that in this example

$$M(L) = \begin{pmatrix} 1-\phi_1 L & -\phi_2 \\ 0 & 1 \end{pmatrix} , \quad H(L) = \begin{pmatrix} 1 & 0 \\ 0 & 1 \end{pmatrix}$$

$$\omega_{yx_{-1}}^{(1)} = \gamma\omega_{yx}^{(1)} + \beta_0^{(1)} \omega_{xx_{-1}}^{(1,1)} + \beta_1^{(1)} (\omega_{xx}^{(1,1)} - \sigma_{\delta\delta}^{(1)})$$

$$\omega_{yx_{-\tau}}^{(1)} = \gamma\omega_{yx_{-\tau+1}}^{(1)} + \beta_0^{(1)} \omega_{xx_{-\tau}}^{(1,1)} + \beta_1^{(1)} \omega_{xx_{-\tau+1}}^{(1,1)} , \qquad \tau > 1 ,$$

$$\omega_{yx}^{(2)} = \beta_0^{(1)} \omega_{xx}^{(1,2)} + \beta_1^{(1)} \omega_{xx_{-1}}^{(1,2)} + \beta_0^{(2)} (\omega_{xx}^{(2,2)} - \sigma_{\delta\delta}^{(2)})$$

$$\omega_{yy} = \gamma\omega_{yy_{-1}} + \beta_0^{(1)} \omega_{yx}^{(1)} + \beta_1^{(1)} \omega_{yx_{-1}}^{(1)} + \beta_0^{(2)} \omega_{yx}^{(2)} + \sigma_{uu} + \sigma_{\varepsilon\varepsilon}$$

$$\omega_{yy_{-1}} = \gamma(\omega_{yy} - \sigma_{\varepsilon\varepsilon}) + \beta_0^{(1)} \omega_{y_{-1}x}^{(1)} + \beta_1^{(1)} \omega_{yx}^{(1)}$$

$$\omega_{xx}^{(1,1)} = \phi_1\omega_{xx_{-1}}^{(1,1)} + \phi_2\omega_{xx}^{(1,2)} + \sigma_{\delta\delta}^{(1)} + \sigma_{bb}^{(1)}$$

$$\omega_{xx_{-\tau}}^{(1,1)} = \phi_1\omega_{xx_{-\tau+1}} , \qquad \tau > 0$$

$$\omega_{xx}^{(1,2)} = \phi_1\omega_{xx_{-1}}^{(2,1)} + \beta_2^{(2)} (\omega_{xx}^{(2,2)} - \sigma_{\delta\delta}^{(2)})$$

$$\omega_{xx}^{(2,2)} = \sigma_{bb}^{(2)} + \sigma_{\delta\delta}^{(2)}$$

can be solved for the γ, β, ϕ and σ-parameters. Notice that in the present case, due to the crosscovariances between the exogenous variables, the crosscovariance equation corresponding to the variable $\zeta_t^{(i)}$ includes some of the $\beta^{(j)}$-parameters, for $i \neq j$.

Therefore, the crosscovariances between the exogenous variable seem to provide another type of information that affects the state of identification of a shock-error model. As we have been concerned with the effects of dynamic stochastic assumptions, we shall not further pursue this issue at the present time. Yet the analysis of how the dynamic assumptions interact with the effects due to the existence of crosscovariances, as the ones implied by simultaneous equations models (see Geraci [1977]), seems a natural extension of the present research. 3/

3/ Some general results are reported in Hsiao [1976], [1977].

2. NON STATIONARITY

All of our previous results were derived under the assumption that the stochastic processes involved were stationary. In this section we shall relax this assumption for the case of model I; in particular, we shall assume that the endogenous variable follows an homogenous nonstationary process. We consider model I with η_t replaced by $\nabla^d \eta_t$, where $\nabla^d = (1-L)^d$. Thus the variable:

$$\nu_t = \nabla^d \eta_t$$

follows a stationary process. 4/

2.1 An Example

The model analyzed in section 1.1 of Chapter II, with one exogenous variable and one lag per variable, was found to be underidentified. We shall see how this result is affected if the stationarity assumption for the endogenous variable is changed. Let the model be described by the equations:

$$x_t = \zeta_t + \delta_t$$

$$y_t = \eta_t + \varepsilon_t$$

$$\nu_t = \nabla \eta_t = \eta_t - \eta_{t-1}$$

$$\nu_t = \gamma \nu_{t-1} + \beta_0 \zeta_t + \beta_1 \zeta_{t-1} + u_t \quad .$$

Similarly to the model considered in Chapter II, we shall assume that $-1 < \gamma < 1$, and that δ, ε, u and ζ are independent white-noise variables.

In terms of the unobservable variables, the covariance equations for this model are given by:

$$\sigma_{\nu\zeta} = \beta_0 \sigma_{\zeta\zeta}$$

$$\sigma_{\nu\zeta_{-1}} = \gamma \sigma_{\nu\zeta} + \beta_1 \sigma_{\zeta\zeta}$$

4/ This class of homogenously non-stationary models is in accordance with the ones proposed by Yaglom [1958] and the ARIMA models in Box-Jenkins [1970].

$$\sigma_{\nu\zeta_{-\tau}} = \gamma\, \sigma_{\nu\zeta_{-\tau+1}} \,, \qquad \tau > 1$$

$$\sigma_{\nu\nu} = \gamma\, \sigma_{\nu\nu_{-1}} + \beta_0\, \sigma_{\nu\zeta} + \beta_1\, \sigma_{\nu\zeta_{-1}} + \sigma_{uu}$$

$$\sigma_{\nu\nu_{-1}} = \gamma\, \sigma_{\nu\nu} + \beta_1\, \sigma_{\nu\zeta}$$

$$\sigma_{\nu\nu_{-\tau}} = \gamma\, \sigma_{\nu\nu_{-\tau+1}} \,, \qquad \tau > 1 \,,$$

Define the variables:

$$z_t = \nabla y_t$$

$$e_t = \nabla \varepsilon_t \,.$$

If follows that

(7.4) $$z_t = \nu_t + e_t \,.$$

Therefore, for $\tau = 0, 1, 2, \ldots,$

$$\sigma_{\nu\zeta_{-\tau}} = E(z_t - e_t)(x_{t-\tau} - \delta_{t-\tau}) = E(z_t\, x_{t-\tau}) = \omega_{zx_{-\tau}}$$

Now, equation (7.6) and the fact that ε and η are independent imply

(7.5) $$\omega_{zz} = \sigma_{\nu\nu} + \sigma_{ee} \,,$$

where $\sigma_{ee} = E(\varepsilon_t - \varepsilon_{t-1})^2$. Thus $\sigma_{ee} = 2\sigma_{\varepsilon\varepsilon}$, and (7.5) becomes:

(7.6a) $$\sigma_{\nu\nu} = \omega_{zz} - 2\sigma_{\varepsilon\varepsilon} .$$

Similarly:

$$\omega_{zz_{-1}} = \sigma_{\nu\nu_{-1}} + \sigma_{ee_{-1}} \,,$$

where $\sigma_{ee_{-1}} = E(\varepsilon_t - \varepsilon_{t-1})(\varepsilon_{t-1} - \varepsilon_{t-2}) = -\sigma_{\varepsilon\varepsilon}$. Thus

(7.6b) $$\sigma_{\nu\nu_{-1}} = \omega_{zz_{-1}} + \sigma_{\varepsilon\varepsilon}$$

As $\sigma_{ee_{-\tau}} = 0$ for $\tau > 1$, it follows that

(7.6c) $$\sigma_{\nu\nu_{-\tau}} = \omega_{zz_{-\tau}} \,, \text{ (for } \tau > 1).$$

Substituting (7.6a, b and c) in the covariance equations, the following system of equations is obtained:

(7.7a) $\omega_{zx} = \beta_0(\omega_{xx} - \sigma_{\delta\delta})$

(7.7b) $\omega_{zx_{-1}} = \gamma\,\omega_{zx} + \beta_1(\omega_{xx} - \sigma_{\delta\delta})$

(7.7c) $\omega_{zz} = \gamma\,\omega_{zz_{-1}} + \beta_0\,\omega_{zx} + \beta_1\,\omega_{zx_{-1}} + (2 + \gamma)\sigma_{\varepsilon\varepsilon} + \sigma_{uu}$

(7.7d) $\omega_{zz_{-1}} = \gamma\,\omega_{zz} + \beta_1\,\omega_{zx} - (1 + 2\gamma)\sigma_{\varepsilon\varepsilon}$

(7.7e) $\omega_{zz_{-2}} = \gamma\,\omega_{zz_{-1}} + \gamma\,\sigma_{\varepsilon\varepsilon}$

(7.7f) $\omega_{zz_{-3}} = \gamma\,\omega_{zz_{-2}}$,

plus a set of equations where γ is the only parameter explicitly appearing. We shall prove that the Jacobian of this system of equations with respect to the parameters β_0, β_1, γ, $\sigma_{\delta\delta}$, $\sigma_{\varepsilon\varepsilon}$, σ_{uu} is non singular (a.e.). This Jacobian is given by the matrix:

$$\begin{pmatrix} 0 & \omega_{xx} - \sigma_{\delta\delta} & 0 & -\beta_0 & 0 & 0 \\ \omega_{zx} & 0 & \omega_{xx} - \sigma_{\delta\delta} & -\beta_1 & 0 & 0 \\ \omega_{zz_{-1}} + \sigma_{\varepsilon\varepsilon} & \omega_{zx} & \omega_{zx_{-1}} & 0 & 2+\gamma & 1 \\ \omega_{zz} - 2\sigma_{\varepsilon\varepsilon} & 0 & \omega_{zx} & 0 & -1-2\gamma & 0 \\ \omega_{zz_{-1}} + \sigma_{\varepsilon\varepsilon} & 0 & 0 & 0 & \gamma & 0 \\ \omega_{zz_{-2}} & 0 & 0 & 0 & 0 & 0 \end{pmatrix}$$

with determinant equal to

$$\gamma\beta_1\,\omega_{zz_{-2}}\,\omega_{zx}\,(\omega_{xx} - \sigma_{\delta\delta}) ,$$

which is different from zero. Therefore the model is identified.

2.2. The General Case

Consider Model I, with η_t substituted by $\nu_t = \nabla^d \eta_t$ (i.e., we assume the model to be stationary for the $d^{\underline{th}}$ difference of the endogenous variable). Defining $z_t = \nabla^d y_t$ and $e_t = \nabla^d \varepsilon_t$, we have

$$z_t = \nu_t + e_t ,$$

so that

$$\omega_{zz_{-\tau}} = \sigma_{\nu\nu_{-\tau}} + \sigma_{ee_{-\tau}} , \quad \tau = 0, 1, 2, \ldots$$

Considering that

$$\sigma_{ee_{-\tau}} = E(e_t \, e_{t-\tau}) ,$$

and that

$$e_t = \varepsilon_t - d\varepsilon_{t-1} + \binom{d}{2} \varepsilon_{t-2} + \ldots + (-1)^d \varepsilon_{t-d} ,$$

it is easily seen that:

For $\tau \leqq d$, $\sigma_{\nu\nu_{-\tau}} = \omega_{zz_{-\tau}} - c_\tau \sigma_{\varepsilon\varepsilon}$

For $\tau > d$, $\sigma_{\nu\nu_{-\tau}} = \omega_{zz_{-\tau}}$,

where c_τ is an integer, different from zero. 5/ Thus the only difference between

---

5/ To see an example, consider a model stationary in the second difference, $\nu_t = \nabla^2 \eta_t$. Then:

$$\omega_{zz_{-\tau}} = \sigma_{\nu\nu_{-\tau}} + E(e_t \, e_{t-\tau}), \quad (\tau = 0, 1, 2, \ldots),$$

where $z_t = \nabla^2 y_t$, $e_t = \nabla^2 \varepsilon_t$

Now:

$$E(e_t)^2 = E(\nabla^2 \varepsilon_t)^2 = E(\varepsilon_t - 2\varepsilon_{t-1} + \varepsilon_{t-2})^2 = 6 \, \sigma_{\varepsilon\varepsilon}$$

$$E(e_t \, e_{t-1}) = E(\varepsilon_t - 2\varepsilon_{t-1} + \varepsilon_{t-2})(\varepsilon_{t-1} - 2\varepsilon_{t-2} + \varepsilon_{t-3}) = -4 \, \sigma_{\varepsilon\varepsilon}$$

$$E(e_t \, e_{t-2}) = E(\varepsilon_t - 2\varepsilon_{t-1} + \varepsilon_{t-2})(\varepsilon_{t-2} - 2\varepsilon_{t-3} + \varepsilon_{t-4}) = \sigma_{\varepsilon\varepsilon}$$

$$E(e_t \, e_{t-\tau}) = 0 \text{ for } \tau > 2.$$

Thus $c_0 = 6$, $c_1 = -4$, $c_2 = 1$, $c_\tau = 0$ for $\tau > 2$.

the system of covariance equations corresponding to Model I and to the nonstationary model we are considering lies in the following fact: For the stationary case (Model I), the τ-lag autocovariance equation includes the parameter $\sigma_{\varepsilon\varepsilon}$ for $\tau = 0, 1, \ldots,$ p. When stationarity affects the dth difference of the exogenous variable, the parameter $\sigma_{\varepsilon\varepsilon}$ appears in the τ-lag autocovariance equation as long as $\tau \leqq p + d$. This consideration suggests the following result.

Theorem 10:

Consider Model I, when stationarity is achieved through the dth difference of the endogenous variable (i.e., with η_t in the structural equation substituted for $\nabla^d \eta_t$). The model is identified if and only if the conditions of Theorem 2 are satified, with p substituted for by $p' = p + d$.

Proof of Theorem 10: The proof of the Theorem is the same as the proof of Theorem 2, with the following modification: The vector $\underline{\gamma}^*$ in (2.15) of Chapter II is changed to:

$$\underline{\gamma}^* = \begin{cases} -(\gamma_1', \gamma_2', \ldots, \gamma_{n+1}') & \text{if } p + d \geqq n + 1 \\ -(\gamma_1', \ldots, \gamma_{p+d}', 0, \ldots, 0) & \text{if } p + d < n + 1, \end{cases}$$

where

$$\gamma_i' = \begin{cases} c_i + \gamma_i & \text{if } i \leqq p \\ c_i & \text{if } i > p, \end{cases}$$

and c_i, $(i = 1, 2, \ldots, p + d)$, is a non-zero integer.

Therefore, as far as identification of model I is concerned, nonstationarity of the type we have considered has the same effect as increasing the size of the autoregressive polynomial operating on the endogenous variable. 6/

6/ Notice that if in the equation

$$G_p(L)\, \nabla^d\, \eta_t = \sum_{i=1}^{n} B_{q_i}^{(i)}(L)\, \zeta_t^{(i)} + u_t$$

The analysis could be extended to cover other types of nonstationarity. In particular, it would be interesting to study the identification effects of nonstationarity in the exogenous variables and/or in the shock of the structural equation. 7/

3. A PRIORI ZERO RESTRICTIONS IN THE COEFFICIENTS (SEASONAL MODELS)

So far all the models we have considered were characterized by the fact that the only constraints affecting the coefficients of the equations were the ones implied by the stationarity and invertibility conditions of assumptions 1, 4b, and 5b. Thus, in particular, each one of the γ_j (j=1, ..., p) and $\beta_j^{(i)}$ (j=0, 1, ..., q_i; i=1, ..., n) coefficients of the structural equation were assumed different from zero. Yet, on occasions, the model may contain a priori information concerning these parameters. For the case of dynamic models, an example is provided by the ones that incorporate seasonal effects. For instance, let the ith exogenous variable in a monthly model reflect an annual (seasonal) effect. Then the polynomial $B_{q_i}^{(i)}(L)$ is given by an expression of the form:

$$B_{q_i}^{(i)}(L) = \beta_0^{(i)} + \beta_1^{(i)} L^{12} + \beta_2^{(i)} L^{24} + \ldots + \beta_{q_i}^{(i)} L^{12q_i} ,$$

so that the coefficients corresponding to a power of L not a multiple of 12 are constrained to be zero.

The existence of these a priori zero constraints for the coefficients may have drastic effects, as far as identification is concerned. The following example illustrates the point.

6/ (continued)

we expand $\nabla^d \eta_t$, we obtain a new equation with an AR polynomial of order (p + d). But as the model expressed in terms of the variable η_t is not stationary it is not anymore true that, for example,

$$E(\eta_t \, \eta_{t-\tau}) = E(\eta_{t+k} \, \eta_{t+k-\tau}) ,$$

for $k \neq 0$. Thus the nonstationary model we have considered cannot be seen simply as a particular case of Model I, and Theorem 10 is not a particular case of Theorem 1.

7/ A different approach to the analysis of nonstationarity in dynamic model with errors of measurement is contained in Aigner [1966].

In Section 1, Chapter II, we considered the model

$$\eta_t = \gamma\eta_{t-1} + \beta_0\zeta_t + \beta_1\zeta_{t-1} + u_t$$

where u and ζ are independent white-noise variables, and the variables η and ζ are measured with error, according to equations (1.1b) and (1.1c). We concluded that the model was underidentified.

Consider now the model

$$\eta_t = \gamma\eta_{t-t^0} + \beta_0\,\zeta_{t-t_0} + \beta_1\,\zeta_{t-t_1} + u_t, \tag{7.8}$$

where t^0, t_0 and t_1 are positive integers, and $t_0 < t_1$. Let c be a positive integer such that $c > 1$ and $ct^0 > t_1$. The τ-lag autocovariance equation for $\tau = ct^0$ yields

$$\omega_{yy_{-ct^0}} = \gamma\omega_{yy_{-(c-1)t^0}} \tag{7.9}$$

Thus the coefficient γ is identified. For the complete model to be identified, a subsystem of the covariance equations (not including (7.9)) has to provide a solution for the parameters β_0, β_1, $\sigma_{\delta\delta}$, $\sigma_{\varepsilon\varepsilon}$, and σ_{uu}.

Consider now the following facts:

a) The parameter σ_{uu} appears only in the 0-lag autocovariance equation:

$$\omega_{yy} = \gamma\omega_{yy_{-t^0}} + \beta_0\,\omega_{yx_{-t_0}} + \beta_1\,\omega_{yx_{-t_1}} + \sigma_{\varepsilon\varepsilon} + \sigma_{uu}. \tag{7.10a}$$

b) The parameter $\sigma_{\varepsilon\varepsilon}$ appears only in this last autocovariance equation, and in the τ-lag autocovariance equation for $\tau = t^0$:

$$\omega_{yy_{-t^0}} = \gamma(\omega_{yy} - \sigma_{\varepsilon\varepsilon}) + \beta_1\,\omega_{yx_{-t^0+t_1}} \tag{7.10b}$$

c) The parameter β_0 appears only in equation (7.10a) and in the τ-lag crosscovariance equation for $\tau = t_0$,

$$\omega_{yx_{-t_0}} = \beta_0\,(\omega_{xx} - \sigma_{\delta\delta}) \tag{7.10c}$$

d) The parameter $\sigma_{\delta\delta}$ appears only in equation (7.10c) and in the τ-lag crosscovariance equation for $\tau = t_1$:

$$\omega_{yx_{-t_1}} = \gamma\omega_{yx_{-t_1+t^0}} + \beta_1\,(\omega_{xx} - \sigma_{\delta\delta}) \tag{7.10d}$$

As (7.10d) is also the only crosscovariance equation containing the parameter β_1, for the model to be identified this parameter has to appear in some τ-lag autocovariance equation. To see when this will happen, consider the τ-lag autocovariance equation:

$$\omega_{yy_{-\tau}} = \gamma\omega_{yy_{-t^0+\tau}} + \beta_1 \omega_{yx_{-t_1+\tau}} ,$$

where use has been made of the fact that $\omega_{yx_{-t_0+\tau}} = 0$, since equation (7.8) implies:

(7.11) $\omega_{yx_{-\tau}} = 0$ for $\tau < t_0$.

Thus for equation (7.10e) to contain β_1 it has to be that

(7.12) $\omega_{yx_{-t_1+\tau}} \neq 0$.

As the final form of equation (7.8) is given by the expression:

$$\eta_t = (1 - \gamma L^{t^0})^{-1} \; [(\beta_0 + \beta_2 L^{t_1-t_0}) \zeta_{t-t_0} + u_t]$$

$$= [\beta_0 + \sum_{j=1}^{\infty} \gamma^j \beta_0 L^{jt^0} + \sum_{j=0}^{\infty} \gamma^j \beta_1 L^{jt^0+t_1-t_0}] \zeta_{t-t_0} + v_t ,$$

where $v_t = (1 - L^{t^0})^{-1} u_t$, it follows that for (7.12) to hold, it has to be that

(7.13a) $t_1 - \tau = t_0$,

or

(7.13b) $t_1 - \tau = t_0 + jt^0$, for $j = 1, 2, \ldots$

If $t^0 = t_1 - t_0$ the only positive values of τ that satisfy (7.13a) or (7.13b) are:

$$\tau = 0 \text{ and } \tau = t_1 - t_0 = t^0 .$$

Thus, if $t^0 = t_1 - t_0$, the only τ-lag autocovariance equations that include the coefficient β_1 are the ones corresponding to $\tau = 0$ and $\tau = t^0$. When this is the case, the five parameters β_0, β_1, $\sigma_{\varepsilon\varepsilon}$, $\sigma_{\delta\delta}$ and σ_{uu} appear only in four covariance equations (equations (7.10a, b, c, and d)), and the model is not identified.

If $t^0 \neq t_1 - t_0$, the τ-lag autocovariance equation for $\tau = t_1 - t_0$ becomes:

$$\omega_{yy_{-t_1+t_0}} = \gamma\omega_{yy_{-t^0+t_1-t_0}} + \beta_1 \omega_{yx_{-t_0}}$$

and the Jacobian of the system of this equation plus equations (7.10a, b, c and d), with respect to the parameters β_0, β_1, $\sigma_{\delta\delta}$, $\sigma_{\varepsilon\varepsilon}$ and σ_{uu} is given by the matrix:

$$J = \begin{pmatrix} 0 & \omega_{yx_{-t_0}} & 0 & 0 & 0 \\ \omega_{yx_{-t_0}} & \omega_{yx_{-t_1}} & 0 & 1 & 1 \\ 0 & \omega_{yx_{-t^0+t_1}} & 0 & -\gamma & 0 \\ \omega_{xx}-\sigma_{\delta\delta} & 0 & -\beta_0 & 0 & 0 \\ 0 & \omega_{xx}-\sigma_{\delta\delta} & -\beta_1 & 0 & 0 \end{pmatrix}$$

Since (in absolute value) $\det J = \gamma\beta_1\, \omega_{yx_{-t_0}} (\omega_{xx}-\sigma_{\delta\delta}) = \gamma\beta_1\, \beta_0\, (\omega_{xx}-\sigma_{\delta\delta})^2$, it follows that J is nonsingular and the model is identified.

Therefore, under our assumptions, the necessary and sufficient condition for the model with structural equation (7.8) to be identified is $t^0 \neq t_1 - t_0$. The extension of the analysis to more complicate models with n exogenous variables and any number of zero constraints on the coefficients requires a similar approach; to determine under which conditions a system of covariance equations can be solved for the parameters. In the same way that a covariance equation can be characterized by the set of parameters appearing in the equation, each parameter can be associated to the set of covariance equations where the parameter appears. If it is possible to assign, for each parameter, a different (linearly independent) covariance equation, the model will be identified. It can be seen that this approach may be formalized with the use of a field of combinatoral mathematics known as "Transversal Theory". [8/] But this extension lies beyond the scope of the present analysis, and may represent one of the natural directions for further research.

8/ See, for example, Mirsky [1971]. The relationship between Transversal Theory and Identification of econometric models has been pointed out by Geraci [1974, p. 48], in the context of "contemporaneous" shock-error models.

4. AUTOCORRELATED ERRORS OF MEASUREMENT

Throughout the previous chapters we have analysed the identification effects of different stochastic assumptions for the exogenous and endogenous variables and for the shock. All the models considered have assumed the errors of measurement, ε and $\delta^{(i)}$, to be distributed as white-noise. In this section we consider the effect of autocorrelated error of measurement for the example of Section 1, Chapter II, where the structural equation is given by:

(7.14a) $$\eta_t = \gamma\eta_{t-1} + \beta_0 \zeta_t + \beta_1 \zeta_{t-1} + u_t \quad .$$

The errors-in-variables equations are, as before,

(7.14b) $$y_t = \eta_t + \varepsilon_t$$

(7.14c) $$x_t = \zeta_t + \delta_t \quad .$$

The variable ε_t is assumed white-noise, but δ_t, the error affecting the exogenous variable, is assumed to be the outcome of a first order autoregressive process:

(7.14d) $$\delta_t = \mu\delta_{t-1} + g_t \quad ,$$

where $-1 < \mu < 1$ and g_t is white-noise, independent of ε, ζ and u.

In Section 1, Chapter II, we concluded that, when δ is white-noise, the model is not identified. We shall see that if, instead, δ is assumed to follow the process (7.14d), the complete model is identified.

As ζ is assumed white-noise, independent of δ, the autocovariance equations for (7.14c) are:

(7.15a) $$\omega_{xx} = \sigma_{\zeta\zeta} + \sigma_{\delta\delta}$$

(7.15b) $$\omega_{xx_{-\tau}} = \sigma_{\delta\delta_{-\tau}} \qquad \tau > 0$$

Considering (7.14d), equation (7.15b) can be rewritten:

$$\omega_{xx_{-\tau}} = \frac{\mu^\tau}{1-\mu^2}\,\sigma_{gg}$$

Now, letting $\tau = 1$ and 2, the system of two autocovariance equations obtained has a Jacobian with respect to the parameters μ and σ_{gg} given by the matrix:

$$J = \begin{pmatrix} \frac{1+\mu^2}{(1-\mu^2)^2}\sigma_{gg} & \frac{\mu}{1-\mu^2} \\ \frac{2\mu}{(1-\mu^2)^2}\sigma_{gg} & \frac{\mu}{1-\mu^2} \end{pmatrix}$$

Since det $J = \frac{\mu^2(1-\mu)^2}{(1-\mu^2)^3}\sigma_{gg}$, the Jacobian is nonsingular, which implies that the parameters μ and σ_{gg} are identified. Therefore the parameter $\sigma_{\delta\delta}$ is identified also, since

$$\sigma_{\delta\delta} = \frac{\sigma_{gg}}{1-\mu^2} .$$

The parameter γ is identified through the 2-lag autocovariance equation for (7.14a):

$$\omega_{yy_{-2}} = \gamma\omega_{yy_{-1}}$$

Consider now the covariance equations: 9/

9/ These covariance equations are obtained as follows: First, multiplying both sides of equation (7.14a) by ζ_t, and performing the same operations for ζ_{t-1}, η_t and η_{t-1}, after taking expectations, the following equations are obtained.

$$\sigma_{\eta\zeta} = \beta_0\sigma_{\zeta\zeta}$$

$$\sigma_{\eta\zeta_{-1}} = \gamma\sigma_{\eta\zeta} + \beta_1\sigma_{\zeta\zeta}$$

$$\sigma_{\eta\eta} = \gamma\sigma_{\eta\eta_{-1}} + \beta_0\sigma_{\eta\zeta} + \beta_1\sigma_{\eta\zeta_{-1}} + \sigma_{uu}$$

$$\sigma_{\eta\eta_{-1}} = \gamma\sigma_{\eta\eta} + \beta_1\sigma_{\eta\zeta} .$$

Considering the relationships between the unobservable and observable covariances:

$$\omega_{xx} = \sigma_{\zeta\zeta} + \sigma_{\delta\delta}$$

$$\omega_{yx_{-\tau}} = \sigma_{\eta\zeta_{-\tau}} , \qquad \tau \geqq 0$$

$$\omega_{yy} = \sigma_{\eta\eta} + \sigma_{\varepsilon\varepsilon}$$

$$\omega_{yy_{-\tau}} = \sigma_{\eta\eta_{-\tau}} \qquad \tau \geqq 0$$

the system of equations (7.16) is obtained.

$$
(7.16)\quad
\begin{aligned}
\omega_{yx} &= \beta_0 (\omega_{xx} - \sigma_{\delta\delta}) \\
\omega_{yx_{-1}} &= \gamma\omega_{yx} + \beta_1 (\omega_{xx} - \sigma_{\delta\delta}) \\
\omega_{yy} &= \gamma\omega_{yy_{-1}} + \beta_0\, \omega_{yx} + \beta_1\, \omega_{yx_{-1}} + \sigma_{\varepsilon\varepsilon} + \sigma_{uu} \\
\omega_{yy_{-1}} &= \gamma(\omega_{yy} - \sigma_{\varepsilon\varepsilon}) + \beta_1\, \omega_{yx} .
\end{aligned}
$$

The Jacobian of this system with respect to the parameters β_0, β_1, $\sigma_{\varepsilon\varepsilon}$ and σ_{uu} is given by the matrix:

$$
\begin{pmatrix}
\omega_{xx} - \sigma_{\delta\delta} & 0 & 0 & 0 \\
0 & \omega_{xx} - \sigma_{\delta\delta} & 0 & 0 \\
\omega_{yx} & \omega_{yx_{-1}} & 1 & 1 \\
0 & \omega_{yx} & -\gamma & 0
\end{pmatrix}
$$

with determinant equal to $[\gamma(\omega_{xx} - \sigma_{\delta\delta})^2]$. Therefore, when the error of measurement δ_t follows an AR(1) process, the complete model is identified.

On the other hand, it can be verified that if the error δ_t is assumed to follow a first order moving average process, the model is not identified. A more general analysis of the identification effects of the stochastic assumptions concerning the errors of measurement seems to be also a natural extension of the present research. 10/

10/ Some results are reported in Nowak [1977].

CHAPTER VIII

SUMMARY

Our analysis has concentrated on the problem of identification of a sequence of dynamic shock-error models. The shock-error model is characterized by the fact that the structural econometric equation is perturbated by a random shock, and the exogenous and endogenous variables are observed with error. The dynamics of the model are reflected, on the one hand, in the presence of distributed lags in the structural equation. On the other hand, possible autocorrelations between the exogenous variables and the shock are explained by autoregressive-moving average processes.

The first chapter describes the equations and assumptions of the model and presents the methodology followed in the analysis of identification. The main assumptions are that the variables are normally distributed (with zero mean), that the ARMA processes generating the shock and the exogenous variables are stationary and invertible, and that the implied stochastic process for the endogenous variable is also stationary. (Under these assumptions, it is seen that, when no errors of observation are present, the model is identified.)

These stochastic assumptions imply some restrictions on the parameters of the equations; the restrictions define the admissible parameter space. Also, our assumptions imply that all the observational information is contained in the auto and crosscovariance functions of the variables that can be observed.

The concept of identification can then be formulated in terms of our models. For a given model, each point in the admissible parameter space defines a structure. The model is identified if and only if no two (or more) structures are observationally equivalent. Thus identification is achieved when all the parameters of the model can be uniquely determined from the elements of the observable auto and crosscovariance functions. These elements can be expressed in the form of covariance equations. Therefore, identification of a model can be formulated in terms of the latter: if there exists a system of covariance equation which can be solved uniquely for the unknown parameters of the model (as functions of the observable covariances), the model is identified. Inversely, the model is not identified if no such system exists. We confine our analysis to the existence of locally isolated solutions to systems of covariance equations. In this way, the model is (locally) identified if and only if a system of covariance equations has a Jacobian with respect to the parameters of the model which is nonsingular. It is interesting to notice that, whenever the model is identified, the solution to the system of covariance equations expresses the parameters as functions of observable covariances. For a given time series, if these observable covariances are replaced by their sample estimates, consistent estimates of the parameters are obtained. This is mentioned as a side result; we do not concern ourselves with estimation of the models.

In the next chapters, the method we have outlined was applied to a sequence of models. By this we intent to capture the isolated effects of each one of the different dynamic assumptions. For each model, necessary and sufficient conditions for identification are found. In all cases, these conditions only involve the orders of the lag polynomials appearing in the equations, and their computation is trivial.

Chapter II considers the case in which the shock and each one of the exogenous variables are independent white-noises. The necessary and sufficient conditions for identification can be expressed as follows: consider the maximum lags with which the exogenous and the endogenous variables appear in the structural equation (i.e., the number p, q_1, ..., q_n of equation (1a)). Arrange these numbers in an increasing sequence and let q_i^* be the one occupying the ith position in the sequence. The model is identified if and only if $q_i^* \geq i$, for $i = 1, 2, \ldots, n+1$.

Chapter III considers models in which the shock is autocorrelated. If this autocorrelation is explained by a (finite) moving average process of order s the condition becomes $q_i^* \geq i+s$, for $i=1,2,\ldots,n+1$. Alternatively, when the shock follows an autoregressive process of order r, the condition reads $q_i^* \geq i-1$. Thus while autoregressive processes "help" to identify a model, moving average processes have the opposite effect (yet the two effects are not mirror images of each other). The two cases are somewhat combined in the next chapter. Chapter IV considers models where the shock follows a mixed autoregressive-moving average process of orders r and s, respectively. It is seen that the combined effect depends on the relative values of r and s. When r > s, the condition for identification is $q_i^* \geq i-1$; while, if $r \leq s$, the condition is $q_i^* \geq i+s-r$, for i = 1, 2, ..., n+1.

Next, the effect of autocorrelation in the exogenous variables is analysed. Chapter V considers a model where each one of the exogenous variables follows some kind of moving average, autoregressive, or mixed process. To isolate the effect of autocorrelation in the exogenous variables from the one due to autocorrelated shock, the latter is assumed to be white-noise. We find that, when each one of the exogenous variables presents some sort of autocorrelation, with independence of the type of process that generates it, the necessary and sufficient condition for identification simply becomes $p \neq 0$. Thus autocorrelation in the exogenous variables always helps identification.

Chapter VI brings together the results of the previous chapters. First, a model is considered where the shock and each one of the exogenous variables are autocorrelated. The model is identified if and only if $p + r > s$ (independent of the relative values of r and s). Second, the more general case is considered, in which any number of exogenous variables as well as the shock may or may not be autocorrelated. The necessary and sufficient conditions for the model to be identified can be expressed as follows: let n_1 ($\leq n$) be the number of white-noise exogenous variables. Consider only the maximum lags with which these variables appear in the structural equation (i.e., the numbers $q_1, q_2, \ldots, q_{n_1}$). Arrange the numbers p, $q_1, \ldots, q_{n_1}$ in a nondecreasing sequence and let q_i^{**} denote the one occupying the ith position in the sequence. When $r > s$ the model is identified if and only if $q_i^{**} \geq i-1$; otherwise the condition is given by $q_i^{**} \geq i+s-r$, for $i = 1,2,\ldots n_1+1$. It is easily seen that each one of the results obtained before can be derived as a particular case of the last one.

Finally, Chapter VII considers some extensions of the analysis when applied to models where some of the assumptions presented in Chapter I are violated. First, a model is considered where the exogenous variables are crosscorrelated (and possibly autocorrelated also). These variables are assumed to follow jointly a multivariate ARMA process. The implication of our analysis is that the existence of crosscorrelation helps identification. Second, effects due to nonstationarity are analysed. A model is considered in which the endogenous variable is homogenously nonstationary. It is seen that this type of nonstationarity also helps the state of identification. Third, by means of an example, we show how the analysis can be extended to models in which additional prior information on the parameters is available. This information states that some of the parameters for intermediary lags in the structural equation are equal to zero (seasonal models present this feature). It is suggested that "transversal theory" may provide a convenient framework for the analysis of such models. The last extension considers a model with autocorrelated errors of observations. Similarly to the case of autocorrelated shock, it is seen that different patterns of autocorrelation may have opposite effects as far as identification of the model is concerned.

APPENDIX A

1. Proof that the Jacobian J_I of (2.15) is Nonsingular

We shall prove that if the conditions $q_j^* \geq j$, $j = 1, \ldots, n+1$ are met, the matrix, J_I, of expression (2.15) is nonsingular, except on a zero measure set on the admissible parameter space.

The admissible parameter space is only constrained by the stationarity conditions and by the nonnegativity constraints on the variances. Therefore, considering (2.18), for $|J_I|$ to be zero, it has to be that

(A.1) $$\sum_{i_1=1}^{q_1} \sum_{i_2=1}^{q_2} \cdots \sum_{i_n=1}^{q_n} \beta_{i_1}^{(1)} \beta_{i_2}^{(2)} \cdots \beta_{i_n}^{(n)} \det D_{i_1 i_2 \ldots i_n} = 0$$

We shall prove that if $q_j^* \geq j$, $j = 1, \ldots, n+1$, then one of the elements of the above summation involves a function of the parameters that:

a) will be nonzero, and

b) will not cancel out with the other elements of the summation.

Once this is proved, it will follow that equation (A.1) cannot be true, so that J_I has to be nonsingular.

Consider two different cases:

1. $p > n$

The condition $q_j^* \geq j$ implies, in this case:

$q_1 \geq 1$, $q_2 \geq 2$, $q_n \geq n$, $p \geq n + 1$.

Setting $i_1 = 1$, $i_2 = 2$, $\ldots$, $i_n = n$ in expression (2.19), the matrix $D_{1,2,\ldots,n}$ becomes the $(n + 1) \times (n + 1)$ matrix:

$$(\underline{d}_1^{(1)}, \underline{d}_2^{(2)}, \ldots, \underline{d}_n^{(n)}, -\underline{\gamma}^*) = \begin{pmatrix} \omega_{yx}^{(1)} & \omega_{yx_{-1}}^{(2)} & \cdots & \omega_{yx_{-n+1}}^{(n)} & -\gamma_1 \\ 0 & \omega_{yx}^{(2)} & \cdots & \omega_{yx_{-n+2}}^{(n)} & -\gamma_2 \\ \vdots & \vdots & & \vdots & \vdots \\ 0 & 0 & & \omega_{yx}^{(n)} & -\gamma_n \\ 0 & 0 & & 0 & -\gamma_{n+1} \end{pmatrix}$$

Thus,

(A. 2) $\det D_{1,2,\ldots,n} = -\gamma_{n+1} \prod_{i=1}^{n} \omega_{yx}^{(i)} = -\gamma_{n+1} \prod_{i=1}^{n} (\beta_0^{(i)} \sigma_{\zeta\zeta}^{(1)})$, where use has been made of the fact that $\omega_{yx}^{(i)} = \beta_0^{(i)}(\omega_{xx}^{(i)} - \sigma_{\delta\delta}^{(i)}) = \beta_0^{(i)}\sigma_{\zeta\zeta}^{(i)}$. If follows that, corresponding to det $D_{1,2,\ldots,n}$, one of the summation terms in (A.1) will be given by

(A.3) $-\gamma_{n+1} \prod_{i=1}^{n} (\beta_i^{(i)} \beta_0^{(i)} \sigma_{\zeta\zeta}^{(i)})$, which is different from zero.

If $q_i = i$, $i = 1,\ldots, n$, then using (2.16) and (2.17), it is easily seen that no vector $\underline{d}_\ell^{(i)}$ with $\ell > i$ will appear in the $D_{yx}^{(i)}$ matrices. It follows that all determinants in expression (A.1), except the one given by (A.2), will be determinants of upper triangular matrices with some zeroes in the main diagonal, and hence zero. Then, $|J_I| \neq 0$ q.e.d. On the other hand, suppose $q_i > i$ for some $0 \leq i \leq n$. Then, any determinant in expression (A.1), except the one given by (A.2), that is nonzero will be the determinant of a matrix that includes a column of the form $\underline{d}_{i+\ell}^{(i)}$ for $i \leqq n$ and $\ell > 0$. Therefore, the corresponding term in the summation (A.1) will include the coefficient $\beta_{i+\ell}^{(i)}$. But this coefficient will not appear in expression (A.3). It follows that the summation term given by (A.3) will cancel out only on a set of zero measure in the parameter space (i.e. when some of the β-coefficients are equal). Since (A.3) is different from zero so will the determinant $|J_I|$.

2. $\underline{p \leq n}$

Without loss of generality, let $q_1 \leq q_2 \leq \ldots \leq q_{j_0-1} \leq p \leq q_{j_0} \leq \ldots \leq q_n$. The conditions $q_j^* \geq j$, $j = 1, \ldots, n+1$ can be rewritten:

(A.4) $q_1 \geq 1,\ q_2 \geq 2,\ \ldots,\ q_{j_0-1} \geq j_0-1,\ p \geq j_0,\ q_{j_0} \geq j_0 + 1,\ \ldots,\ q_n \geq n + 1.$

For $i_1 = 1$, $i_2 = 2$, ..., $i_{j_0-1} = j_0-1$, $i_{j_0} = j_0 + 1$, ..., $i_n = n + 1$, the matrix given by (2.19) becomes the (n+1) x (n+1) matrix:

(A.5) $(\underline{d}_1^{(1)}, \underline{d}_2^{(2)}, \ldots, \underline{d}_{j_0-1}^{(j_0-1)}, \underline{d}_{j_0+1}^{(j_0)}, \ldots, \underline{d}_{n+1}^{(n)}, -\underline{\gamma}_*) =$

$$\begin{pmatrix}
\omega_{yx}^{(1)} & \omega_{yx_{-1}}^{(2)} & \cdots & \omega_{yx_{-j_0+2}}^{(j_0-1)} & \omega_{yx_{-j_0}}^{(j_0)} & \cdots & \omega_{yx_{-n}}^{(n)} & -\gamma_1 \\
0 & \omega_{yx}^{(2)} & & \omega_{yx_{-j_0+3}}^{(j_0-1)} & \omega_{yx_{-j_0+1}}^{(j_0)} & \cdots & \omega_{yx_{-n+1}}^{(n)} & -\gamma_2 \\
\vdots & \vdots & & \vdots & \vdots & & \vdots & \vdots \\
\cdot & \cdot & & \omega_{yx}^{(j_0-1)} & \omega_{yx_{-2}}^{(j_0)} & & \cdot & \cdot \\
\cdot & \cdot & & 0 & \omega_{yx_{-1}}^{(j_0)} & \cdots & \cdot & -\gamma_p \\
\cdot & \cdot & & 0 & \omega_{yx}^{(j_0)} & & \cdot & 0 \\
\vdots & \vdots & & \vdots & \vdots & & \vdots & \vdots \\
0 & 0 & & 0 & 0 & \cdots & \omega_{yx}^{(n)} & 0
\end{pmatrix}$$

Direct inspection of the matrix shows that it can be written in upper triangular form, with determinant equal (in absolute value) to

(A.6) $$\det D_{1,2,\ \ldots,\ j_0-1,\ j_0+1,\ \ldots,\ n+1} = \gamma_p \prod_{i=1}^{n} \omega_{yx}^{(i)} = \gamma_p \prod_{i=1}^{n} \beta_0^{(i)} \sigma_{\zeta\zeta}^{(i)}$$

so that one of the summation terms in (A.1) will be given by:

(A.7) $$\gamma_p \prod_{i=1}^{j_0-1} (\beta_i^{(i)} \beta_0^{(i)} \sigma_{\zeta\zeta}^{(i)}) \prod_{i=j_0}^{n} (\beta_{i+1}^{(i)} \beta_0^{(i)} \sigma_{\zeta\zeta}^{(i)}),$$ which is different from zero.

The rest of the proof follows as in the previous case: if the expressions in (A.4) are strict equalities, then the only determinant in (A.1) not equal to zero is the one given by (A.6). On the other hand, if:

(a) for some $i < j_0$, $q_i > i$, and/or

(b) for some $i \geq j_0$, $q_i > i+1$,

then any nonzero determinant appearing in (A.1) has to include a column of the form $\underline{d}_{i+\ell}^{(i)}$ and/or a column of the form $\underline{d}_{i+\ell+1}^{(i)}$ for $\ell > 0$. Thus, any nonzero summation term in (A.1), apart from the one given by (A.7), will include a coefficient $\beta_{i+\ell}^{(i)}$, and/or a coefficient $\beta_{i+\ell+1}^{(i)}$, for $\ell > 0$. As these coefficients will not appear in expression (A.7), this last summation term will be different from zero and will not cancel out, except on a zero measure set in the parameter space. Thus, $|J_I| \neq 0$, which finishes the proof.

2. An Example

An example will illustrate the proof of Theorem 1. Consider the model:

$$\eta_t = \gamma_1\eta_{t-1} + \gamma_2\eta_{t-2} + \beta_0^{(1)}\zeta_t^{(1)} + \beta_1^{(1)}\zeta_{t-1}^{(1)} + \beta_2^{(1)}\zeta_{t-2}^{(1)} + \beta_0^{(2)}\zeta_t^{(2)} + \beta_1^{(2)}\zeta_{t-1}^{(2)} + \beta_2^{(2)}\zeta_{t-2}^{(2)} + \beta_3^{(2)}\zeta_{t-3}^{(2)} + u_t , \tag{A.8}$$

where $\zeta^{(1)}$, $\zeta^{(2)}$, and u are white-noise variables, independent of each other. The errors-in-the-variables equations (1.1d) and (1.1e) are assumed to hold, together with assumptions 1, 2, 3, 4a and 5a. Lemma 1 states that the autoregressive parameters, γ_1 and γ_2, can be determined through the covariance equations:

$$\omega_{yy_{-4}} = \gamma_1\,\omega_{yy_{-3}} + \gamma_2\,\omega_{yy_{-2}}$$

$$\omega_{yy_{-5}} = \gamma_1\,\omega_{yy_{-4}} + \gamma_2\,\omega_{yy_{-3}}$$

To find out whether the conditions of the theorem are satisfied, we notice that $p = 2$, $q_1 = 2$, $q_2 = 3$. Thus, $q_j^* \geq j$ for $j = 1, 2, 3$, and the model is identified. We shall check the result and, at the same time, illustrate the proof of the sufficiency part of the theorem.

Consider the cross-covariance equations:

$$\omega_{yx_{-\tau}}^{(i)} = \sum_{j=1}^{2}\gamma_j\omega_{yx_{-\tau+j}}^{(i)} + \beta_\tau^{(i)}\left(\omega_{xx}^{(i)} - \sigma_{\delta\delta}^{(i)}\right), \tag{A.9a}$$

for $\tau = 0, 1, 2$ when $i = 1$; and $\tau = 0, 1, 2, 3$ when $i = 2$. Consider also the autocovariance equations:

$$\omega_{yy_{-1}} = \gamma_1(\omega_{yy} - \sigma_{\varepsilon\varepsilon}) + \gamma_2\omega_{yy_{-1}} + \sum_{j=1}^{2}\beta_j^{(1)}\omega_{yx_{-j+1}}^{(1)} + \sum_{j=1}^{3}\beta_j^{(2)}\omega_{yx_{-j+1}}^{(2)} \tag{A.9b}$$

$$\omega_{yy_{-2}} = \gamma_1\omega_{yy_{-1}} + \gamma_2(\omega_{yy} - \sigma_{\varepsilon\varepsilon}) + \beta_2^{(1)}\omega_{yx}^{(1)} + \sum_{j=2}^{3}\beta_j^{(2)}\omega_{yx_{-j+2}}^{(2)} \tag{A.9c}$$

$$\omega_{yy_{-3}} = \gamma_1\omega_{yy_{-2}} + \gamma_2\omega_{yy_{-1}} + \beta_3^{(2)}\omega_{yx}^{(2)} . \tag{A.9d}$$

If the system of equations (A.9a to d) can be solved for the β, $\sigma_{\varepsilon\varepsilon}$, and $\sigma_{\delta\delta}$-parameters the model is identified. The Jacobian of this system of equations with respect to the parameters $\beta_0^{(1)}$, $\beta_1^{(1)}$, $\beta_2^{(1)}$, $\beta_0^{(2)}$, $\beta_1^{(2)}$, $\beta_2^{(2)}$, $\beta_3^{(2)}$, $\sigma_{\delta\delta}^{(1)}$, $\sigma_{\delta\delta}^{(2)}$, and $\sigma_{\varepsilon\varepsilon}$ is given by the matrix:

$$\begin{pmatrix}
\sigma_{\zeta\zeta}^{(1)} & 0 & 0 & 0 & 0 & 0 & 0 & -\beta_0^{(1)} & 0 & 0 \\
0 & \sigma_{\zeta\zeta}^{(1)} & 0 & 0 & 0 & 0 & 0 & -\beta_1^{(1)} & 0 & 0 \\
0 & 0 & \sigma_{\zeta\zeta}^{(1)} & 0 & 0 & 0 & 0 & -\beta_2^{(1)} & 0 & 0 \\
0 & 0 & 0 & \sigma_{\zeta\zeta}^{(2)} & 0 & 0 & 0 & 0 & -\beta_0^{(2)} & 0 \\
0 & 0 & 0 & 0 & \sigma_{\zeta\zeta}^{(2)} & 0 & 0 & 0 & -\beta_1^{(2)} & 0 \\
0 & 0 & 0 & 0 & 0 & \sigma_{\zeta\zeta}^{(2)} & 0 & 0 & -\beta_2^{(2)} & 0 \\
0 & 0 & 0 & 0 & 0 & 0 & \sigma_{\zeta\zeta}^{(2)} & 0 & -\beta_3^{(2)} & 0 \\
0 & \omega_{yx}^{(1)} & \omega_{yx_{-1}}^{(1)} & 0 & \omega_{yx}^{(2)} & \omega_{yx_{-1}}^{(2)} & \omega_{yx_{-2}}^{(2)} & 0 & 0 & -\gamma_1 \\
0 & 0 & \omega_{yx}^{(1)} & 0 & 0 & \omega_{yx}^{(2)} & \omega_{yx_{-1}}^{(2)} & 0 & 0 & -\gamma_2 \\
0 & 0 & 0 & 0 & 0 & 0 & \omega_{yx}^{(2)} & 0 & 0 & 0
\end{pmatrix}$$

This is the matrix J_I of expression (2.15) for model (A.18); and if this matrix has full rank, the model will be identified. Expanding by the elements of the first row, the determinant of this matrix is given by

$$\text{(A.10)} \quad J_I = (\sigma_{\zeta\zeta}^{(1)})^2(\sigma_{\zeta\zeta}^{(2)})^3[\beta_1^{(1)}\ \beta_1^{(2)} \det D_{11} + \beta_1^{(1)}\ \beta_2^{(2)} \det D_{12} + \beta_1^{(1)}\ \beta_3^{(2)} \det D_{13} + \beta_2^{(1)}\ \beta_1^{(2)} \det D_{21} + \beta_2^{(1)}\ \beta_2^{(2)} \det D_{22} + \beta_2^{(1)}\ \beta_3^{(2)} \det D_{23}],$$

Which corresponds to expression (2.18). In (A.10), the notation is as follows:

$$D_{j\ell} = (\underline{d}_j^{(1)}\ ,\ \underline{d}_\ell^{(2)}\ ,\ -\underline{\gamma}_*)\ ,\ \underline{\gamma}_* = (-\gamma_1\ ,\ -\gamma_2\ ,\ 0)'\ ,$$

and

$$\underline{d}_1^{(1)} = \begin{pmatrix} \omega_{yx}^{(1)} \\ 0 \\ 0 \end{pmatrix} \quad \underline{d}_1^{(2)} = \begin{pmatrix} \omega_{yx}^{(2)} \\ 0 \\ 0 \end{pmatrix}\ ,\ \underline{d}_2^{(1)} = \begin{pmatrix} \omega_{yx_{-1}}^{(1)} \\ \omega_{yx}^{(1)} \\ 0 \end{pmatrix},\ \underline{d}_2^{(2)} = \begin{pmatrix} \omega_{yx_{-1}}^{(2)} \\ \omega_{yx}^{(2)} \\ 0 \end{pmatrix},$$

$$\underline{d}_3^{(2)} = \begin{pmatrix} \omega_{yx_{-2}}^{(2)} \\ \omega_{yx_{-1}}^{(2)} \\ \omega_{yx}^{(2)} \end{pmatrix}$$

which corresponds to expressions (2.16) and (2.17) with $\sigma^{(1)}_{\zeta\zeta} = \omega^{(1)}_{xx} - \sigma^{(1)}_{\zeta\zeta}$ and $\sigma^{(2)}_{\zeta\zeta} = \omega^{(2)}_{xx} - \sigma^{(2)}_{\zeta\zeta}$. According to (A.10), for J_I to vanish it has to be that

(A.11) $$\sum_{j=1}^{2} \sum_{\ell=1}^{3} \beta^{(1)}_j \beta^{(2)}_\ell \det D_{j\ell} = 0,$$

which corresponds to expression (A.1).

For this particular model, p = 2 and n = 2, thus we are in the case when $p \leq n$. Consider then the (3x3) matrix:

$$D_{13} = (\underline{d}^{(1)}_1, \underline{d}^{(2)}_3, -\underline{\gamma}_*) = \begin{pmatrix} \omega^{(1)}_{yx} & \omega^{(2)}_{yx_{-2}} & -\gamma_1 \\ 0 & \omega^{(2)}_{yx_{-1}} & -\gamma_2 \\ 0 & \omega^{(2)}_{yx} & 0 \end{pmatrix}$$

which corresponds to expression (A.5). The determinant of D_{13} is equal (in absolute value) to the determinant of the diagonal matrix $(\underline{d}^{(1)}_1, -\underline{\gamma}_*, \underline{d}^{(2)}_3)$. Thus (in absolute value)

$$\det D_{13} = \omega^{(1)}_{yx} \gamma_2 \omega^{(2)}_{yx} = \gamma_2 \beta^{(1)}_0 \beta^{(2)}_0 \sigma^{(1)}_{\zeta\zeta} \sigma^{(2)}_{\zeta\zeta},$$

which is equivalent to (A.6). Therefore, one of the summation terms in (A.11) will be equal to:

(A.12) $$\gamma_2 \beta^{(1)}_1 \beta^{(2)}_3 \beta^{(1)}_0 \beta^{(2)}_0 \sigma^{(1)}_{\zeta\zeta} \sigma^{(2)}_{\zeta\zeta}$$

which corresponds to (A.7) and is different from zero. Consider now the rest of the summation terms in (A.11). It is easily seen that the determinants of D_{11}, D_{12}, D_{21}, D_{22} vanish. That leaves

$$D_{23} = \begin{pmatrix} \omega^{(1)}_{yx_{-1}} & \omega^{(2)}_{yx_{-2}} & -\gamma_1 \\ \omega^{(1)}_{yx} & \omega^{(2)}_{yx_{-1}} & -\gamma_2 \\ 0 & \omega^{(2)}_{yx} & 0 \end{pmatrix}$$

Substituting for $\omega^{(i)}_{yx_{-k}}$ by using the equations in (A.9a), we find

$$\det D_{23} = [\gamma_2\beta_1^{(1)}\beta_0^{(2)} + \gamma_2\gamma_1\beta_0^{(1)}\beta_0^{(2)} - \gamma_1\beta_0^{(1)}\beta_0^{(2)}]\ \sigma_{\zeta\zeta}^{(1)}\ \sigma_{\zeta\zeta}^{(2)}$$,which

will be different from zero. The summation term in (A.11) that involves $\det D_{23}$ is given by

$$\beta_2^{(1)}\ \beta_3^{(2)}\ \det D_{23}$$

Since this expression contains $\beta_2^{(1)}$, which is not included in (A.12), it follows that the only two nonzero terms will not cancel out. Thus $|J_I| \neq 0$ and the model is identified.

REFERENCES

Aigner, D.J. [1966], "Errors of Measurement and Least Squares Estimation in a Simple Resursive Model of Dynamic Equilibrium" Econometrica, vol. 34, pp. 424-432, 1966

Anderson, T.W. [1971], The Statistical Analysis of Time Series, John Wiley and Sons, New York, 1971

Box, G.E.P., Hillmer, S.C. and G.C. Tiao [1976], "Analysis and Modeling of Seasonal Time Series". Presented at the NBER/Bureau of the Census Conference on Seasonal Analysis, Washington, D.C., Sept. 76

Box, G.E.P. and Jenkins, G.H. [1970], Time Series Analysis, San Francisco, Holden Day, 1970

Brewer, K.R.W. [1973], "Some Consequences of Temporal Aggregation and Systematic Sampling for ARMA and ARMAX Models," Journals of Econometrics, vol. 1, June 1973

Dhrymes, P.J. [1971], Distributed Lags: Problems of Estimation and Formulation, San Francisco, Holden Day, 1971

Espasa, A. [1977], The Spectral Maximum Likelihood Estimation of Econometric Models with Stationary Errors. Vandenhoeck and Ruprecht, 1977

Fisher, F.M. [1966], The Identification Problem in Econometrics, New York: McGraw Hill Book Co., 1966

Geraci, V.J. [1977], "Identification of Simultaneous Equations Models with Measurement Errors," In Latent Variables in Socio-economic Models, eds. D.J. Aigner and A.S. Goldberger, North-Holland Pu. Co., 1977

__________, [1974]; Simultaneous Equations Models with Measurement Errors" Ph.D. Dissertation, Department of Economics. The Univ. of Wisconsin, Madison, 1975.

Goldberger, A.S. [1964], Econometric Theory, J. Wiley and Sons, New York, 1964

______________, [1972], "Structural Equation Methods in the Social Sciences", Econometrica, vol 40, Nov. 1972

______________, [1974], "Unobservable Variables in Econometrics" In Frontiers of Econometrics, ed. P. Zarembka. Academic Press, N.Y. 1974.

Graupe, D. [1972], Identification of Systems, Van Nostrand Reinhold Co., New York, 1972

Grether, D.M. and Maddala, G.S. [1973], "Errors in Variables and Serially Correlated Distributed Lag Models," Econometrica, vol. 41, no. 2, March 1973

Griliches, Z. [1974], "Errors in Variables and Other Unobservables," Econometrica, vol. 42, no. 6, Nov. 1974

___________, [1967], "Distributed Lags: A Survey," Econometrica, vol. 35, no. 1, Jan. 1967

Hadley, G. [1961], Linear Algebra, Addison-Wesley Pu. Co. Reading, Mass. 1961

Hannan, E.J. [1971], "The Identification Problem for Multiple Equation Systems with Moving Average Errors," Econometrica, vol. 39, Sept. 1971

__________, [1976], "The Identification and Parameterization of Armax and State Space Forms." Econometrica, vol. 44, July 1976

Haugh, L.D. and G.E.P. Box [1977] "Identification of Dynamic Regression (Distributed Lag) Models Connecting Two Time Series". JASA, vol. 72, no. 357, March 1977

Hsiao, C. [1975], "Identification for a Linear Dynamic Simultaneous Error-Shock Model," International Economic Review. vol. 18, no. 1, Feb. 1977

________, [1976], "Measurement Error in a Dynamic Simultaneous Equations Model with Stationary Disturbances," Institute of Business and Economic Research, University of California, Berkeley, Rev. Aug. 1976

Hurwicz, L. [1949], "Some Results on Identification in Lagged Shock-Error Models," Cowles Commission Discussion Papers: Statistics, no. 324, 1949

__________, [1950], "Variable Parameters in Stochastic Processes: Trend and Seasonality" In Statistical Inference in Dynamic Economic Models, ed. T.C. Koopmans. John Wiley and Sons, N.Y., 1950

Johnston, J. [1963], Econometric Methods. McGraw-Hill Book Co., N.Y., 1963

Joreskog, K.G. and Goldberger, A.S. [1973], "Estimation of a Model with Multiple Indicators and Multiple Causes of a Single Latent Variable," JASA, vol. 70, no. 351, Sept. 1975

Karni, I. and Weissman, I. [1974], "A Consistent Estimator of the Slope in a Regression Model with Errors in the Variables," JASA, vol. 69, no. 345, March 1974

Koopmans, T.C. [1953], "Identification Problems in Economic Model Construction." In Studies in Econometric Method, ed. W.C. Hood and T.C. Koopmans. Yale University Press, New Haven, 1953

Maravall, A. [1974], "Identification in Shock-Error Univariate Autoregressive Distributed Lag Models," Social Systems Research Institute, The University of Wisconsin, Madison, Dec. 1974

Maravall, A. and D.J. Aigner [1977], "Identification of the Dynamic Shock-Error Model: The Case of Dynamic Regression". In Latent Variables in Socio-economic Models. Eds. D.J. Aigner and A.S. Goldberger-North-Holland Pu. Co. 1977

Mehra, R.K. [1974], "Identification in Control and Econometrics: Similarities and Differences," Annals of Economic and Social Measurement, vol. 3, no.1, Jan.1974

Mirsky, L. [1971], Transversal Theory, Academic Press, New York and London, 1971

Nerlove, M. [1967], "Distributed Lags and Unobserved Components in Economic Time Series," Cowles Foundation Discussion Paper, no. 221, Yale University, March 1967

Nowak, Eugen [1977], "Identification of the Dynamic Shock-Error Model with Autocorrelated Errors", Unpublished manuscript, 1977

Pandit, S.M. [1973], "Data Dependent Systems: Modeling Analysis and Optimal Control via Time Series," Doctoral Dissertation, The University of Wisconsin, Madison, Oct. 1973

Pierce, D.A. [1976], "Seasonal Adjustment when both Deterministic and Stochastic Seasonality are Present". Presented at the NBER, Bureau of the Census Conference on Seasonal Analysis, Washington, D.C., Sept. 1976

Quenouille, M.H.[1968], The Analysis of Multiple Time-Series, 2nd Ed. Griffin, London, 1968

Reiersol, O. [1950], "Identifiability of a Linear Relation Between Variables which are Subject to Error," Econometrica, 18, pp. 345-389, 1950

Rothenberg, T.J. [1971], "Identification in Parametric Models," Econometrica, vol. 39, May 1971

Sorenson, H. [1966], "Kalman Filtering Techniques". In Advances in Control Systems, ed. C. Leondes. Academic Press, N.Y., 1966

Spiegel, M.R. [1971], Finite Differences and Difference Equations, McGraw-Hill Book Co., New York, 1971

Telser, L. [1967], "Discrete Sample and Moving Sums in Stationary Stochastic Processes," JASA, vol. 62, pp. 484-99, 1967

Whittle, P. [1963], Prediction and Regulation by Linear Least-Square Methods, The English University Press Ltd., London 1963

Williamson, J.H. [1962], Lebesgue Integration, Holt, Rinehart and Winston, N.Y., 1962

Yaglom, A.M. [1958], "Correlation Theory of Processes with Stationary Random Increments of Order n," American Mathematical Society Translations, series 2, vol. 8, 1958

Zellner, A. [1970], "Estimation of regression relationships containing unobservable variables. International Economic Review, vol. 11, pp. 441-454

__________, [1971], An Introduction to Bayesian Inference in Econometrics, New York: John Wiley and Sons, 1971

Zellner, A. and Palm, F. [1974], "Time Series Analysis and Simultaneous Equation Econometric Models," Journal of Econometrics, vol. 2, pp. 17-54, 1974

Vol. 59: J. A. Hanson, Growth in Open Economies. V, 128 pages. 1971.

Vol. 60: H. Hauptmann, Schätz- und Kontrolltheorie in stetigen dynamischen Wirtschaftsmodellen. V, 104 Seiten. 1971.

Vol. 61: K. H. F. Meyer, Wartesysteme mit variabler Bearbeitungsrate. VII, 314 Seiten. 1971.

Vol. 62: W. Krelle u. G. Gabisch unter Mitarbeit von J. Burgermeister, Wachstumstheorie. VII, 223 Seiten. 1972.

Vol. 63: J. Kohlas, Monte Carlo Simulation im Operations Research. VI, 162 Seiten. 1972.

Vol. 64: P. Gessner u. K. Spremann, Optimierung in Funktionenräumen. IV, 120 Seiten. 1972.

Vol. 65: W. Everling, Exercises in Computer Systems Analysis. VIII, 184 pages. 1972.

Vol. 66: F. Bauer, P. Garabedian and D. Korn, Supercritical Wing Sections. V, 211 pages. 1972.

Vol. 67: I. V. Girsanov, Lectures on Mathematical Theory of Extremum Problems. V, 136 pages. 1972.

Vol. 68: J. Loeckx, Computability and Decidability. An Introduction for Students of Computer Science. VI, 76 pages. 1972.

Vol. 69: S. Ashour, Sequencing Theory. V, 133 pages. 1972.

Vol. 70: J. P. Brown, The Economic Effects of Floods. Investigations of a Stochastic Model of Rational Investment. Behavior in the Face of Floods. V, 87 pages. 1972.

Vol. 71: R. Henn und O. Opitz, Konsum- und Produktionstheorie II. V, 134 Seiten. 1972.

Vol. 72: T. P. Bagchi and J. G. C. Templeton, Numerical Methods in Markov Chains and Bulk Queues. XI, 89 pages. 1972.

Vol. 73: H. Kiendl, Suboptimale Regler mit abschnittweise linearer Struktur. VI, 146 Seiten. 1972.

Vol. 74: F. Pokropp, Aggregation von Produktionsfunktionen. VI, 107 Seiten. 1972.

Vol. 75: GI-Gesellschaft für Informatik e.V. Bericht Nr. 3. 1. Fachtagung über Programmiersprachen · München, 9.–11. März 1971. Herausgegeben im Auftrag der Gesellschaft für Informatik von H. Langmaack und M. Paul. VII, 280 Seiten. 1972.

Vol. 76: G. Fandel, Optimale Entscheidung bei mehrfacher Zielsetzung. II, 121 Seiten. 1972.

Vol. 77: A. Auslender, Problèmes de Minimax via l'Analyse Convexe et les Inégalités Variationelles: Théorie et Algorithmes. VII, 132 pages. 1972.

Vol. 78: GI-Gesellschaft für Informatik e.V. 2. Jahrestagung, Karlsruhe, 2.–4. Oktober 1972. Herausgegeben im Auftrag der Gesellschaft für Informatik von P. Deussen. XI, 576 Seiten. 1973.

Vol. 79: A. Berman, Cones, Matrices and Mathematical Programming. V, 96 pages. 1973.

Vol. 80: International Seminar on Trends in Mathematical Modelling, Venice, 13–18 December 1971. Edited by N. Hawkes. VI, 288 pages. 1973.

Vol. 81: Advanced Course on Software Engineering. Edited by F. L. Bauer. XII, 545 pages. 1973.

Vol. 82: R. Saeks, Resolution Space, Operators and Systems. X, 267 pages. 1973.

Vol. 83: NTG/GI-Gesellschaft für Informatik, Nachrichtentechnische Gesellschaft. Fachtagung „Cognitive Verfahren und Systeme", Hamburg, 11.–13. April 1973. Herausgegeben im Auftrag der NTG/GI von Th. Einsele, W. Giloi und H.-H. Nagel. VIII, 373 Seiten. 1973.

Vol. 84: A. V. Balakrishnan, Stochastic Differential Systems I. Filtering and Control. A Function Space Approach. V, 252 pages. 1973.

Vol. 85: T. Page, Economics of Involuntary Transfers: A Unified Approach to Pollution and Congestion Externalities. XI, 159 pages. 1973.

Vol. 86: Symposium on the Theory of Scheduling and its Applic tions. Edited by S. E. Elmaghraby. VIII, 437 pages. 1973.

Vol. 87: G. F. Newell, Approximate Stochastic Behavior of n-Serv Service Systems with Large n. VII, 118 pages. 1973.

Vol. 88: H. Steckhan, Güterströme in Netzen. VII, 134 Seite 1973.

Vol. 89: J. P. Wallace and A. Sherret, Estimation of Produc Attributes and Their Importances. V, 94 pages. 1973.

Vol. 90: J.-F. Richard, Posterior and Predictive Densities f Simultaneous Equation Models. VI, 226 pages. 1973.

Vol. 91: Th. Marschak and R. Selten, General Equilibrium wi Price-Making Firms. XI, 246 pages. 1974.

Vol. 92: E. Dierker, Topological Methods in Walrasian Economic IV, 130 pages. 1974.

Vol. 93: 4th IFAC/IFIP International Conference on Digital Con puter Applications to Process Control, Part I. Zürich/Switzerlan March 19–22, 1974. Edited by M. Mansour and W. Schaufelberge XVIII, 544 pages. 1974.

Vol. 94: 4th IFAC/IFIP International Conference on Digital Cor puter Applications to Process Control, Part II. Zürich/Switzerlan March 19–22, 1974. Edited by M. Mansour and W. Schaufelberge XVIII, 546 pages. 1974.

Vol. 95: M. Zeleny, Linear Multiobjective Programming. X, 220 page 1974.

Vol. 96: O. Moeschlin, Zur Theorie von Neumannscher Wach tumsmodelle. XI, 115 Seiten. 1974.

Vol. 97: G. Schmidt, Über die Stabilität des einfachen Bedienung kanals. VII, 147 Seiten. 1974.

Vol. 98: Mathematical Methods in Queueing Theory. Proceedin 1973. Edited by A. B. Clarke. VII, 374 pages. 1974.

Vol. 99: Production Theory. Edited by W. Eichhorn, R. Hen O. Opitz, and R. W. Shephard. VIII, 386 pages. 1974.

Vol. 100: B. S. Duran and P. L. Odell, Cluster Analysis. A Surve VI, 137 pages. 1974.

Vol. 101: W. M. Wonham, Linear Multivariable Control. A Ge metric Approach. X, 344 pages. 1974.

Vol. 102: Analyse Convexe et Ses Applications. Comptes Rendu Janvier 1974. Edited by J.-P. Aubin. IV, 244 pages. 1974.

Vol. 103: D. E. Boyce, A. Farhi, R. Weischedel, Optimal Subs Selection. Multiple Regression, Interdependence and Optim Network Algorithms. XIII, 187 pages. 1974.

Vol. 104: S. Fujino, A Neo-Keynesian Theory of Inflation an Economic Growth. V, 96 pages. 1974.

Vol. 105: Optimal Control Theory and its Applications. Part I. Pr ceedings 1973. Edited by B. J. Kirby. VI, 425 pages. 1974.

Vol. 106: Optimal Control Theory and its Applications. Part II. Pr ceedings 1973. Edited by B. J. Kirby. VI, 403 pages. 1974.

Vol. 107: Control Theory, Numerical Methods and Comput Systems Modeling. International Symposium, Rocquencourt, Ju 17–21, 1974. Edited by A. Bensoussan and J. L. Lions. VIII, 757 page 1975.

Vol. 108: F. Bauer et al., Supercritical Wing Sections II. A Han book. V, 296 pages. 1975.

Vol. 109: R. von Randow, Introduction to the Theory of Matroic IX, 102 pages. 1975.

Vol. 110: C. Striebel, Optimal Control of Discrete Time Stochas Systems. III. 208 pages. 1975.

Vol. 111: Variable Structure Systems with Application to Economi and Biology. Proceedings 1974. Edited by A. Ruberti and R. R. Mohl VI, 321 pages. 1975.

Vol. 112: J. Wilhelm, Objectives and Multi-Objective Decision Maki Under Uncertainty. IV, 111 pages. 1975.

Vol. 113: G. A. Aschinger, Stabilitätsaussagen über Klassen v Matrizen mit verschwindenden Zeilensummen. V, 102 Seiten. 19

Vol. 114: G. Uebe, Produktionstheorie. XVII, 301 Seiten. 1976.

Vol. 115: Anderson et al., Foundations of System Theory: Finitary and Infinitary Conditions. VII, 93 pages. 1976

Vol. 116: K. Miyazawa, Input-Output Analysis and the Structure of Income Distribution. IX, 135 pages. 1976.

Vol. 117: Optimization and Operations Research. Proceedings 1975. Edited by W. Oettli and K. Ritter. IV, 316 pages. 1976.

Vol. 118: Traffic Equilibrium Methods, Proceedings 1974. Edited by M. A. Florian. XXIII, 432 pages. 1976.

Vol. 119: Inflation in Small Countries. Proceedings 1974. Edited by H. Frisch. VI, 356 pages. 1976.

Vol. 120: G. Hasenkamp, Specification and Estimation of Multiple-Output Production Functions. VII, 151 pages. 1976.

Vol. 121: J. W. Cohen, On Regenerative Processes in Queueing Theory. IX, 93 pages. 1976.

Vol. 122: M. S. Bazaraa, and C. M. Shetty,Foundations of Optimization VI. 193 pages. 1976

Vol. 123: Multiple Criteria Decision Making. Kyoto 1975. Edited by M. Zeleny. XXVII, 345 pages. 1976.

Vol. 124: M. J. Todd. The Computation of Fixed Points and Applications. VII, 129 pages. 1976.

Vol. 125: Karl C. Mosler. Optimale Transportnetze. Zur Bestimmung ihres kostengünstigsten Standorts bei gegebener Nachfrage. VI, 142 Seiten. 1976.

Vol. 126: Energy, Regional Science and Public Policy. Energy and Environment I. Proceedings 1975. Edited by M. Chatterji and P. Van Rompuy. VIII, 316 pages. 1976.

Vol. 127: Environment, Regional Science and Interregional Modeling. Energy and Environment II. Proceedings 1975. Edited by M. Chatterji and P. Van Rompuy. IX, 211 pages. 1976.

Vol. 128: Integer Programming and Related Areas. A Classified Bibliography. Edited by C. Kastning. XII, 495 pages. 1976.

Vol. 129: H.-J. Lüthi, Komplementaritäts- und Fixpunktalgorithmen in der mathematischen Programmierung. Spieltheorie und Ökonomie. VII, 145 Seiten. 1976.

Vol. 130: Multiple Criteria Decision Making, Jouy-en-Josas, France. Proceedings 1975. Edited by H. Thiriez and S. Zionts. VI, 409 pages. 1976.

Vol. 131: Mathematical Systems Theory. Proceedings 1975. Edited by G. Marchesini and S. K. Mitter. X, 408 pages. 1976.

Vol. 132: U. H. Funke, Mathematical Models in Marketing. A Collection of Abstracts. XX, 514 pages. 1976.

Vol. 133: Warsaw Fall Seminars in Mathematical Economics 1975. Edited by M. W. Loś, J. Loś, and A. Wieczorek. V. 159 pages. 1976.

Vol. 134: Computing Methods in Applied Sciences and Engineering. Proceedings 1975. VIII, 390 pages. 1976.

Vol. 135: H. Haga, A Disequilibrium – Equilibrium Model with Money and Bonds. A Keynesian – Walrasian Synthesis. VI, 119 pages. 1976.

Vol. 136: E. Kofler und G. Menges, Entscheidungen bei unvollständiger Information. XII, 357 Seiten. 1976.

Vol. 137: R. Wets, Grundlagen Konvexer Optimierung. VI, 146 Seiten. 1976.

Vol. 138: K. Okuguchi, Expectations and Stability in Oligopoly Models. VI, 103 pages. 1976.

Vol. 139: Production Theory and Its Applications. Proceedings. Edited by H. Albach and G. Bergendahl. VIII, 193 pages. 1977.

Vol. 140: W. Eichhorn and J. Voeller, Theory of the Price Index. Fisher's Test Approach and Generalizations. VII, 95 pages. 1976.

Vol. 141: Mathematical Economics and Game Theory. Essays in Honor of Oskar Morgenstern. Edited by R. Henn and O. Moeschlin. XIV, 703 pages. 1977.

Vol. 142: J. S. Lane, On Optimal Population Paths. V, 123 pages. 1977.

Vol. 143: B. Näslund, An Analysis of Economic Size Distributions. XV, 100 pages. 1977.

Vol. 144: Convex Analysis and Its Applications. Proceedings 1976. Edited by A. Auslender. VI, 219 pages. 1977.

Vol. 145: J. Rosenmüller, Extreme Games and Their Solutions. IV, 126 pages. 1977.

Vol. 146: In Search of Economic Indicators. Edited by W. H. Strigel. XVI, 198 pages. 1977.

Vol. 147: Resource Allocation and Division of Space. Proceedings. Edited by T. Fujii and R. Sato. VIII, 184 pages. 1977.

Vol. 148: C. E. Mandl, Simulationstechnik und Simulationsmodelle in den Sozial- und Wirtschaftswissenschaften. IX, 173 Seiten. 1977.

Vol. 149: Stationäre und schrumpfende Bevölkerungen: Demographisches Null- und Negativwachstum in Österreich. Herausgegeben von G. Feichtinger. VI, 262 Seiten. 1977.

Vol. 150: Bauer et al., Supercritical Wing Sections III. VI, 179 pages. 1977.

Vol. 151: C. A. Schneeweiß, Inventory-Production Theory. VI, 116 pages. 1977.

Vol. 152: Kirsch et al., Notwendige Optimalitätsbedingungen und ihre Anwendung. VI, 157 Seiten. 1978.

Vol. 153: Kombinatorische Entscheidungsprobleme: Methoden und Anwendungen. Herausgegeben von T. M. Liebling und M. Rössler. VIII, 206 Seiten. 1978.

Vol. 154: Problems and Instruments of Business Cycle Analysis. Proceedings 1977. Edited by W. H. Strigel. VI, 442 pages. 1978.

Vol. 155: Multiple Criteria Problem Solving. Proceedings 1977. Edited by S. Zionts. VIII, 567 pages. 1978.

Vol. 156: B. Näslund and B. Sellstedt, Neo-Ricardian Theory. With Applications to Some Current Economic Problems. VI, 165 pages. 1978.

Vol. 157: Optimization and Operations Research. Proceedings 1977. Edited by R. Henn, B. Korte, and W. Oettli. VI, 270 pages. 1978.

Vol. 158: L. J. Cherene, Set Valued Dynamical Systems and Economic Flow. VIII, 83 pages. 1978.

Vol. 159: Some Aspects of the Foundations of General Equilibrium Theory: The Posthumous Papers of Peter J. Kalman. Edited by J. Green. VI, 167 pages. 1978.

Vol. 160: Integer Programming and Related Areas. A Classified Bibliography. Edited by D. Hausmann. XIV, 314 pages. 1978.

Vol. 161: M. J. Beckmann, Rank in Organizations. VIII, 164 pages. 1978.

Vol. 162: Recent Developments in Variable Structure Systems, Economics and Biology. Proceedings 1977. Edited by R. R. Mohler and A. Ruberti. VI, 326 pages. 1978.

Vol. 163: G. Fandel, Optimale Entscheidungen in Organisationen. VI, 143 Seiten. 1979.

Vol. 164: C. L. Hwang and A. S. M. Masud, Multiple Objective Decision Making – Methods and Applications. A State-of-the-Art Survey. XII, 351 pages. 1979.

Vol. 165: A. Maravall, Identification in Dynamic Shock-Error Models. VIII, 158 pages. 1979.

GPSR Compliance

The European Union's (EU) General Product Safety Regulation (GPSR) is a set of rules that requires consumer products to be safe and our obligations to ensure this.

If you have any concerns about our products, you can contact us on ProductSafety@springernature.com

In case Publisher is established outside the EU, the EU authorized representative is:

Springer Nature Customer Service Center GmbH
Europaplatz 3
69115 Heidelberg, Germany

Batch number: 10844827

Printed by Printforce, the Netherlands